Something Abundant

Growing from a child of God
to the bride of Christ

Angie Nichols

PRESS

DEDICATION

To my parents

Roy Henry Grunden (1953-1988)
Your short life and long absence are for a better ending.
I will miss you until I see you again.

Barbara Ann (Law) Adams
You nurtured me in every pain and joy of this birth.
Blood and Spirit made us mothers, daughters, sisters, brides.

I love you both.

ACKNOWLEDGEMENTS

This message is a labor of many people's love. I am deeply thankful...

First and foremost, to Chris. Best friend and husband, you make my dreams come true, provide a safe place to feel and ponder this life, and speak encouragement over my wildest plans. Thank you for letting God turn us, two broken kids, into a more accurate reflection of His holy design of Bridegroom and Bride.

Most importantly, to Mycah. Baby girl, only child of my flesh, this is your story. God used your cancer to save your momma from a life of fear. I am so very sorry for the suffering, but find none of it worth comparing to the glory He continues to reveal of Himself in you. I pray you always **know** how much Jesus loves you—and how much I do, too.

To my extended family, who supported this message and ministry with your prayers, your finances, and your encouragement.

To Amy Grigg, for counseling me through every doubt, fear, and excuse I've ever felt, but never allowing a single one to exalt above the Name. You know the nightmare of your baby's cancer and all our failures in handling this call, but are *known* by the One who calls you "bride." I am ever grateful to you and Donnie.

To Joel Wier. You set the words in my heart to the song in yours. Only God can take a vineyard and a field and connect them as puzzle pieces, even before we knew this life worth living. May the land yield a great harvest of glory for Jesus. I count it all joy to know you and Teresa.

To all the ladies who persevered with me as God conceived the message week by week, the Wednesday morning and Wednesday night ladies Bible study classes at FBC Midlothian. You gobbled this study up when it was a "homemade cake" prepared by a well-meaning, but clueless, baker.

To those who helped handle each letter, word, dot, line, and space by editing and formatting — Beth Johnson, Barbara Goins, Diana Bryan, and Barbara Adams; and graphic design — Daniel Champagne. You saved me from that awkward moment when the words "on the homemade cake" are misspelled, inaccurate, or ugly.

To those who opened doors I never could. Like jewels in a crown set in fine gold, you are a royal diadem in the hand of your God. Melinda Nix, Judy Davis, Ramey Hutson, Kathryn Greene, Missi Perkins, Stephanie Oliver, Cynthia Hopkins, John Greene, Bruce Prindle, and last, but never least, the Beulah Registry.

INTRODUCTION

Dear Reader,

Thank you for picking up this book and for flipping it open. Thank you for lingering here to read simple words in a world addicted to fast information and quick results. I am convinced you have not done so by accident. No, I believe in the still, small voice of a Lover who continually, gently guides you into all truth, who allows you to slow down and hear Him if you choose. I believe in a Lover who takes His time to develop the love story He has for you.

God desires for you to know His Son Jesus as Bridegroom. He is an eternal Husband who desires intimacy with His Bride. Does that thought freak you out a little? A lot? It did me once, too.

See, the enemy of Love has attacked our perception of intimacy in order to malign a precept meant to bring us into a powerfully complete state with Christ through the Holy Spirit. Satan has an entire arsenal of evil directed toward this all-important experience. And as in the Eden garden, the woman seems to be his primary target. The beauty given women by a holy God is under brutal attack. Like Eve, we fall to deception and sin. Our view of intimacy is often twisted long before we even get a chance to learn or practice a pure version of it. Therefore when Christ calls us to an intimate spiritual relationship, we don't know how to react. Our painful, pressured, or even shameful physical experiences color the perception we have of His spiritual intentions.

Welcome to *Something Abundant*. Perhaps this is your time. Perhaps you've come to this place for such a time. To know. . .really KNOW Jesus in your spirit. As a wife knows her husband in their bed.

Intimately.

If this is your time, know that it is going to take time. Maturing from a child of God to the bride of Christ doesn't happen overnight for most. It is a process He designs for our good and His glory. While there are twelve chapters, do not think you are on a twelve week timetable to complete bridal success. I still find myself needing reminders, review, and reasons for remembering. Until we see Jesus face to face, we will be in process.

With the freedom to know we will not get it perfect, we should balance a motivation to persevere nonetheless. As one who knows Jesus intimately, I will tell you He is worth it.

This is both a book and a Bible study. The front of the book has twelve chapters of text, immediately followed by twelve chapters of Bible study and homework corresponding to the text. Though the book may be read in isolation of the homework, I feel the homework is a powerful tool to introduce you to the intimacy available in personal relationship with Jesus. Because, really, in the end. . .it is just you and Him. That is the essence of intimacy. However, it doesn't mean you have to study or walk alone. This book and Bible study are a great resource for women to use in groups. It facilitates discussion, but ultimately points learners back to their one-on-one relationship with Jesus.

As you read and study, know there is a team of ministry partners—brides—who've completed the study and are committed to praying for those who follow. If you received this book from one of them, you are much blessed. Perhaps in time, you will pass the truths you discover through this book onto another, birthing life into a spiritual daughter to the glory of God the Father.

God had precise reasons for His commands on marriage because they signify a powerful spiritual precept. When we have access to a perfect and complete union with Christ, we are empowered to accomplish mountain-moving works for His Kingdom. May the Lord bring you a spiritual harvest, reader. And May the Bride of this generation hasten the blessings, favor, and return of the Bridegroom. Amen.

CONTENTS

"It is my pleasure to tell you about the miraculous signs and wonders that the Most High God has performed for me." (Daniel 4:2)

Chapter 1

My "Once Upon A Time..."

"Something is wrong with her bone marrow."

His voice hesitated. He looked at the white sheet of paper he held in his hands absently, fidgeting with black numbers printed on stark white. He knew the interpretation from many years of medical training, but seemed to struggle with the telling. Clearing his throat, he willed his eyes to lock on mine. "Something is wrong with her bone marrow. All of her blood counts are extremely low. There could be a number of explanations, but I feel it best to get her quickly to a hospital more capable of handling her critical state. I have an ambulance waiting to take you and your daughter to Dallas. When you get to Children's Hospital, an oncologist will see her." While his eyes revealed a worrisome concern and sincere compassion, nothing about the tall emergency room doctor's words comforted.

I struggled to find air in my lungs and breathed a string of stammered questions laced with unbelief. "Low blood counts? What does that mean? Why an oncologist? What are you saying?"

"Something is wrong with her bone marrow. . ." Then, as he said a lot of other things, my ears only heard the shatter of my life to the score of a real-time nightmare. I woke to his voice again when he said the word "cancer" and my daughter's name in the same sentence. "I feel cancer might be the reason for Mycah's dangerously low blood counts." Those words ripped with each syllable. I stood in the corridor of that emergency room feeling as if the skin had been torn from my body. I doubled over, unable to stand upright.

Something is wrong with her bone marrow. Seven words and I knew. I knew. I always knew this someday lurked deep in hidden denial. This dark night of reckoning came like a thief and the world I fashioned, controlled, manipulated, and fiercely protected tumbled with a clamoring whisper. Like a child's heart breaks over a toy tower's collapse, I sat amongst the shattered facade rubble, helpless to prevent or repair it.

"No. Not Mycah. Not her. Anything, Lord. Just not her." Bent in defeat, the frantic words I cried into vice fists vanished against the ambulance engine's roar, the beeps of machines that looked alien, and the deafening silence of EMTs. I wondered if the shouting whispers pounded out by my soul resounded in the heavenly realms.

In one night, God spoke as clear as the darkness stretched long. My only child did not belong to me. She is His. I stared down at my four-year-old obsession dressed in downy-sweet flowered pajamas. She was scared and sick. I was scared sick. In a matter of days, she faded from a bubbly and twirling girl, in love with all critters great and small, to a pale-white remnant of her former vibrancy. Within the chaotic tangle of thoughts coiling in my mind, I saw her, just last week, dressed in a ballet tutu and pink tights squatting in our back-yard. With a sly smirk on her lips, she gingerly held up the toad she wrangled from its hiding place. How did she now lay listless, hooked to machines and monitors? Her eyes looked to me for answers over the Mickey Mouse surgical mask covering her tiny nose and colorless lips. But in an ambulance bound for the big city children's hospital, sufficient explanations escaped me. I knew nothing of practical salvation.

Two medical professionals tended to Mycah's transport, my husband followed the ambulance in our family's car, my mother and other family members raced from out of state to meet us, and many friends back in our hometown already prayed. But I never felt more alone, awash in the weight of an eternal black sea.

Then a conversation I neither spoke aloud nor heard with my own ears, struck more authentic than any other of the previous 20 years. God spoke like thunder over cold hard stone.

"God, I can't do this. You know I can't do this."

"Is she mine, Angie?"

"Yes, God, I told You again and again. She is Yours. But God. I can't. Please. You can have anything. Take my home, my money, my marriage, my dreams, my life. Just not Mycah."

"Even her."

"But I'm so scared."

"I know. I've come to set you free."

The exchange rang with an honest but terrifying throb. How can a good God deal in such contrasts? Where is freedom in shards? And what do I need of freedom when my only child's life drained away? I couldn't survive losing her.

Something was wrong with her bone marrow. That is all I knew of her physical condition. I held her tiny hand little knowing her physical condition mirrored my own spiritual disease. As painful and devastating as the news sounded ringing over and over again in my ears, I think a celebration of a coming rescue already swelled— albeit unheard by any ear this side of Heaven. The dark wind carried a melody of Divine engagement.

Growing up, my family looked a bit like a story-book photograph. A family of five—father, mother, and three healthy children—I held the position of darling girl sandwiched in the middle of two blonde, strapping boys. By no means rich, we did own an Atari, a basketball goal in the driveway, bicycles, and the superhero Underoos of our choice. My dad worked hard, ambitious almost to a fault. He started his career as a medic in the Air Force and worked his way into hospital administration, earning nursing degrees and promotions for management positions to better life for our family. Coach of my brother's little league baseball team, beloved Boy Scout troop leader, Sunday school teacher, and die-hard Denver Broncos football fan, he played as hard as he worked.

A homemaker, my mother employed her gifts and talents creatively in all her chores and duties. Active in church, she served as the chair of the Hostess Committee, led a prison ministry, planned the arts and crafts for Vacation Bible School, and honored the forgotten older members of our church through a nursing home ministry. She served supper as my dad came through the door after work at 5:00 pm sharp. Each night following the nightly news, our family tended to yard work or played a game of basketball in the driveway. My daddy made time to push me on the swing set between baseball or football catches with my brothers. After homework and baths, both parents tucked us into clean sheets. Dad whispered sweet secrets in each ear and Mom bounced us in our beds amidst squealing laughter and protests of "do it again!" in a game of "Gorilla Mommy!" The routine of love gave us confidence all was right in the world. Every night, without fail, my heart soared with the sound of my daddy's whisper in the curve of my ear, "You are so special. You are so beautiful. I love you." The apple of his eye — I found such a pretty identity of myself in the reflection of his blue.

When I was eleven years old, our young family of five relocated to another town, leaving behind extended family, friends, and the familiarity of all a small Texas hometown offers. My dad accepted a new position as the Director of Nurses in another small Texas town about a three hour's drive from the home we knew for most of my life. In this new place, our family grew even closer. Between the everyday details of dirty clothes, school Christmas programs, church fellowships, bumps, bruises, and bedtime stories, our family looked, to me, very much the picture of a modern day fairytale.

Until one day.

On a June evening, we just returned home from a summer vacation to Disney World that my parents worked very hard to plan and afford. My dad spared few expenses to ensure we shared an experience of memories to last a lifetime. I wonder now if, in some prophetic sense, he knew they needed to last that long.

Our entire family gathered in my parents' bedroom. We tucked my dad in on this particular night because he had to attend a medical

19

conference in Austin the next day. He and some colleagues were set to leave in the early morning hours on one of the doctor's private planes. An early bedtime was necessary for him, but not for us since we were out of school for the summer. All of us bounced and giggled on their bed, a bliss of tangled kids with mom and dad playfully in love. In the rightness of that night is a sweet feeling I recall with absolute clarity, even today.

The next morning, my mom, my younger brother and I ran about town on errands. My older brother, thirteen years old at the time, stayed home—too cool to tag along with the family to tote groceries and choose new friends for the fish tank at the pet store. We pulled into the driveway of our home around lunch time to see several members of our church standing in the front yard. My mother immediately suspected something was very wrong. My younger brother and I, not as savvy to the ways of tragedy, climbed out of our station wagon, he carrying a bag of water and tiny fish with careful kindergarten hands. Crossing the front lawn, the music minister from our church ushered my mom aside and spoke words unheard by me. Then I saw her body slump limp. Had he not held her up within his embrace, she might have been a heap on the grass. "No. . ." I heard her whisper in a tone I never heard from her before and then she sobbed short, quiet breaths into her hands. Not loud or hysterical, her sounds carried silent like trembling leaves blowing in the gale of an approaching storm. I am certain she intended to protect her watching children from the torrent of screams she concealed. But still, seeing her shoulders tremble in softened timbre tore through my body like jagged, rusted steel.

I sent my pony tail in flight, turning quickly to my Sunday school teacher. Her voice hesitated while her eyes revealed a worrisome concern and sincere compassion. I demanded she tell me what she knew but wasn't saying. Reluctantly, slowly, her eyes locked on mine. "On the way to Austin, the plane your dad was in crashed. No one survived. I am so sorry, Honey."

And just like that, I stood in the front yard of my home with my skin torn from my body. This child knew nothing of the word disillusionment. I knew only a life-sized bleeding wound and that my nurse daddy wasn't there to prevent or fix it.

In the ensuing hours, the fish found their way into the tank. In the ensuing days, months, and years, our family of four found a way to move on in a new reality. We moved back to the hometown we knew and loved to live among extended family. By God's grace, my mother raised three children on her own, making decisions like both a mother and a father. Holidays, driver's licenses, first dates, graduations, and even my wedding took place without my daddy.

But a part of my heart still stood in that front yard bleeding and exposed because of a pain too savage to explain. A part of my former soaring-heart remained wrecked and unmoved in the reality of an eleven year old girl who missed her daddy's whisper, "You are so special. You are so beautiful. I love you." The pretty identity I found in his eyes burned up in that smashed airplane. Unable to heal, I determined to never let that kind of pain touch me again. And so began the controlling and manipulation of all things dangerous or risky. "What if" became the mantra I sang to a string of idols.

At first, I obsessed over my mother. Every night I insisted the door be open between our bedrooms to listen to her breathing. So afraid she'd die too, I found comfort only in her near presence.

When I married, I obsessed over my husband. Bless his heart, Chris loved me, but he could not predict the fierce hold with which I gripped him once he asked for my hand in marriage. My fears persisted, "What if he dies?" Determined to ensure he didn't, I forbade anything dangerous. He said I forbade anything fun.

Convinced my worry and planning provided a safety net for my wounded heart, motherhood required an even greater effort. The minute the doctor placed Mycah's slippery body on my chest in the delivery room, I knew I could never survive losing her. I cared for her meticulously, toiled over her safety, and if necessary, I would have walked through fire to save her one moment's pain. I followed every law, rule, guideline, and precaution. I researched every sniffle and memorized every inch of her to spot potential abnormalities in an instant. She was life itself.

While I arranged, researched, and prevented pain from touching our lives, all my choices were made in fear because if the object of my obsession slipped away, I'd surely die. My actions built a wall of distrust in the One True God. Shackles locked my unbelieving hands and feet to a prison of counterfeit safety found in doing things my way. But someday drew closer.

In September 2007 Chris and I moved our tiny family of three to a new community for his new job. Mycah, four years old at the time, was growing up to be the smart, fun, vibrant child we hoped her to be. I took a part-time job coordinating the curriculum at the Mother's Day Out program at our church and Mycah attended pre-school there as well. The elements of our lives once again pieced together with responsible and careful planning. Meanwhile I fought fear's attempt from strangling the red blood from my life. But trouble took hold even while I believed nothing escaped my watchful eye.

Mycah developed a low-grade fever a few weeks into the school year. A couple of doctor visits revealed nothing beyond the normal suspects of an ear infection or virus. However the fever persisted even after a round of antibiotics. It unsettled me when she slept undisturbed by the cubbies in her classroom even as moms and classmates hustled and bustled at the end of the school day to gather backpacks and craft projects. But my concerns overtook me the next night. She slept most of the day and by bedtime appeared pale and lethargic. I took her temperature and discovered a new terror when the thermometer read 104 degrees. Wrought with worry, Chris and I drove our precious bundle wrapped in her favorite pastel flannel blanket to the hospital emergency room near our home.

I knew something was very wrong when the nurse ushered us back to the triage area ahead of people who sat holding their precious bundles for many hours. Before I processed what might be happening, a whirl of people and sterile equipment muddled cognitive thoughts. X-rays, blood tests, and an I.V. scared Mycah to tears and panicked me to sickened silence.

Savvier to the ways of tragedy, I saw the ER doctor walking toward me with blood test results in his hand and felt the urge to turn and run. "Something is wrong with her bone marrow," he said. And in a moment, the unhealed wound of an eleven year old girl stung new again. It felt so cruel. How could God allow savagery the likes of childhood cancer to enter my well-planned life? I wanted desperately to believe a loving God for the protection from experiencing that sort of shredded wound again. But what access did I have to the mercy of a loving God when I forsook Him to worship at the altar of idols?

In hindsight I realize, my mother, my husband, my child — certainly I should love them, favor them above others, care for them. But they should never take the high and exalted position rightfully belonging to God alone in my life. Not even out of damaged understanding caused by a fallen airplane and a dead daddy. Here is the thing about finding life in anything other than God's Son. He calls that idolatry. *For the LORD is your life. . .*(Deuteronomy 30:20 emphasis added) *"Do not worship any other god, for the LORD, whose name is Jealous, is a jealous God."* (Exodus 34:14) While God never wanted me to feel that sort of pain again and patiently loved me in my brokenness, He is absolute on His first and most important command. *"You shall have no other gods before me.* (Exodus 20:3)

It felt cruel. But for my good, for my protection, for my true salvation I must learn: Safety is not found in the absence of danger, but in the presence of God. He loved me too much to allow me to live one more day as an exposed, bleeding child imprisoned by fear. Despite my best efforts, fear cannot be fought without God's peace. Something was wrong in my soul's marrow. Cancerous fear diseased the life He planned for me. He intended to heal this thirty-something year old girl and set her free through her daughter's blood cancer.

One of God's most incredible abilities is His sovereignty causing savagery to display His beauty in its violent wake. This book is the story of that journey. It is the rescue story of one hurting girl who grew from a child of God into the bride of Christ. I became a Christian as a young girl, taught on my daddy's knee. I knew I was a child of God, and I wanted salvation and eternal life in heaven someday — it seemed a better outcome than the alternative. But when my daddy's plane crashed and burned, my desire to know the God who allowed such pain faded like smoke. Stuck in the very early stages of spiritual maturity for decades, Mycah's cancer diagnosis forced me into spiritual ICU. Her cancer treatment lasted two and a half years. In that time, God opened His Word to me in a way that exposed old wounds and shed light on the brokenness I fostered by conceiving my own plan for getting by in life. He tended to my spiritual illness even as I walked through the unthinkable tragedy of my only child's cancer.

"As a mother comforts her child, so will I comfort you. . ." (Isaiah 66:13a)

His Word proved true. As I helped Mycah through her cancer treatment, I found comfort in the arms of my Father. He is Healer—both for a mother and a child. But I will also tell you without hesitation, the healing was nothing short of a miracle by way of messy, hard work and received Grace. By walking with me through my worst nightmare, I found God to be more than all I ever dreamed.

But this book is also much more. It is indeed impossible for me to highlight the Biblical precepts in this book apart from my personal story. I lived, walked, and breathed each step of the process presented in the chapters of this book. However, it is much more than my story. It is yours too, sweet sister. No matter your testimony, no matter your walk with Christ, no matter your failures, God intends for each of his children to grow up in their salvation. (1 Peter 2:2) And while this book is by no means a formula or a twelve step program, it is based on Biblical truth. There is a plan for your eternity *as well as* for your daily reality as the life-bearing bride of Jesus Messiah.

When a person accepts Jesus into her heart, she is immediately sealed with the Holy Spirit and becomes a child of God. He intends for the relationship to be purposeful, powerful, and highly personal. As believers we are collectively the children of God, but we are to be an individual child of God with all-encompassing submission of our entire life to His will. Individually we maintain a personal one-on-one relationship with the Almighty Father through the Holy Spirit. I am suggesting when we grow up in our salvation our relationship can and should grow into something more as well. Scripture points to the Church as the Bride of Christ. (Ephesians 5:25-27, Revelation 19:6-8) As believers, having been cleansed through the blood of Jesus and reconciled to God through the death of His Son, our relationship as the bride of Christ is to be personal and individual. It is essential we not be stunted in our growth, becoming content in being a child forever. God desires to chose and present you and I to His Son as a mature and flawless beauty fit for marriage. (2 Corinthians 11:2)

I think it is especially appealing for women to consider a committed and passionate relationship with Jesus in terms of a bridegroom coming for his bride. In childhood, girls dream of a white dress, flawless beauty, marriage's first kiss, the man of her dreams against the backdrop of a magnificent sunset. It is simply impossible to think of marriage as anything but a relationship of personal intimacy. The desire to be the heroine in an epic love story is woven as gold thread into the fabric of the female heart by the God who created romance. God, the weaver of your desires, intends to tie you with chords of love to His Son in an eternal covenant. The role of Christ's bride fits each of us willing to obey ourselves to maturity perfectly — like garments of splendor given by the Bridegroom who knew our form in the secret place. It is fitting to think of yourself as the bride of Christ on a personal and individual basis just as you think of a relationship with God as His child as personal and individual.

Think for a moment how it might change the way you live if you believed down to the tips of your toes you are the chosen bride of Christ. Think about what it would mean to realize that since before the creation of the world, God chose you to be the flawless virgin, uniquely gifted and destined to unite in covenant relationship with His Son for all eternity.

I wonder if you know Jesus deeply enough to be turned-on by the notion. I did not. Between the years of my dad's death and the healing that took place after Mycah's cancer diagnosis (mind you that was about 20 years!), I was one twisted sister, dysfunctional and sick down to the deepest place of my soul. My actions betrayed my heart and revealed the truth about my feelings of Jesus. Too much of a pleaser (and coward) to be outright rebellious, I learned subconsciously to cover my pain with fake obedience and socially acceptable falseness. I married, became a teacher, had a child and worked in my church and attended regularly. I prayed in my alone moments, but I approached Jesus as if He were passive, weak, and uninvolved. And if I am really honest, I didn't believe He had the ability or desire to cause good in and for me. An eternity in Heaven sounded nice when I taught it to the preschoolers in our church, but in the dark and secret places of my inner-most heart, it sounded boring at best and scary at worst. I never longed for His touch on my life, an eternity with Him, nor fathomed an intimate moment for Him to love me uniquely and completely. In reality, He was not attractive to me. My heart was too hurt to let Him near it, let alone to offer it freely to His healing. If someone proposed the notion of being the bride of Christ, I think I would have responded, "No, thanks."

The life-threatening illness of my daughter finally caused my stubborn knees to bend. In a desperate search for the object of my obsession—healing for Mycah—I found no other option than to get real naked, real quick—spiritually speaking. I took off every pretense, confessed every sin I could frantically recall, got on my face and begged. Healing was my focus, even if it meant being slain for all my mistakes. In what is still unimaginable to me, something happened that forever changed me marrow deep. Jesus, The Redeemer, stepped in and covered me—taking my dirty rags and exchanging them for clean, fine linen purchased with His own life. He didn't condemn, He saved instead. Suddenly all the things I heard growing up in church about Jesus dying for sin made sense in my daily devastated reality. He rescued me in a personal time and place, speaking directly to all my doubts and fears. My heart fell madly and deeply for my Rescuer and in doing so, Mycah and her healing—the former object of my obsession—became second to the love I experienced in Him. Christ alone stood as the uncontested God above all in my life. Only then could He give me my heart's desire –precisely because I finally realized who I am in Him. I am His bride—the object of *His* obsession.

I don't want to give you the wrong idea. The process was any-thing but romantic at times. A hard, gut-wrenching, ugly mess in a season of threshing and sifting almost convinced me to quit. But through submission and obedience, God showed me the beauty of the threshing floor, purchased my soul through His Son's death, and then proceeded to build a temple out of my heart on the very threshing floor on which I proved true. He betrothed me forever in righteousness, justice, love and compassion to know the LORD. (Hosea 2:19-20) Please do not put this book down now because the concepts of threshing, sifting, threshing floors, and betrothal are spiritual words and concepts meaning little to you. They didn't mean a thing to me either. In fact, my Biblical knowledge was like a toddler's grasp of environmental geology when I ran face first into The Rock who broke my foolish beliefs to bits. But that is precisely why this book is such a miraculous work of Christ. He took a broken and foolish child and made Himself evident to her through His Word. I am not a learned or theologically trained woman. But I have been with Jesus. He taught me about Himself, and He will take delight to teach you as well. So I ask you to stay tuned.

Perhaps you've been devastated in a relationship, were abused, betrayed, victimized, or are oppressed, or depressed. Perhaps you've messed up, really messed up or failed big. Perhaps you are just so regular you hurt inside. I am certain the enemy ensures no one escapes this life without receiving a devastating wound to her most inner heart and soul. I wonder if Satan targeted Eve in the garden precisely because she was the bride—the prize of her husband and the prophetic symbol of God's love for His people—making her utmost in value to his evil plot.

Because of my victory over the enemy in Jesus, I feel called to strengthen my sisters on the other side of my season of sifting. The chapters of this book will lead you to the Scriptures God showed me to bring understanding of His desire. We will go together to the threshing floor and glean true seed useful for planting and grinding into spiritual food. We will study God's temple and His activity in it to learn how He will move in our hearts for His glory. Together we will look into the rich treasure of the ancient Jewish betrothal and wedding customs to see God's plans for your relationship with His Son. It is my pleasure to lead you to a more intimate and passionate reality with your First Love. For me, to serve and strengthen the bride of Christ is to serve and strengthen my sisters. I believe, with all that is in me, we will never be powerful and effective as a body until we are passionately enthralled in a relationship with Christ individually. Nothing would please my soul more than for your eyes to open to the incredible story He is weaving in you right now.

You are reading these words by His appointment. Are you ready to begin a new journey? Are you ready to prepare yourself for The Bridegroom? He wants nothing more than the sincere offering of your heart. Even if it is broken, mishandled, victimized, sinful or wounded beyond recognition—He wants to turn it into a home for Himself—where His glory will be powerfully at work in and through you for His Kingdom on earth as it is in heaven.

He is the Way, the Truth and the Life. (John 14:6 emphasis added) Yes, His truth is alive and it is treasure but I would be remiss to not warn you. Beware, reader. Make no mistake—the Kingdom is glorious—but the way is hard on the flesh. Once you know the truth of Jesus and His offer of abundant life, you will be accountable for what you did with it. So I beg you to move ahead. He is worth every risk.

Can you hear the melody of divine engagement? It may be inaudible to your ears, but your heart was created to recognize His eternal song. If you choose to read on, get ready. This is your cue.

Here comes the bride. . . .

Listen, O daughter, consider and give ear: Forget your people and your father's house. The King is enthralled by your beauty; honor Him, for He is your LORD." (Psalm 45:10-11)

As the rain and the snow
Come down from heaven,
And do not return to it
Without watering the earth
And making it bud and flourish,
So that it yields seed for the sower and bread for the eater,
So is my word that goes out from my mouth:
It will not return to me empty,
But will accomplish what I desire
And achieve the purpose for which I sent it. (Isaiah 55:10-11)

Chapter 2

Preparing Your Field for an Abundant Harvest

C hildress, the town in which I grew up, was a small Texas main-street community—primarily agricultural in industry and lifestyle. Our town's annual "Old Settler's" parade and celebration was marked largely by tractors and flat bed trailers decorated with streamers and various assortments of children waving and throwing candy at most of the town's adult population—as the bulk of the children were all somewhere on a tractor or flat-bed trailer. Many of my friends were born and bred in farming families and lived "in the country." And since I grew up in an agricultural community, I knew about the vital importance of producing a good crop to sustain a family's living. However, mine was an "in-town" family, and we knew very little about the details of producing a crop or a farmer's daily life.

So when my widowed mother re-married a farmer after I graduated from high school and left home for college, the change was dramatic and even comical. Her new husband, a high school teacher by day and a farmer by blood still lived and worked on the land belonging to his late father. I will never forget the first time I visited my mother in her new home on the farm. The property is rural to be certain, a remote plot of land in southwest Oklahoma about an hour's drive from our hometown of Childress. The house is unreachable by any paved surface. As I attempted the muddy one mile stretch of road in my little Ford Escort, I wondered how in the world my mother was able to stand living in such a place. Then I saw her teal green Mercury Cougar parked beside the old farm house. The pair looked as mismatched as stiletto heels with denim cover-alls. I could not keep from rolling my eyes and releasing a sigh of dismay.

The two-story farm house, constructed in 1900 when things were built to last, was the strong tower where my step-father's family lived since before his birth. Mildly convinced, in its day, the house might have been quite cozy and cute, in a country sort of way, the years took a crippling toll on the structure. And as I first laid eyes on the exterior walls, where siding shingles swung diagonal and the ancient grey lumber lay exposed through fading paint, I worried my mother made a huge mistake, and I should make haste to come to her rescue. The whole scene made me think of the Beverly Hillbillies *before* ol' Jed went shooting for some food and up from the ground came that bubblin' crude.

As I stepped out of my car, an assortment of feathered and furry critters greeted me with wet noses and muddy paws. I proceeded to navigate the dozen or so steps to the small front porch of the house where my mom stood arms wide to welcome me. I honestly promise I had no idea how squishy and slippery mud could be on a farm.

I expected to tip-toe lightly across the furrows and puddles, just soiling the tiniest bottom portion of my new clean, white Nike tennis shoes. However, I soon received my first lesson in slippery farm mud. Let's just say, only Jesus Himself could have made those fifteen steps without sinking ankle deep in sludge.

I hugged my mom and fought the urge to drag her back into my car and escape the God-forsaken home she obviously unknowingly inherited in her new union. Instead I smiled and covered my shock and awe as best I could. Half-way joking I asked, "So. . . .do you have electricity and running water out here?" To which she replied, "Don't be silly. Of course we do. But we don't have central heating and air conditioning." I didn't know what she even meant by that. But I soon learned, because I walked into the house on a balmy, warm spring day and found the weather inside to be much the same as the weather outside, apart from the heavy breeze from several humming floor fans. She apologized for the uncomfortable climate in the house and then commented how she got used to it quickly, and I would as well. Again, I faked an unaffected demeanor and with a laughing smile joked how it would be like camping. "Camping is fun," I lied. Really, I wondered if she lost her mind entirely.

Perhaps she saw something in the muddy farm that I didn't. I hoped so.

By the time night fell and I cuddled into the pull-out sofa sleeper with an old hand-made quilt for covers, the sounds of the farm were actually beginning to tug at the strings of my heart. I noticed a magnificent array of stars above my head from the window in the front door and felt a cool breeze beginning to blow through unseen openings in the drafty old house. Perhaps my mother wasn't insane.

I might even understand the draw of this farm in the mud. But when I heard the buzz of some sort of invisible bug and discovered fireflies twinkling in the room with me and not in the outdoor distance as I first thought, the feeling quickly fled.

This was just like camping. I don't enjoy camping.

But the farm has grown on me as the years have passed. Of course, things got much better when my mom and step-dad built a new house down the road a bit from the old two-story homestead. It even has central heat and air conditioning—Praise God!

At any rate, my mom is enthralled by the beauty and simplicity of the life and nature in her new home. Truly she traded her panty hose and high-heels for Carhartt coveralls. She cares for the animals, learned to birth livestock and never misses an opportunity to witness the miracle of new life. She embraced old-time traditions with both hands and taught herself to grind wheat and bake bread, even milking goats in order to make the most amazing home-made soap. She has taught my daughter the beauty of a mother hen teaching her chicks to peck seeds and how a sunset is an original work of God to be cherished every evening.

Mycah adores all the critters great and small, feathered and furry—goats, horses, cows, chickens, cats, dogs, and even peacocks. The farm calls to her soul and she prefers a day of feeding a goat stalks of wheat by hand, one at a time, than a day at Disney World. If my husband, Chris, can get his hands and pants dirty doing some type of outdoor man-project like welding a trailer, wrangling goats, building fence, hunting wild boar, or riding the dirt bike he is in man-heaven on earth.

For me, an early summer evening on the front porch of the new farmhouse, looking out on a ripe, swaying wheat field, easily makes my "top ten list" of most peaceful places. If not for my mother's muddy farm, I would have only viewed a wheat field from the window of a speeding car travelling down a paved highway. Her new home allowed me the opportunity to experience the amazing greenness of a wheat crop's early growth, the amber waves of grain at harvest time, and the sensual feel of pure seed sliding through my fingers after being threshed and cleaned. The practice of sowing and reaping is very prevalent in the Bible as these were concepts with which the people of the time could easily identify. Now that I have a small amount of experience because of my mother's new life, I've found beauty and value in them as well.

But for the record, I still buy my flour at the local grocery store. Additionally, I usually only purchase one five pound bag every other year. You see, my need for flour is a rare occasion. There are several aisles of bread loaves, prepared and prepackaged baked goods at a variety of markets in and near my city. You will rarely catch me in the kitchen with flour on my face from baking something homemade.

I am as far from being an expert on cultivating wheat as Old MacDonald was an expert on the Disney Princesses, the current toy collectibles inside Happy Meals, or the proper technique of cutting crust off a PB&J sandwich; all areas in which I could hold a Ph.D. at the moment. But because of Mycah's cancer, I have also recently spent a season on a spiritual threshing floor, been tossed, sifted, and shaken to my core. I have first-hand experience and on-the-job training in gleaning true seed from trashy chaff and bringing forth a harvest after months of watering the field of my heart with tears.

The intention of this study is to learn about what God has to say regarding the precepts of sowing, reaping, threshing, sifting, and using the seed of His Word to possess the abundant life He promises. So take heart, my sister, if you are not one interested in cultivating crops, grinding your own wheat or baking home-made bread. If you are, this book most likely will leave you severely wanting. However, if you are hungry for a sustaining word for your weary heart, if you want to learn about God's intentions toward your personal seasons of threshing and sifting, if you want to feast on the true Bread of Life, it is my intention to serve you a big fresh batch of whole-Word truths. Truths I would have surely missed if not for a personal season of sifting I thought I might never survive that led to an abundant harvest I never imagined. With all that is in me, I invite you to take a seat at His table, my friend. You will never hunger again.

Blessed are those who hunger and thirst for righteousness, for they will be filled. (Matthew 5:6)

The Parable of the Sower in Matthew Chapter 13 is a terrific place to start looking for hearty truths in the Word. I love stories, don't you? Jesus told a lot of stories, or parables. It just so happens today He is telling one from which we can glean a wealth of truth pertaining to our desire for abundance. We'll find Him sitting in a boat on a lake. Let's take a seat on the shore and listen.

"A farmer went out to sow his seed. As he was scattering the seed, some fell along the path, and the birds came and ate it up. Some fell on rocky places, where it did not have much soil. It sprung up quickly, because the soil was shallow. But when the sun came up, the plants were scorched, and they withered because they had no root. Other seed fell among thorns, which grew

up and choked the plants. Still other seed fell on good soil, where it produced a crop—a hundred, sixty, or thirty times what was sown. He who has ears, let him hear." (Matthew 13: 3b-8)

I hope I am not the only one sitting on this shore having a hard time enjoying this story—it sounded more like a riddle to me. Let's go listen to the conversation Jesus is having with His disciples. I have ears, and I heard the story, but I want the kind of hearing Jesus is speaking of. I want to understand with my heart. You? Shhhhh. He's speaking again.

"Listen then to what the parable of the sower means: When anyone hears the message about the kingdom and does not understand it, the evil one comes and snatches away what was sown in his heart. This is the seed sown along the path. The one who received the seed that fell on rocky places is the man who hears the word and at once receives it with joy. But since he has no root, he lasts only a short time. When trouble or persecution comes because of the word, he quickly falls away. The one who received the seed that fell among the thorns is the man who hears the word, but the worries of this life and the deceitfulness of wealth choke it, making it unfruitful. But the one who received the seed that fell on good soil is the man who hears the word and understands it. He produces a crop, yielding a hundred, sixty, or thirty times what was sown." (Matthew 13: 18-23)

Wow. I am sure glad we stuck around to hear the meaning of the story. Let me see if I can get this straight.

Seed = the Word

Soil = the heart

Bird = Satan

Rocks = no root

Thorns = worries and greed.

Seed on the path = one who hears the message of the kingdom and has no understanding. Satan steals what was sown in his heart.

Seed on the rocky places = one who hears the word and receives it with joy but lasts only a short time then falls away.

Seed falling among the thorns = one who hears the word but the worries and greed of life choke it.

Seed on good soil = one who hears and understands the word and produces an abundant crop.

That seems to make a lot more sense now that we have the correct code to the secret message. I don't know about you, but if I were taking a multiple choice quiz on the parable of the sower, I would have to go with answer D. I want an abundant crop. In fact, I would like to order the" hundred times" what was sown, please. Why go with sixty or thirty times, when you can have "a hundred times what was sown?" I just love that God allows us to be greedy with Himself. Yes, I definitely want to be the seed planted in good soil. If conditions exist in which I can have a crop yielding WAY more than what was sown, that is the condition I want to strive toward. Since it is impossible for God to lie (Hebrews 6:18), we can be sure this riddle is actually a promise. So let's find out more about how to be good soil and start doing some seed sowing.

I love the Old Testament book of Hosea. Hosea was the first prophet to associate the relationship between God and His people to the relationship of husband and wife. Before you get all huffy that your husband is in no way a god, and you are in no way "his person," let me encourage you to stay tuned. You will see just how beautiful God's ways are when we tune our hearts to listen and obey.

God commanded Hosea to marry a prostitute. "What?" you might say. I know. I could hardly believe it myself. There was a long time that I thought the Bible was all about perfect people written for perfect people and I found little to no use for it since I was not perfect. Now I shout, "Glory!" The Bible is full of messed-up people, and God works His glory in and through the midst of them. I can get into that!

God commands Hosea to marry an adulterous wife who has even bore children of unfaithfulness. God does this to show that the land of His people is guilty of the vilest adultery in departing from the LORD while turning to worship idols and false gods. Hosea's wife continues in her adultery and either sells herself into slavery, or is in debt and paying her creditors with the only ability she possesses. Either way, God commands Hosea to purchase her back for himself and instructs her to live with Hosea and stop her prostitution. This was to show that God's people would be purchased back and should return to His loving care. Hosea is full of prophesy, judgment and punishment for unrepentant Israel. But in the end, there is a promise of healing and blessing for their repentance.

I can imagine few things more difficult to forgive than the unfaithfulness of a spouse. The book of Hosea is using the example of a prostituting wife to demonstrate God's tremendous, enduring, and forgiving love for His people. It would be easy for me to say that since I have never been physically unfaithful to my husband or prostituted my body for actual money, that I am righteous according to the book of Hosea. It would also be wrong. While I have never been with a man outside of my marriage, I have left my First Love (God) to worship other gods (my own desires and things of this world).

The meaning of the book of Hosea is about the love of God for his people much more than a lesson on earthly marriage. It is meant to demonstrate the great love God has for His people—no matter how badly they mess up. I want you to know that no matter the sin, no matter the rebellion, no matter the unfaithfulness, the book of Hosea promises God wants to purchase you back with the blood of His Son. He wants you to turn away from sin and live in righteousness through Christ, offering your whole heart to His authority. It is not because He is unjustly demanding. It is because the safest, most blessed place to be is with Him. It is for your good.

Now that we have a grasp on what the book of Hosea is about and its message, I would like to pull out a key verse for our purpose, to really examine the truth and apply it for our abundant good.

Hosea Chapter 10, verse 12:

Sow for yourselves righteousness,
Reap the fruit of unfailing love,
And break up your unplowed ground;
For it is time to seek the LORD,
Until he comes
And showers righteousness on you.

According to this Scripture, when we plant righteousness for ourselves, we will reap the fruit of unfailing love. That sounds good. I could use some unfailing love. What about you? I have tried to make other people or earthly things my god, and I have been left wanting every single time. Not that the people were not worthy of my deep love and affection. My mother, my husband, and my daughter have all occupied the position of a god in my personal circumstance at one time or another. They certainly loved me back, but couldn't possibly fulfill my need for God Himself. Nor can money, food, sex, alcohol, drugs, or any other material possession or earthly addiction we may try to use as an unfailing source of life. God alone is worthy of our sincere and devout worship, because He is the only source of unfailing love. In Isaiah 42:8 God leaves no doubt about His authority to require it. *"I am the LORD; that is my name! I will not give my glory to another or my praise to idols. . ."* So if we want to sow for ourselves righteousness and reap the fruit of unfailing love from the worthy God, what do we do? How do we do it?

I love the next part of Hosea 10:12: *"and break up your unplowed ground."* Some Biblical translations use the phrase, "fallow ground" or "the hard ground of your hearts." Fallow ground is land that has been used for planting but is left unseeded for a season or more. It is by definition inactive and unproductive.[1] In a fallow condition, the land is not ready for planting due to several reasons. Fallow land is easily overtaken by thorns and weeds. It is also too hard for water to penetrate the hard surface and so it runs off quickly instead of being absorbed for the good of the seed. And in its hard condition, seed is not able to take root deeply enough to establish thriving plants. In essence, fallow ground has the same properties and risk of detrimental outcomes as the conditions of which Jesus warned in the parable of the sower. Hosea 10:12 tells us the remedy for fallow ground. The remedy is to break it up.

I wonder about the condition of your heart. I know my own had been neglected and left fallow for way too long. After the wound of my father's death, instead of allowing God to heal it, I hid it away. Soon decisions were made in fear rather than trust, and it began to harden. I placed people in God's position, and sin began to separate my heart from the life-giving seed of God's Word and His loving maintenance. In my experience a neglected heart soon becomes hardened by sin. And a hard heart soon begins to sin all the more until it is easier to judge, condemn, spew bitterness and harbor ill for not only others, but God, than to face and repent of the sin. The thing about a wounded, broken heart is that it can never heal or be whole again on its own. It just hardens with furrows and cracks where the thorns and weeds of this sinful world can quickly take hold.

The remedy to fallow ground is to break it up by seeking the LORD.

". . .for it is time to seek the LORD, until he comes and showers righteousness on you." (Hosea 10:12)

If it is your heart's desire to grow up into the mature and flawless bride of Christ, you have to know how to cooperate with God's plan in order to prepare yourself for the abundance He intends to bring forth in your life. A crusty-dusty heart will never be able to produce the type of fruit that will allow others to see and know Jesus in you. The Psalmist has some great insight into the type of heart offering God will bless.

*"You do not delight in sacrifice, or I would bring it; you do not take pleasure in burnt offerings. The sacrifices of God are a broken spirit; a **broken***

44

and contrite heart, O God, you will not despise." (Psalm 51:16, 17 emphasis added)

Has your heart been truly broken for your Redeemer? Have you stood among the dry and cracked furrows of your heart and bent your knees in brokenness before your God? Contrite is defined as feeling regret and sorrow for one's sins or offenses; sincere remorse. Have you been contrite with Him?

I can recall with photographic detail the moment I finally confessed my sins after a long season of socially acceptable rebellion. That may be the worst kind of sin. Many who knew me and observed me in public would have never suspected the type of deadness concealed in my false version of a safe reality. Now I realize that a person who wears the label of Jesus outwardly, but contains only the slightest resemblance of Him inwardly is a dangerous soul indeed. It leads to the profession of a false-Christ in our witness as one who darkens His counsel with words she knows not (see Job 38). Eventually, God questioned me out of the storm and waited for an answer.

It was about two weeks after Mycah's leukemia diagnosis, when the pressure of holding things together in my own strength proved to be too much. I collapsed in a heap of tears on my bathroom floor behind closed doors. God let me feel the full weight of fear for my daughter's life. I needed Him like never before, but He was unable to intervene for me because my sin separated me from His Holy help. The feeling that He wanted to rush to my rescue was overwhelming. But He was also unable to come near due to my un-confessed sin. God's Spirit leaned heavily upon my conscience. *"Arise, cry out in the night, as the watches of the night begin; pour out your heart like water in the presence of the Lord. Lift up your hands to him for the lives of your children. . ."* (Lamentations 2:19) After making the excuses of a victim, pleading that the situation was not my fault, and pointing my finger in all directions but my own, I felt Him ask me, "Angie, do you think I am unaware? I view the ends of the earth and I see everything under the heavens." He saw my broken heart and the sin I held onto for cover. He saw everything and wanted me to offer it all to Him. He saw my crusty heart and wanted it anyway. It was absolutely required to restore His ability to work in my circumstance. And then a torrent, held back by my own feeble hands, finally broke forth. Tears from the deep well of a broken and contrite spirit fell and began to soak the bathroom rug and the surface of my fallow heart.

The volume of my tears scared me. They were certainly cleansing and a reprieve to the drought. But to my surprise, they weren't enough. I could have stayed and cried for days on end. I emptied the well of this sinful woman completely, and it didn't make a difference. My tears served just to darken the surface. Here is a true statement: Friend, you cannot cry enough tears, you cannot beat yourself up adequately, you cannot grieve the guilt long enough. Your own contrite spirit and tearful expression of brokenness will never be enough to water the fallow fields of your heart. Make no mistake, they are pre-requisite. He would never despise them. In fact they are absolutely precious to God. He holds each tear in His holy hands. The New Living Translation of Psalm 56:8 says it like this: *"You keep track of all my sorrows. You have collected all my tears in your bottle. You have recorded each one in your book."* But the tears of a broken spirit are useless in bringing forth meaningful healing.

Psalm 34:18 brought great comfort to me, and I hope it speaks to you as well. Let it fall afresh like the autumn rains in season. *"The LORD is close to the brokenhearted and saves those who are crushed in spirit."* I will never forget the peace and inconceivable relief that exhaled through my body when I perceived His ear bent low to hear my every contrite confession. My brokenness was precious to Him, like music to His Holy ears. Finally, my desire was to return to the LORD, and He was waiting right where He had been all along. . .anxiously waiting to powerfully heal me. (Psalm 107:20)

I had strong motivation to seek God in the moment I finally knelt before His cross and asked for forgiveness. My daughter's life was threatened and in the throes of an all out battle with blood cancer. Not knowing the outcome but fearing the worst, I knew she would never be fully whole again without miraculous divine intervention—and I was finally realizing that neither would I.

I don't have the first clue about your past, your circumstances, or your failures. It may be that you are caught up in a terrible mess from a sinful stronghold. You may be depressed and unproductive, or bitter and full of poison and thorns. Perhaps this world and its lies have choked and stolen the life out of you. It may also be that you see yourself as so ordinary you cannot imagine a situation where your heart would bear the type of fruit in which this study teaches. You may feel your life and testimony could never be used in such a gloriously rich way. If so, you've bought into a lie and are living in the sin of unbelief. Sin is sin and it all separates us from our calling in Christ Jesus.

I don't know the condition of your heart, but I don't need to. God uses all manner of things to prepare the field. A contrite heart looks different in every woman and measuring oneself against another is stony ground. Because of the authority of God's Word, I am confident of this: You are not without sin (1 John 1:8) nor have you sinned more than He is willing and able to forgive (Jeremiah 33:8). And you do not possess the only heart in which He cannot bring forth an abundant harvest. He is bent low to hear your heart's honest and contrite confessions, and I am convinced He can hardly stand waiting to shower down His righteousness over you. He is near the broken and contrite heart. He is near. *"In your distress you called and I rescued you, I answered you out of a thundercloud. . ."* (Psalm 81:7a)

When I finally believed Him for the forgiveness He so freely gave, I found the furrows of my heart fully saturated and the ridges leveled, drenched in Living Water. I felt the soil of my heart soften, even down to the darkest depths, with streams of flowing Grace. The blood and water from Jesus' side cleansed my soul and changed my heart from a hard, cracked, and thorny wasteland into the humus of humility, where future abundance could be sown with seeds of hopeful promise.

"Who can tip over the water jars of the heavens when the dust becomes hard and the clods of earth stick together?" (Job 38:37b)

Hosea 10:12 states that only the rain of righteousness from The Lord Himself can soften a hard heart and produce enough moisture to loosen the soil for tilling and prepare your heart for an abundant harvest.

Dear one, the path from an adulterous wife, who has wandered from the fold of her First Love, to the flawless virgin bride Christ desires, originates in the fallow fields of your heart. It leads you to the cross where dry brokenness is watered with the contrite tears of your own soul. When they are not enough, lift your eyes to heaven. Notice the sudden clouds of an approaching storm. With it, the fragrance of righteous redemption will stir your senses as the hot, dusty soil begins to mix with the first sprinkles. Breathe deeply the scent of thirsty earth bathed by Living Water. The LORD Our Righteousness, will lift you from your knees and turn your parched and withered heart into a fertile field ready to receive His seed and bring forth a hundred times what is sown. Break up your unplowed ground. Seek the LORD *until* — until He showers righteousness on you.

Yes, my mom undoubtedly saw something in the muddy farm that I did not. She saw promise where I saw filth. She saw life where I saw mire. Beloved, God sees something in your heart that perhaps you do not. Where there are furrows, He sees the potential for abundant glory. Where there is brokenness, He is reminded of His Son's body nailed to a cross. Call out to Jesus. Pray for rain and don't be afraid to fall on your knees. Because sister, if you offer your broken, sin-hardened heart to Jesus, He will shower it with His righteousness. Don't be discouraged if you find yourself in what appears to be a soggy mess. Your thirst has found the Healer. Your dry and weary land has received its flood. Lift your hands awash in praise! There is hope for abundance in you. . .and it begins with mud.

There is hope in the mud.

"You heavens above, rain down righteousness; let the clouds shower it down. Let the earth open wide, let salvation spring up, let righteousness grow with it; I, the LORD, have created it." (Isaiah 45:8)

Be glad, O people of Zion,
Rejoice in the LORD your God,
For he has given you
the autumn rains in righteousness.
He sends you abundant showers,
Both autumn and spring rains, as before.
The threshing floors will be filled with grain. . . (Joel 2:23, 24)

Chapter 3

Cultivating an Abundant Harvest

Mycah was three years old when our little family moved to the growing Dallas-Ft. Worth suburb that is the setting for this story of my real-life season of sifting. A small but typical American family, we hoped to find a quiet life in the 'burbs. Since the housing market was in full boom, with scores of builders competing for buyers, we decided to purchase a half acre lot instead of a pre-existing home and worked with a builder to tweak pre-planned blue prints for our needs. The quiet and friendly neighborhood seemed like a safe place for a young family to settle. And in the years we called it home, we found it to be just that. Our home was not fancy but simply small and cozy. It had everything we could ever need as a family of three and suited us like baby bear's chair suited Goldilock's rear. . .just right.

The yard needed a bit more work, however. Our builder had included only a front yard of sod and little else in the way of landscaping. We moved in during the month of November as the Texas growing season was coming to an end, with a pocketbook suffering from too many expenses related to the experience. Circumstances dictated we hold off on pricey landscaping projects. Instead, we decided to move the newly laid sod from the front edge of the house and relocate it along the side and back of the house where the ground was left bare. Envisioning a flowerbed on each side of the front door, it made sense to remove the sod and put it to good use somewhere else. We put some garden edging in place to outline the borders of the future flowerbeds, deciding to wait until spring to fill them with permanent plants.

After a few weeks of looking at the muddy bleakness at the front of the house, I decided it might be a good idea to purchase some mulch to cover the dirty mess. While pushing Mycah in a squeaky cart through the home improvement mega-store, Chris and I passed a pallet of spring bulbs. In a moment of brilliance, I exclaimed, "we could plant some bulbs!" Chris knew I had never planted bulbs, and the shade of my green thumb is more of a pale yellow. He witnessed the times I killed patio pots of petunias and trashed house plants after only a few weeks of their residence in our home. Good man that he is, he still slowed the basket and endured my enthusiastic plans for color in the front of our new home come spring. The way I figured, we could plant spring bulbs and then put off having to buy permanent landscaping until early summer. The house would have some colorful plants to beautify the front yard, and we would buy ourselves a bit more time to recover our budget. "Genius, don't you think, babe?"

He knew me too well to argue. I quickly scanned the labels of the bulbs. I had no idea how to pick out good bulbs. They all looked the same to me—crusty and dead—one probably as good as the next. So in my moment of brilliance, I decided to purchase the bags with the greatest quantity of bulbs for the price. That way, we would be sure to have a lush flowerbed full of. . .well, whatever type of flowers these bulbs would produce—the names of the flowers meant little to me. The pictures on the labels looked lovely and in my imagination, the front of the house looked glorious on a very skinny budget.

We spent the rest of the afternoon digging small holes in the muddy mess in front of the house. Mycah even helped by dropping bulbs, one at a time, into the designated places, pointed out by her well-intentioned, but ill-informed mother. Once the bulbs were planted randomly, Chris covered the flowerbeds with mulch.

March came in like a lion and April showers arrived as expected. By May, many of the neighbors had already enjoyed many weeks of colorful blooms from their bulbs. We had nothing. Sorely disappointed, I wondered if I bought dud bulbs or if we were hasty in planting them without reading the instructions. No matter, my brilliance was wasted, and I wanted *something* pretty to grow in the front flowerbeds. Our house looked as inviting as the Munster's for goodness sake! So Chris and I purchased a few shrubs and a flowering tree or two. It certainly wasn't enough to accomplish the scene in my mind's eye for the space, but it would be better than nothing.

In the middle of the summer I noticed a new, tender plant beginning to poke through the mud and mulch. I spotted it as I knelt, pulling dandelion weeds and stray grass from the front flower beds. Immediately I thought it must be one of the bulb plants I had given up on back in the spring. Giddy, I crawled closer to inspect the new arrival. I called Mycah over to admire it and reminded her of the afternoon we spent tossing crusty bulbs into holes. This was finally one of the bulbs growing! We decided immediately to water it gently.

In just a matter of a few weeks, the plant stood almost as tall as three-year-old Mycah and the stalk expanded to a couple inches in diameter. Even if most of the bulbs were a bust, this one miraculously grew. I loved that we had at least one. Mycah and I tried to predict what type and color the bloom might be. To save my life, I couldn't recall what kind of bulbs we bought, and the labels were long since gone in the trash. The element of surprise made it all the more exciting.

In a weekly phone conversation with my mom, I told her about the one miraculous bulb that managed to survive the winter and bloom with the spring. She is an avid lover of nature and always has a beautiful display of carefully tended plants and flowers around her Oklahoma farmhouse. I described its appearance to her over the phone, thinking she might be able to tell me what type of plant we had. She couldn't think of what it could be, but she was coming to visit soon. She would look at it for me and hopefully identify it then.

I will never forget as long as I live and breathe. On the day of her visit, she got out of her car and hugged my neck in the front yard. We exchanged greetings and chatted. As we walked toward the house together, I pointed out the plant I so carefully nurtured. I loved how it welcomed our special guest, beckoning us to the front door. Mom inspected it for a moment, even taking its leaves into her fingers. In a moment, she looked right at me and spoke the truth in love.

"Oh, honey...that's not a bulb flower. You've been tending a weed!"

"What? No!" I refused to accept her verdict.

She wasted not a single second. Kneeling down on one knee over my miracle plant, she tugged on it at the base. "Yes, Angie. This is a spindly, no good weed. And it's a tough booger." She continued to rock the base of it back and forth as her bent body pushed and pulled. I looked on in horror as finally the thick stalk along with a mature root system tore out of the dirt.

"There!" she said out of breath, holding the poor thing like a dead snake. Seeing my horrified expression, she spoke in a comforting tone to cover her chuckles, "Awww, don't worry. You just didn't know any better."

Hebrews 6:7-8 says,

Land that drinks in the rain often falling on it and that produces a crop useful to those for whom it is farmed receives the blessing of God. But land that produces thorns and thistles is worthless and is in danger of being cursed. In the end it will be burned.

This truth in Scripture was certainly true of the state of my heart at the time. Living blissfully unaware of my impending great and dreadful day of the Lord, I tended weeds where He intended blessing. Life in Christ can be very similar to my story of nurturing a weed. We want the abundant fruit that the Bible tells us is found in Jesus. But often we don't take the time to read God's instructions or seek His Word through Scripture to know a weed from fruit. If we find growth in our lives apart from Him, it may look like fruit, but in reality, it isn't. When we don't know any better, it is easy to nurture something that looks like life to us. All the while, it is nothing more than a no-good weed to be burned in the fire. If we are after a mature relationship with Jesus, we might have to learn some hard lessons—even if we have to let go of the very things that look like life.

In the previous chapter, we looked at the importance of preparing the field of our hearts to bring forth an abundant harvest for the glory of God. By breaking up the fallow ground, offering a broken and contrite spirit, and allowing the Lord to rain down His righteousness, the once hardened heart transforms into workable soil where seed of promise is sown. There is great hope in mud. We should not assume the mud a curse but rather a good place where God wants to plant abundant glory. If we desire to cultivate abundance, we must seek God's instruction for sowing, maintaining, and reaping.

In our current time and culture, it is difficult to understand the concepts of sowing and reaping enough food for an entire family. I am sure you may live a lot like my family. When we need bread, we go to the grocery store and buy it. Even in difficult economic times, food can be obtained without having to plant a crop and wait for it to produce the harvest needed to eat and survive. For the people of the Old Testament, sowing and reaping were essential to sustain life. Let's try to imagine walking a mile in those sandals.

Bread was the main staple of a family's diet, with bread-making being a daily activity in an ancient Israeli home. Storage rooms were built as part of the home and used to preserve a surplus of seed. A farmer needed to harvest enough grain to feed his family, plant the next year's crop, as well as reserve some to sustain the family in years of poor harvest. Planting began in the fall with harvest taking place in the late spring and early summer months.[2] Indulge me for a moment and imagine yourself living in the days of the Bible.

When the harvest came in this year you sang and danced with the family. However, privately you worried. You thought about the years past when there had been much less seed in the storehouse, but you also thought about the past years when there had been much more. This year, it had taken much creativity to stretch the flour to feed the increasing and growing hungry mouths at the table. Somehow you had been able to make each day's ration sufficient. However, today the clay jar in the house is empty of flour. You know the remnant of seed left in the storehouse will never last until next year's harvest. The remaining seed is to use when the crop is insufficient. This was surely such a time. But it would be six more months until the next harvest. The amount couldn't last that long. Not wanting to worry your husband, you hesitated to tell him of the seriousness of the short supply. Instead, you hope somehow there might be enough. But today the reality of the deficit is too extreme to deny. You have to let him know because he is headed to the muddy field.

He was up before the sun to begin planting. You spot him leaning a bit as he walks slowly, the bag around his shoulder full and heavy with the seed set aside for sowing next year's harvest. Quickly, you run out after him holding the hems of your skirts. Just as he begins to toss the first handful of seed into the muddy rows, you hear your own voice exclaim, "Wait!" Through choked tears you tell him there is no more flour for today's breakfast and no seed except the remnant in the storehouse. With six months until the seed in his sack will grow into wheat for a new harvest, how could he throw it into the earth? What if the seed is eaten by birds, there isn't enough rain, or the locusts devour the growing plants? What if by sowing the seed into the ground, it is just thrown away in a fruitless waste, starving the family while waiting for harvest time? Perhaps it would be better to keep the seed, eat and sustain for the moment. But what would happen when there is no harvest next year at all?

Awash in a fitful sea of if only's and what if's you wonder if you should have just kept your mouth shut and let things be. But you told him. He is aware, and now he must decide. To eat now or to sow that you might eat later? Eat or sow?

You walk back toward the house wondering and weeping, despising the desperate situation. He shouts directions for you to use the remnant of seed in the storehouse for breakfast as he releases a fist full of life into the mud. Looking back, you see him push away tears with an empty hand.

It is hard to imagine having to make such a decision. Eat or sow? Seed equaled life in those times. It was necessary to plant a new crop every year to sustain a family. When times were especially difficult and seed was in short supply, it would be painful to decide. Eat or sow?

I feel very strongly the LORD asks His people to make decisions of similar magnitude even today. Perhaps not with wheat seed and a family's physical hunger, but make no mistake, He is the same yesterday, today, and tomorrow. In order to grow up and mature in our faith, we will face a choice — to hold on in fear, or let go in faith.

I am certain when godly families of the Old Testament made the choice to sow in faith, Psalm 126:5-6 was never far from their thoughts, prayers, or tongues. Let it fall fresh on you as well.

"Those who sow in tears
will reap with songs of joy.

He who goes out weeping,

carrying seed to sow,

will return with songs of joy,

carrying sheaves with him."

Have you faced a decision like that? Maybe God asked you to let go of something. Many things can look like life to us: an addiction or sinful secret, a person or relationship, a grudge or anger toward another, material possessions, reputation, beauty, status, money, fame, self, and the like. We tend to hold on to them with a white-knuckle grip. I know only because the color has just recently returned to my own fingers.

As I have shared, from the time I fist knew Mycah was growing in my womb, she was my treasured possession. Giving little to no thought toward God's will for her life or mine, I went about arranging our lives myself. She became my life. And I held on to her with a death grip, confident that losing her would be the end of me.

I have also shared the moment, soon after Mycah's diagnosis, when I finally came to the foot of the cross and repented of the sin which separated me from God's ability to intervene in my circumstances. I knew nothing short of His hand in our circumstance could see us through such an intensely devastating time. Highly motivated to save Mycah's life, I wanted Him to be near like never before.

Very soon, I found my heart softened toward Him. His Word came alive to me. I started to believe He was speaking directly to me through words written by men thousands of years ago, and I found it euphoric. I expected that once I had "gotten right" with God, everything would be instantly made right. He indeed touched my heart with His forgiving righteous hand, and I expected to see immediate fruit. I hoped to find Mycah miraculously healed, our active lives restored, and the whole cancer diagnosis a misunderstanding. . .a bad dream. When the circumstances of life remained, I wondered if it had been worth it. Was there really any point in seeking God and desiring forgiveness, if it didn't change the reality of a really messed-up, difficult, and painful life? If He forgave me in an instant, why didn't I see my desires fulfilled just as quickly?

It is not that God does not ever immediately rescue His children. I have read and heard testimonies of miraculous and immediate rescues. God reserves the right to intervene for His children at any time and in any way He desires. However, I learned in this particular season, God was asking me to release Mycah to Him in faith and then wait for Him while remaining in Him.

A few days after my bathroom floor break down, Mycah endured some very painful and difficult treatments. The chemo regiment she followed distorted not only her appearance but her personality. She quickly changed from a twirling wisp of pink sunshine to a remnant of her former self, lying around listless and unresponsive. Her innocent trust seemed to be eradicated along with the cancer cells as the price paid for her treatment. When anyone came near her, she believed they might poke her with needles or ask her to swallow nasty medicine. She became fearful of even my touch. The worst part, I hardly even recognized her. She was severely swollen, bald, pale, and mean. People who knew her very well would not have known her if she passed them on the street. I remember showing her a photo I took of her and she looked at the image on the digital camera and then looked at me and asked, "Where's me?" She didn't even recognize herself. And when I pointed her out in the photo, she turned and grimaced at what she saw. I grieved for the four year old innocent child I once knew. I missed her terribly. My softened heart, touched by God's forgiveness felt torn apart. I wondered where He was in the pain. Why would He not make it stop?

Day after day, the treatment proved more wearisome and dreadful for Mycah and for me as I seemed to feel her pain as my own. Unable to bring relief to either one of us, my frustrations caused a type of distress within my soul I had never experienced. I couldn't eat and couldn't sleep because I felt my daughter slipping away slowly. I held on to her –the memory of the old her—with a grip so fierce it brought exhaustion to my body, mind, and spirit. Again in a desperate moment, I fell at the feet of Jesus. This time I sat alone in the bathtub, allowing the roaring water flowing from the tap to muffle the sound of my uncontrolled sobbing. I asked Him why all the pain? Why all the treatments? It felt like torture, and it felt like He was standing by just watching. Are You really there? Are You asleep? Why would You let this happen? Was I not repentant enough? Is this Your way of punishing me for the years of unbelief and rebellion? What? What, LORD? I want to fix this! Why won't You fix this?

I threw a fit like a toddler. And when the heaving sobs and flailing stopped from pure exhaustion, He whispered into my heart words that comforted my soul but troubled my mind. It went something like this:

"Angie, I know the desires of your heart. I have placed them there. I know you love Mycah. I love her more. You want to fix her. You never could. You have to give her to Me or you will surely lose her. Release your grip and give her to Me. Trust Me. I AM that I AM."

61

I opened my Bible and immediately my eyes fell on Jeremiah 31:15-17:

This is what the LORD says:

"A voice is heard in Ramah, mourning and great weeping, Rachel weeping for her children and refusing to be comforted, because her children are no more." This is what the LORD says: "Restrain your voice from weeping and your eyes from tears, for your work will be rewarded," declares the LORD. "They will return from the land of the enemy. So there is hope for your future," declares the LORD. "Your children will return to their own land."

It felt as if the words might have been penned in that moment for just my circumstance. I was overwhelmed with the reality of His Word. Was He talking to *me*? He WAS talking to me. In that very moment, Scripture became beautiful, breathing life. God was not dead nor was He asleep. I wanted so badly for my child to return. I missed her so much. If I dared to believe the Scripture, I would find great comfort in it. He asked me to let Him have her, and the request came with a promise; "your work will be rewarded."

"Those who sow in tears, will reap with songs of joy. . ." (Psalm 126:5)

But Mycah was everything. She was, to me, life itself. To release her, felt as if it would kill me. The promise of the Scripture brought me comfort, but the promise came without specific details of whether her return would be in the here and now life of earth or the eternal life in heaven. But our feelings often have little to do with God's ways.

Luke 9:24 quotes Jesus Himself, *"For whoever wants to save his life will lose it, but whoever loses his life for me will save it."* He was teaching me His way. If I wanted to save the very one who was life to me, I would have to let her go completely for His sake.

In my flesh it seemed too high a price. I am her mother, after all. Mothers are supposed to protect their children at all cost. It is my responsibility to fight for her, to find the best doctors, the best treatment. No one else could love and protect her like I could. How could it be wrong to do so? I am her mother!

"And I Am God," He answered. In fact, in the three Scriptures of Jeremiah 31:15-17, there are four times God declares His name with His statement. The words, "This is what the LORD says" and "declares the LORD" are present four times in three little Scriptures. He made Himself crystal clear.

So I had a choice—a painful and tearful choice. Hold on in fear or let go in faith. Spiritual maturing sometimes hurts more than we think we can bear. Letting go felt like death, but His Word says it is life.

The time had come to decide to live according to my own flesh or according to the truth of the Word. Galatians 6:8 puts it like this: *"For the one who sows to his own flesh will from the flesh reap corruption, but the one who sows to the Spirit will from the Spirit reap eternal life."* (NASB)

Over the next few weeks, God put me in front of several Scriptures, teaching me about life according to the truth of His Word.

Deuteronomy 30: 11-20 spells it out very clearly. The Word is near so that we may obey it. He sets before us life and prosperity or death and destruction. To follow His command to love the LORD your God, to walk in His ways, and to keep His commands means we will live and increase and have His blessings. Verse 19 and 20 especially spoke to my circumstance. *"Now choose life, so that you and your children may live and that you may love the LORD your God, listen to His voice, and hold fast to Him.* **For the LORD is your life.** *. . ."*(emphasis added)

How could it be clearer? I had to let go of my death grip on Mycah and hold fast to God. She was not my life. He is life. In doing so, I chose life for myself and also for her. Don't misunderstand. God gives us children as blessings. He was not asking me to forsake her, give up on her fight, or lessen my commitment to do what was best for her. He instead expected me to trust Him with her life and told me to seek the instructions for her welfare in the pages of Genesis to Revelation. I needed to let go of my belief that I could save her apart from trusting completely in Him. Holding on to Mycah for my life kept me from holding on to Him for true life. The time had come. I must let go of her. I prayed for help and then committed her to His care. I laid her at the cross and finally released my death grip. Then I brushed away the tears with my empty hand. Thankfully, He wasted no time in taking my empty hand into His. He never held me tighter.

What about you? I wonder what you might be holding onto for dear life. His Word is crystal clear that anything other than a fast hold onto Him is death—no matter how much it looks like life to our human eyes. He alone is our life. We know that in order to receive eternal life in heaven, we have to lay down our own lives, take up our cross and follow Christ. (Mark 8:34) I think it is also vital to understand that the concept goes beyond our choice for eternal salvation. Anything we hold fast to other than the LORD Himself will result in corruption and even perhaps death (to relationships, career, finances, health) in this life.

Are you holding on to what you believe to be life? Is it something other than God? Does the thought of letting it go make you feel as if you might die? If so, I lovingly advise you to release it. Sow it to the Spirit and reap eternal true life.

Friend, weeping must never stop you from sowing. *"Blessed are those who mourn, for they will be comforted."* (Matthew 5:4) Making a choice to let go in faith and sow to the Spirit what appears to be life to you will be painful. It is sweaty and tearful work. But take comfort. Hold on to the LORD with everything you have. He will never leave you or forsake you. (Deuteronomy 31:6) You will reap with songs of joy. Your work will be rewarded. In a matter of time, you will sing a song of joy. Your arms will be full of the sheaves of real life. An abundant harvest in Christ will be yours. He alone is life. . .and life abundant. He promised.

He made me a promise, and I couldn't wait to see Him fulfill it. But I soon learned—waiting is a must. Sown seed takes time, care, and patience before the sheaves of abundance are harvested. Mycah's cancer treatment would take about two and a half years. I felt confident in the promise of Jeremiah 31:17. *"Your children will return. . ."* But waiting for the promise proved almost overwhelming. The evidence of any type of harvest seemed nowhere to be found. Cancer invaded and took up residence in our daily lives. Day upon day, the work continued and the results were hidden away in what seemed like endless acres of mud.

My eyes saw only the loss of my precious daughter as I once knew her. Just weeks before she was in dance class holding hands with her friends, she was in pre-school creating a finger-painted masterpiece. Just weeks ago I brushed her long silky hair and tied it back with pink ribbons. Just a few weeks ago her giggles were the soundtrack of our family. Now she was covered in the chaos of cancer treatment. I wanted to see signs of harvest, but all I saw was her sweet, bald head and stacks of medicine with toxic warning labels on them. For months on end, her toys went unwanted and her giggles were replaced with fearful cries.

Throughout Mycah's cancer treatment, I found myself back in the bathtub weeping on a regular basis. When I doubted, when I felt scared, when the circumstances appeared that she might never return, I ran back to our secret place to seek God's comfort. But often, comfort's form was only a reminder of the promise. It had to be enough. It was the hardest work I've ever done. I continually sowed the seed, carrying my fears and burying them in the ground, watering them with tears. Waiting and praying for the promised harvest. And just as a seed fights its way out of the ground, Mycah had to fight her way past the cancer while I had to fight my way past the cancerous fear. I wanted so badly to sing a song of joy at the sight of my girl returning even stronger than ever. But the season of waiting had not come to completion. Perseverance leads to maturity. It is the growing pains of abundant life.

Hebrews 10:35-39 became the manna He fed me.

"So do not throw away your confidence, it will be richly rewarded. You need to persevere so that when you have done the will of God, you will receive what he has promised. For in just a little while,

"He who is coming will come and will not delay.

But my righteous one will live by faith.

And if he shrinks back,

I will not be pleased with him."

But we are not of those who shrink back and are destroyed, but of those who believe and are saved."

Also James 1:2-4

"Consider it pure joy, my brothers, whenever you face trials of many kinds, because you know that the testing of your faith develops perseverance. Perseverance must finish its work so that you may be mature and complete, not lacking anything."

God speaks over and over in His word about perseverance, patient enduring, persistence and waiting. This type of waiting means to wait expectantly, to persevere in prayer, continually seek God and watch for His instructions persistently.[3] He was teaching me to mature in Him by waiting. I must learn to seek Him, endure in Him, abide in Him before I could receive what He promised. Seed sown in tears takes time to grow and mature into an abundant harvest.

Perhaps you find yourself in a season of waiting. If you have truly let go of anything apart from the LORD Himself as your life and you've yet to sing songs of joy over the abundant harvest in your life, I encourage you to persevere. Persistently seek Him like an addict seeking her next hit. When you hear things about God and His promises, go to the Word and ask Him for yourself if they are real. Love Him with all your heart, mind, soul, and strength. Follow Him wherever He goes. Obey whatever He commands. Find strength in the manna of His Word until He brings forth a harvest in you so abundant that you will bake bread to feed all those around you. His promise in Leviticus 26 might encourage you as it did me.

"I will look on you with favor and make you fruitful and increase your numbers, and I will keep my covenant (promise) with you. You will still be eating last year's harvest when you will have to move it out to make room for the new. I will put my dwelling place among you, and I will not abhor you." (Leviticus 26:9-11)

There will be a joyous harvest. And you will sing a song of joy.

I can't help but ponder the scene—a coming of age story of a child maturing into a bride. A story of you and me.

Once upon a time a girl found great strength and joy in her precious treasure. One day her Father asked her to bury it in a field of mud with a promise that it would soon return a more valuable reward. Reluctantly and with tears, she obeyed. Sorrowful, she turned her doubting eyes toward Him wondering when she would sing again for joy. In her despair, He responded, "I will uphold you with my righteous right hand. I am your LORD, give me your empty right hand." (From Isaiah 41:10 and 13) He placed His right arm around her, enveloping her in His embrace. Taking her empty right hand into His left, the Father looked down into His child's face. Her eyes wide, she caught a glimpse of the woman reflected in His gaze. In this posture of Daddy-daughter dance, her trust in Him grew strong. She is growing-up and His will is done. One day, the time will come. In her, the Father has found a fitting bride for the Son.

A song of joy quickened and they swayed among the young green sheaves. And for the first time, she found joy not in the life she let go. Not even in the promise of its return. She found her joy and strength in everlasting arms, captivated with the beginning chords of life-abundant harmony.

Dear sister, nothing you could ever hold in your hand is worth missing Him. Stop holding onto what looks like life but is not. Your death grip just might kill it and you. Stop nurturing weeds and seek His Word to plant and maintain the true seed of life. Let go. When you extend an open, empty hand in faith to God, He is pleased to receive it. Now He can lead you in a Father's waltz. Don't worry if you feel like you are falling. Lean back fully in perfect trust. He is dipping you.

"*Search me, O God, and know my heart;*
test me and know my anxious thoughts.
See if there is any offensive way in me,
and lead me in the way everlasting."
(Psalm 139:23-24)

Chapter 4

The Threshing Floor

The threshing floor is absolutely precious to me. . .like the setting of a great love story. Speaking of stories, here is one I have a feeling is about you and me.

Once upon a time. . . .the winter months seemed to pass in slow motion—each day a droning replica of the one before. From the confining walls of her home she saw green life developing in the fields, but somehow, to her, it looked like a mirage. Life should be a cool breath, as light and careless as the sparrows. She knew because it had been. But now it was heavy. Even breathing ached all the way down to her bones. Physical pain would have seemed a welcomed relief to the sorrow she swallowed and carried like a heavy stone inside her soul. On her tongue, a never-ending drumming, the Author's words: *Those who sow in tears will reap with songs of joy Those who sow in tears will reap with songs of joy Those who sow in tears will reap with songs of joy. . .* The promise was her only comfort. Hoping against all hope, she longed for joyful songs of golden sheaves and hummed herself to sleep on scores of spring nights. Until one morning's new mercy brought with it the warm embrace of early summer. Faithful and true to each stroke of His word, God scripted in harvest gold ink onto her heart, "I tell you, open your eyes and look at the fields! They are ripe for harvest." A melody of promise provided the musical score to her gathering abundant ripe sheaves, and she sang along. "I love the harvest of Your faithfulness." Then a question arose. "Is it finished? May I keep it for myself?" His Word, like eternity, is pure love. His answer just. "No, my child, lay it down on the threshing floor."

One of the behavioral side effects of caring full-time for Mycah while she endured the difficult first months of chemo, resulted in her becoming quite used to having us wait on her. You know. . .like unpaid servants we tended to her every need and desire. My husband and I both would have, at times in the early days of treatment, done literal back flips if she asked. We felt helpless in all she endured. She spent days and days on the couch or in bed with an expressionless face, unsatisfied with any number of "normally" desirable suggestions for children. "Mycah, would you like to finger paint? Well, what about decorating cookies? Would you like for me to bring you a puppy? A new toy? A million new toys? Just a drink? Ok. How about juice? I'll squeeze each grape by hand. I'll be *right* back!"

She became accustomed to being the center of our attention. Faithful to His promise, God walked with us through the first months of the hardest chemotherapy. The medicine was applied in His name and we began to see the evidence of the harvest of her returning health that we so desired. She started to feel better, and the effects of the initial, aggressive chemo lessened. Her hair even began to grown back in golden curly locks, as soft and radiant as waves of grain. We were thrilled but soon found altering from complete care and dependence to a new life of independence was an adjustment for her and us. When she clapped her hands over her head, her daddy and I no longer rushed to remove her dinner tray, awaiting our next duty with bated breath. The time had come for her to re-learn to care for herself. The time had come for us to teach her how to mature in her independence.

We started with bath time. I re-taught her to wash her returning short hair with just a tiny bit of shampoo, how to clean inside her ears and to take special care when washing the scar covering her central line where the doctors administered IV chemo each week. One night soon thereafter, she declared her desire to take a bath all on her own from start to finish. She closed the bathroom door, hid herself away for about half an hour, and then presented herself to her daddy and me. She was clean from head to toe and dressed in the pink froggy night gown I laid out for her. Her short locks were smoothed, her teeth brushed and sparkling fresh. We praised her like she won a gold medal in an Olympic bathing event. Then we tucked her in bed, kissed her sweet forehead and left her room feeling ever so proud.

But later, as I passed her bathroom on my way to bed, I got the strange feeling I stumbled into the boy's locker room after a summer camp game of canoe tipping. Dirty clothes littered the floor, a damp towel alongside, a dripping-wet washcloth hung over the side of the tub, toys floated in cold, un-drained water, toothpaste puddles congealed on the counter and Jesus-only-knows-what happened all over the mirror. I gasped and quickly put a hand over my mouth to hold back a scream.

Needless to say, I failed to teach Mycah how to finish the job of bathing herself. She would need to learn that her clean little body did not signify an end to the task. Until the bathroom is picked up, the towel hung on the hook, and her toothpaste is properly closed, the job is not complete. Incidentally, I've heard from some of my friends with teenagers, these tasks are especially hard to teach. Even they are still working on it. I am encouraged. And rightly so. God was moving mightily in the tragic circumstances and I joyfully reaped the harvest of Mycah's cancer remission as well as a powerful spiritual healing within my own heart. But we were not finished yet.

In our study of maturing from a child of God to the bride of Christ, we've done some pretty serious work. And I don't know about you, but I am really excited about a harvest. As well we should be! Carrying sheaves is something to celebrate with songs of joy! As we learned in the previous chapters, preparing the field and sowing seed in faith are very difficult steps in the process of growing. I bet you are sweaty and could use a glass of sweet tea while you look out on the fresh-cut, ripe sheaves of your labor. Perhaps let's sing a few more joyful songs and tarry over the accomplishment of some fruit for once. God has been faithful with a spiritual harvest. He is certainly worthy of all our joyful praise!

However, we will soon see there is work yet to be done.

Ripe wheat stalks are not the sign of a complete harvest. Yes, it is a good start and came at the expense of some tough choices, patient persistence, and painful waiting. But it is not finished. Just because we have some fruit in our lives as a result of preparing the field, sowing seed, and tending the field with care, does not mean we have an abundant harvest. . .yet. Take courage, the LORD is with you, mighty farmer. It is coming. Remember, He promised abundant life. (John 10:10)

Now allow me to introduce you to the threshing floor. Before you groan like Mycah does when I send her back to pick up her dirty panties, let me assure you this step will be well worth our effort. It is a tough concept, will require more faith than we can squeeze from our feeble hands, and might leave us exhausted, but it will be breathless bliss on the other side. It is going to get good, sister. Let's be princesses of perseverance.

In ancient Israel, farmers gathered the wheat harvest in the early summer months. Using sickles, they cut the ripe wheat stalks a few inches from the base and gathered them into bundles, or sheaves, singing songs of joy while doing so I imagine. The sheaves were allowed to dry completely and then workers spread the wheat onto a threshing floor. Threshing floors were typically made of flat stones or packed dirt and located on or near the top of a hill where wind could assist in the winnowing process. In order to separate the wheat seed from the shaft, an animal — most often an ox — pulled a threshing sledge (usually a big plank of wood with stone or metal attached to it) across the wheat stalks. This process crushed the wheat to allow the seed to separate from the stalks. With the stalks sufficiently crushed and the seed rendered from its husk, it was tossed into the air with large winnowing forks. The wind blew the light chaff (stalk) pieces away while the heavier seed fell back to the threshing floor. All of these steps ensured the farmer was left with only the pure, useful seed for eating or sowing. Threshing floors were highly significant in ancient days.[4] They are mentioned in Scripture as highly significant locations and, as we will learn, they hold highly significant spiritual purpose to us as well.

The purpose of threshing and sifting wheat is to remove the useful wheat kernel from the shaft and chaff, the portions minimally useful. Since we are on our way to maturing into the bride of Christ, we want to yield abundant glory for Him in order to become increasingly conformed to the likeness of Him. (Romans 8:29) For this reason, it is important to note that threshing often symbolizes a faith test in the Bible. We will look at a few examples of these faith tests in the Old Testament. Both Abraham and David have much to teach concerning faith and testing and their relationship to the threshing floor. We will glean insight into God's purpose in testing and how He intends to act toward the threshing floors of our hearts.

First let us visit father Abraham in Genesis. You might remember Abraham was a man of great faith and thus earned the name "God's friend." He left his family and home to follow God to a new and unsettled land. (Genesis 12) He and His wife, Sarah, received a son, Isaac, due to a promise God made to Abraham. He became a father at the age of 100. Sarah was 90. (Genesis 17) I can only imagine the type of faith required to bear a child at the age of 90. That fact alone gives me great encouragement. It is never too late to bear fruit for God's glory.

For the purpose of this chapter, we will look especially at Genesis chapter 22. Here we see to what lengths Abraham went to serve and obey God. Isaac is believed by Biblical scholars to be a young man at the time of these events. Verse 1 states it bluntly. No kid gloves here: *"Some time later God tested Abraham."* (v.1) There you have it. God tests His people. Sometimes we want to believe that since God loves us,

He wouldn't test us. Not so. He loves us enough to test us. (Hebrews 12:1-11) It is a primary way we mature in Him. Next we read God's commandment to Abraham. *"Take your son, Isaac, whom you love, and go to the region of Moriah. Sacrifice him there as a burnt offering on one of the mountains I will tell you about."* (v.2)

It is important to pull out a few specifics from God's commandment. First lets all gasp again at the mere thought of it. I have heard and read this commandment many times and it always feels like a bad dream. God tells (not asks, not suggests) Abraham to sacrifice his son—the son who was the incarnate evidence of a very important promise—and burn him on an altar. I find it shocking how God acknowledges the love Abraham has for his son just before He states instructions for him to end Isaac's life. Secondly, it is worth noting the specific instruction of the location where this sacrifice is to take place. God purposefully tells Abraham to go to the region of Moriah to a particular mountain. We will see later how this particular location has great significance then and now.

In the next verses of Genesis 22, we read that Abraham follows God's instructions exactly. Abraham arises early in the morning, takes Isaac and the wood for the burnt offering, and sets out for the place God told him about. Isaac carries the wood on his own back up to the mountain where he is to die. I wonder if this makes you think of another man who carried his own cross up to a hill called Calvary. Father Abraham carried the fire and the knife he would use to slay his son.

Do you even dare think what must be going through Abraham's mind? I imagine Abraham looking at his son, staring at his every move and gesture on the road to the mountain. I think he probably memorized every word the young man spoke, studied his face and expressions, and breathed deeply the scent of his hair as he embraced him. He walked with his son to his death, knowing he was being obedient to God, but hurting so deeply. I wonder if he questioned God. Did he seek confirmation? Surely he doubted his own ears. God hadn't thought this through.

Isaac must have wondered why his father was acting strangely. He might have noticed his father's long stares and troubled demeanor. The Scriptures tell us that Isaac spoke up at one point on their way together asking, *"The fire and wood are here, but where is the lamb for the burnt offering?"* (v.7) Abraham answered in prophetic faith. *"God himself will provide the lamb for the burnt offering, my son."* (v.8) Abraham bound Isaac and laid him on the altar, on top of the wood. Then he reached out his hand and took the knife to slay his son. Suddenly the angel of the LORD called out to him from heaven and instructed him not to lay a hand on the boy. Now God knew Abraham feared Him because he had not withheld from Him his son. (Genesis 22:12)

I don't know about you, but I release a very long exhale of relief when God commands Abraham to hold his hand and saves Isaac from an imminent death. Abraham was going to do it. He really was going to slay his son because he believed God in faith and trusted Him for a plan he couldn't see. He had blind faith even if it meant following God instead of following his own desires. As relieved as we may feel, we cannot miss the next event of this account. It is the most critical aspect. If we look closely with our hearts we will see Jesus.

"Abraham looked up and there in a thicket he saw a ram caught by its horns. He went over and took the ram and sacrificed it as a burnt offering instead of his son." (Genesis 22:13) A sacrifice was still required but

God provided a substitute sacrifice. Many times in the Word, Jesus is referred to and symbolized as a lamb. He indeed was the perfect lamb, without blemish sacrificed for our sins. But in this particular instance the sacrifice was a ram (in Hebrew, "ayil"- a male sheep generally more aggressive and protective of the flock). God was showing Abraham in a very tangible reality, how someday His Son (Jesus) would be provided as a substitute sacrifice for sins. Jesus is characterized here as aggressive and protective of His people. He would be the one and only sacrifice to take the place of any and all others faithful enough to believe Him for the rescue.

God esteems His Son above all else. Jesus is absolutely precious to His Father. When God sees people who resemble His Son, He can't help but bestow mercy. To not, would cheapen what Jesus did on the cross and God just won't allow that. Jesus would someday die instead of Isaac. But until that time, the ram in the thicket symbolized the once-for-all sacrifice to Abraham. Since Abraham trusted God, He spared Isaac. Instead God allowed His Son, Jesus to take the boy's place—symbolically in this Mt. Moriah testing scenario and literally thousands of years later on the cross. When God saw Abraham and Isaac willing to make a sacrifice of such high stakes, he saw the character of His Only Begotten and mercy was inevitable.

God announced the gospel in advance to Abraham. (Galatians 3:8) He placed a circumstance in Abraham and Isaac's reality in order to show Abraham the ultimate importance of His Son, Jesus' sacrifice. Not too long ago, God preached the gospel to me in review by bringing a very similar illustration of the sacrifice of the Lamb to my home, my own heart, my only daughter.

I shared in the previous chapter that I believed God promised if I let go of Mycah as my life in exchange for Him as my life, she would return to us. Although I believed in the promise and trusted Him to fulfill it, I had no idea He would test my faith so quickly and profoundly. In many ways, I feel now that it was a situation very similar to Abraham's. God promised Abraham he would have a son and be the father of nations. But then God told Abraham to kill the son from whom the promise was to come. It made no sense to Abraham, and he had no guarantees of how a dead son could possibly fulfill the promise. Yet Abraham obeyed because He believed in God's power over any circumstance. (Hebrews 11:19) Please do not think I am comparing my faith and obedience with Abraham's. But God did give us a similar command to test our faith just after making a good promise. We didn't know the outcome and found it very difficult to obey.

A month after Mycah's leukemia diagnosis, she was considered to be in remission. The aggressive chemo regiment of the induction phase of her treatment was successful. She suffered with the side effects of the drugs and we hardly recognized her in appearance or personality, but we felt encouraged by the harvest of remission. We really did sing songs of joy. However, we were not finished. Mycah's leukemia treatment came with a two and a half year chemotherapy "road map" as the doctors called it. The road ahead was still very long. As we turned our eyes unto the hills, we were afraid of what lay ahead. We stared at the mountain of the toughest choice we ever had to make. Little did I realize at the time, my feet had come to the threshing floor and soon God leaned so heavily upon me, I felt crushed under the weight of His threshing sledge.

Upon achieving remission, Mycah had to begin a new phase of the treatment protocol. With it, came the offer to enroll her in a nation-wide clinical trial. Leukemia treatment advanced a long way in a relatively short amount of time. Children had a very slim chance of survival before the 1970s, but, at the time of Mycah's treatment, the survival rates reached into the 80 percentile range. However scientists want to continue to develop better means of treating leukemia, the most common type of childhood cancer. The point of this clinical study was to test the effectiveness of increased dosages and increased treatments without having an increase in negative outcomes. Basically, they wanted to see how far they could push the treatment before it proved more harmful than beneficial.

We could enlist her, or we could choose not to. If involved in the study, she would be randomized (like flipping a coin) and placed into one of four treatment plans: the standard treatment (the best known treatment to date), or one of three other more intensified treatment plans with various combinations of increased dosages and increased treatments. We must agree to the study before we knew the outcome of her randomization and we would not receive any type of benefit for choosing to do so. Her treatments would not be free, we would not be paid, and she would be treated by the hospital either way we decided. Compensation or free care never played a role in our decision, but I want to describe the options as we understood them.

Drugs that have terrifying side effects, increased procedures and dosages, and the words "risks yet unknown" sent my mind reeling in a whirl of doubt and fear. What if she needs the increased treatments to heal her? What if the increased treatment causes her unnecessary harm? What do we do? How can we decide what is best for her? My heart and mind were once again awash in a turbulent sea of what ifs and if onlys. When I couldn't stand another ominous computer screen or protocol packet full of jumbled medical terms staring back at me, I went to my knees to the Father. It was a last ditch effort to find an answer that wasn't mine, but left to His sovereignty.

Proverbs 3:5-6 hit me with a new reality. *"Trust in the LORD with all your heart and lean not in your own understanding; in all your ways acknowledge him, and he will make your paths straight."* I promised I wanted to take the straight path on this road map more than anything. Then God immediately commanded me to trust Him regarding His instruction found just a few verses down the page. Proverbs 3:27: *"Do not withhold good from those who deserve it, when it is in your power to act."*

Cancer treatments have come a long way in a short amount of time because other parents have volunteered their children to be studied and "tried" upon. I thought about the parents who struggled with this type of decision before us. I knew Mycah had a fairly good chance to live past cancer because of their sacrifice. I thought about how parents in the future would want me to decide now. Ask yourself what you would have wanted us to decide if you knew your child or grandchild would someday have to fight leukemia. Wouldn't you want the best tested treatment for her? For the good of the deserving children who will follow, God commanded us to place Mycah in the study.

I felt the charge, but doubted my own ears. Surely God didn't mean this for me, not Mycah. I sought confirmation. Did I hear God right? I wondered if God was even aware of the consequences of this decision. Surely He hadn't thought this one through. Perhaps she was placed in an arm of the treatment that caused her to have terrible outcomes. I didn't want to do the study. I wanted to choose "standard treatment" for her. It was a time tested protocol with good results. The risks loomed too high if I offered her to the chance of the study's random determination.

With everything in me, I wanted to say no to God. My instincts, my head, my heart, and even close family members were all against the study. God, through His Word, was the only One pointing to it. I had to decide. When the rubber meets the road, who do I trust? It was a threshing test I thought would kill me or worse, kill Mycah. The choice came without a promise of the specific outcome I desperately wanted. God asked me to come to a place where I trusted Him no matter the outcome. He asked me boldly, "If she is healed completely, will you praise Me? If she dies, will you praise Me? If she lives, but is a remnant of her former self, will you praise Me? Will you trust Me more than your own understanding? Am I God of everything or am I God only when things go the way you think best?" It was the hardest test I ever took and the stakes had eternal consequences. While my mind and heart cried a silent "no," my body and soul answered "yes."

With a mustard seed-sized measure of faith, we went to the cancer clinic on our scheduled appointment date to place Mycah on the altar. I mean in the study. I memorized every word my precious daughter spoke, studied her face and expressions, and breathed deeply the scent of her soft bald head as I embraced her. I knew I had to be obedient to God, but I hurt so deeply. The oncologist entered the room with the necessary paperwork to enlist Mycah in the clinical study. She once again began to explain the four different possible outcomes of the randomization to help us make a decision to enroll Mycah or not. She needed to be certain we understood the significant differences of each of the study's four possible arms, as well as what we were agreeing to do by allowing Mycah to be randomized into one of those study arms. I interrupted her mid sentence with a feeble and choked, "We are going to enroll her in the study. Please just go do the randomization and then tell us only the requirements and risks of the arm of the study she's in. We believe because of our God, there will be nothing random about her placement." I know I must have looked like a woman on death row, making her last request. Surely I was not the living evidence of one convinced of the power of the God she professed. I couldn't even look her in the eye. Our doctor handed us the paperwork and consent forms. We signed it with what felt like the very blood of our child. She left slowly, looking perplexed by our decision and resulting behavior. Silence hung in the air. White hot fear pounded in my weary heart and soon I felt numb. It seemed eternity came to an end while we waited for the doctor to come back with the results of Mycah's random placement. Chris and I didn't speak a word to one another but looked pale as death itself as we felt we stood over our only child with a sacrificial knife in our hands. . . .when suddenly the angel of the LORD intervened.

The doctor entered the room and informed us that Mycah was randomly selected to receive the "standard treatment" arm of the study. She had a 25% chance of receiving the protocol we hoped for (no extra or higher doses of chemo or increased time of treatment). We trusted Him instead of ourselves, and the result was mercy. I couldn't help but wonder if God really deals in random selections. I found the answer in Psalm 16:5. *"LORD, you have assigned me my portion and my cup; you have made my lot secure."* In other words, nothing about Mycah's placement was random. The portion of treatment and chemo were determined by Almighty God—and not by a fearful, faithless mother. And although we didn't know exactly how it would turn out, we knew her road map was maintained and directed by the LORD. He makes paths straight.

I experienced a "ram in the thicket" moment. I held my hand over my daughter ready to sacrifice her life for the ones who will follow her into the nightmare of childhood cancer. Somewhere in the mess of fear and doubt, God saw someone who looked like His Son being offered to Him on an altar. He couldn't help but allow His mercy to flow. Isaiah 54:3 describes the ultimate significance of what Jesus did for me ". . .*He was pierced for my transgressions, He was crushed for my iniquities; the punishment that brought me peace was upon Him.*" (personal paraphrase) When I offered Mycah as a sacrifice, Jesus stepped in as a ram in a thicket and rescued her. . .and me. In that exact moment— upon the threshing floor of my heart – my down-turned eyes lifted to behold His inconceivable beauty. Love at first sight.

God presented the gospel to me in review just as He presented the gospel to Abraham in advance. Jesus is still and always the substitute sacrifice. He took Mycah's place and sacrificed His life in exchange for hers. When the gospel becomes more than a story you've heard in Sunday school and becomes a living breathing reality in your circumstance, it changes you forever. When I saw Jesus offer Himself for me, and became aware of the mercy His love prompted from God, I was captivated and spiritually spent, panting face down on the threshing floor of my heart. I fell for Jesus as the uncontested lover of my soul in that place. The threshing floor is sacred ground. It is where I experienced the crazy mad passion of my Savior. He slays me with His love.

The threshing floor became the turning point for our whole cancer experience. Mycah was never one time re-admitted to the hospital throughout the entire two and a half year treatment period. Not once. She went to clinic for treatment and care but never required a hospital stay. "Extremely rare" is how the doctors described it. "Extremely merciful" is how I do — a straight path. She flew through her protocol, has no evidence of late effects from chemotherapy, and her compassion and understanding for others going through difficult times tenders my heart. I watch her live and move and breathe and I just can't believe all these things have been added unto her. Hallelujah.

Threshing is testing. True faith requires the willing sacrifice of all that you hold precious and dear to your heart. When the sacrifice resonates in God's heart as a likeness to His Son, mercy flows. I released Mycah to God's care, but He wasted little time in putting my trust to a faith test on the threshing floor. He did the same with Abraham, now we will look at how He did it to King David.

Remember how God specifically commanded Abraham go to a particular place on a particular mountain in the region of Moriah to sacrifice Isaac? (Genesis 22:2) Let us visit that very same location again, this time fourteen generations later, where we will see King David face a threshing faith-test. First Chronicles chapter 21 and Second Samuel chapter 24 give the details of the account.

From the text we learn David's pride incited him to sin against God by commanding a census taken of Israel. David acknowledged his sin after the number of fighting men was reported to him. In verse 8 of 1 Chronicles 21 David said to God, *"I have sinned greatly by doing this. Now, I beg you, take away the guilt of your servant, I have done a very foolish thing."* The word of the LORD is made known to David. God asks David to make a choice between three options to be carried out upon him and all of Israel as punishment. One: three years of famine. Two: three months of being swept away by their enemies. Three: three days of the sword of the LORD—days of plague in the land, with the angel of the LORD ravaging every part of Israel.

God offered David a multiple choice test. I imagine David hated to make the decision between any of the three options. Perhaps he should have flipped a coin and decided randomly. As it were, he reasoned punishment at the hand of the LORD is better than falling into the hands of enemies and chose answer number three. So the LORD indeed sent a plague throughout the land and the angel of the LORD was sent to destroy Israel. Seventy thousand of the people from one end of Israel to the other died. In verse 16 and 17 of 2 Samuel 24 we see again mercy flow from a sacrifice resembling Jesus. David's eyes were opened to see the angel striking down the people and he said to the LORD, *"I am the one who has sinned and done wrong. These are but sheep. What have they done? Let your hand fall upon me and my family."* (v.17)

I wonder if all along, God was waiting for David to offer another solution to the test. Answer D, if you will. Because when David asked for the punishment to be upon him instead of the people of Israel, the LORD orders the angel to "stay thy hand." Again we see a hand raised in a position of sacrifice and again we see God command the hand to be withdrawn when the one on the threshing floor displays Christ-like character. When, like Jesus did at the cross, David offers his life in exchange for the ones afflicted, God's mercy flowed with heavy grieving. (2 Samuel 24:16)

Look carefully at the last part of verse 16: *"The angel of the LORD was then **at the threshing floor of Araunah the Jebusite."*** (emphasis added) This particular threshing floor is located on Mt. Moriah and is the *exact same* location where Abraham was commanded to withdraw his hand as he intended to sacrifice Isaac fourteen generations before. It amazes me how consistently God teaches about sacrifice and mercy through the importance of His Son's actions on the cross, all the while, consistently bringing us to a particular location to test and prove faith—the threshing floor. I wonder if the amount of time a soul stays on the threshing floor is related to the amount of time it takes that soul to display the character of Jesus? I am convinced a season of threshing comes to an end when the eyes of our hearts are opened to the inconceivable beauty of the One who takes our place—when we see the ram in the thicket and recognize the sacrificial love of Christ. You will never be more captivated by Him than when you realize just what He did by trading places with you on your own personal threshing floor.

Look down at your own feet in your current circumstance. Are you standing on a threshing floor? Perhaps you feel the threshing sledge on your back and are being beaten, crushed, broken and torn. Is God testing your faith? How far are you really willing to go to obey Him? Maybe you've let go of everything and are holding onto only God. What if He wants to push you even further? I am convinced He wants to teach His people about the importance of His Son's sacrifice in the middle of each one's reality—just as He taught Abraham, David, me, and countless others throughout His story. The more we resemble His Son, the more readily He pours out His mercy. I wonder if He is testing your appearance against the image of Jesus.

Will you lay down your life for another? You will never look more like your Redeemer.

Let this fall hard on your reality: testing is threshing and threshing is painful. The stakes are high and often eternal. The threshing floor of your heart is where God is testing your trust in Him. Prove faithful by resembling His Son's pure love, regardless of the circumstances, regardless of the outcome. You may be exhausted, beaten, and terrified on the threshing floor. Your eyes may be tightly squinted closed as you await the impending sword of sacrifice. But open your eyes and look up, sister. You once were blind, but now you can see His inconceivable beauty. God aims to slay you only with His love. There is a ram in the thicket. He is Jesus –aggressive and protective– and He will take your place. It is what He came to do. You were chosen for this before the creation of the world. Songs of joy sung over sheaves were just the beginning.

The threshing floor is where you first recognize Him as the One who took your place and He first recognizes you — no longer a child — but a pure and faithful woman of the Word. And it is love at first sight. The threshing floor is the setting for the greatest Love story of all time. It is the beginning of your very own "Once upon a time. . ."

"Because [she] loves me, "says the LORD, "I will rescue [her];
I will protect [her], for [she] acknowledges my name. [She] will call upon
me, and I will answer [her]. . .
(Psalm 91:14-15a)

*"I will contend with those who contend with you,
and your children I will save."* (Isaiah 49:25b)

Chapter 5

Sifted as Wheat

Hello, my name is Angie and I am a recovering television addict. I shared with you that at the time Mycah was diagnosed with cancer, I had a storehouse full of unrepentant sins and strongholds from years of hiding my heart from the Healer. Many of them I will not share because frankly, I don't have to. It is private. God knows. But I will tell you of my addiction to television—specifically reality television. "The trashier, the better" was my motto when it came to choosing my nightly entertainment. Twisted morality exploited in cheap one hour portions had me rushing to the sofa most evenings. I won't go into exhaustive detail, because only the LORD needs to know the full extent of my sickness. But I will say that even as I write this book, a new season of *The Bachelor* is on. This is the very first season I have not watched every single one of the "most dramatic rose ceremony ever"s. I have consecrated myself and decided to fast from it that I may be clear-minded and self controlled so I can pray. It is sacrificial beyond my worst nightmare. But yet, I rise in the morning, wash my face and put oil on my head so no one will suspect I am fasting (see Matthew 6:17-18 if you are confused. . .I am making a bit of a joke).

Seriously, though, The LORD and I have done some serious work in this area of my life. Please do not hear me to say watching television is a sin. I don't believe it is. However, my trashy tastes and exhaustive time devotion to it were not beneficial. So the LORD exhorted me to sift those habits from my life. He taught me to not conform any longer to the pattern of this world, but to be transformed by the renewing of my mind that I might know His good, perfect and pleasing will. (Romans 12:2) Filling my mind with the drama of a temptation island or the desperation of housewives from various cities was like hoarding garbage in a palace meant for priceless treasure. Having said all that, I must mention a show I saw on television recently that dropped my jaw to the floor. It is called *Clean House*.[5] Have you ever seen it?

Oh my. If you haven't, let me tell you the premise of this show. It is to highlight a particular family's habit of living in disorganized clutter. A crew of 'professionals' including an interior designer, an organizational expert, a carpenter, and a life coach, descend upon a chosen home to help the homeowners sort through their clutter, filth, chaos, and mayhem. In a matter of days, the home is transformed into a sanitary, organized, and inviting space. I am certainly guilty of being a clean freak (code for control freak) at times so this show almost had my blood pressure to stroke levels the first time I watched it. As it turned out, the television station was running an all day marathon of this program and I sinned by sitting and watching about four episodes in a row. It was as captivating as watching a live train wreck and I couldn't take my eyes off of it.

92

One particular family had an entire house full of what they called "collectibles." It was really junk, newspapers, old magazines, and miscellaneous mess. The show's organizational expert did everything short of standing on her head to help convince them to purge their living space of the massive heaps of collected junk. They refused saying it was all treasure and it added priceless value to their lives. Dejected, the cute and perky organizational girl commenced the mountain task of organizing the mess. Over several days, she sorted through all of it, organized it into thematic categories and stored it in hundreds of large plastic bins with color-coded lids. She stacked the storage bins alphabetically and in rows three to four bins high. The bins consumed almost the entire large upstairs living area.

I had to laugh when the family saw their space in the big "remove your blind folds" moment. The family was elated to see all of their treasures stored in such nifty fashion. The once polished and perky organizational expert now frazzled and frustrated explained how she placed and catalogued each item so they could locate each one easily. She doubted their desire to do so since most of the items she spent days sorting looked as if no one had handled them in decades. But the homeowners insisted their possessions were worth the effort to be stored in such a precise way. If you ask me, the family wasted their joy on garbage. Yes, organized and neatly packaged — but still garbage.

After allowing the family a few moments to delight in the newly organized space, the interior designer opened his laptop computer to show the family a virtual model of what he planned to do with the large living area if they had been willing to part with their "treasures." The plans included a beautiful seating arrangement with new furniture, a big flat panel television, a pool table, and work-out equipment. The looks on the family members' faces were epic as they laid eyes on the impressive plan. You could literally see their elation over stacks of storage bins holding old napkins and celebrity bobble heads morph into lament. Understanding their foolishness was a bitter pill to swallow. They finally realized by holding on to junk, they were forfeiting something not only extravagantly useful and enjoyable, but free of cost to them! The interior designer said, "Here is what I had planned for you, but since you insisted on keeping all of this trash, I was unable to give it to you."

The interviews of the family at the end of the show revealed their regret for their stubborn refusal to part with their belongings. They finally saw the stuff they thought so important for what it was — trash — compared to what they could have enjoyed. I felt a twisted satisfaction when they were disappointed. Ha! That's what you get! I laughed at their foolishness.

But then I was convicted by the Holy Spirit about more than the four hours I spent on the couch watching television. I felt the LORD speak into my heart, "Angie, when you refuse to sift worthless foolishness from your life, you forfeit the treasure I have planned for you." Ouch. A bitter pill to swallow.

1 Corinthians 2:9 says, *"No eye has seen, no ear has heard, no mind has conceived what God has prepared for those who love him."* In the days at hand, I want to see, hear and realize all He has prepared for me. I do not want to leave a single thing unclaimed. Heaven forbid I be so stubborn to refuse the Holy Spirit when He purges meaningless mayhem from my life. An abundant life is His offer and it is foolish to think of missing out on His free gift. Let us look again to the threshing

floor. Adequately broken, now is the time to separate the trash for a life of abundance.

In the previous chapter we learned how ripe sheaves are to be celebrated with songs of joy, but a harvest is not complete until the sheaves are threshed and sifted. Threshing removes the seed from the stalk as a result of being beaten or crushed by a heavy object. Sifting is separating the seed from the chaff. To sift is to sort the trash from the true. In ancient days, once the dry wheat stalks were adequately crushed upon the threshing floor by a threshing sledge, workers tossed the wheat and chaff mixture into the air with large winnowing forks. The wind blew away the light chaff and the grain fell back down to the threshing floor, leaving a heap of harvested seed.

In this chapter, we will be looking specifically at the sifting process. Spiritually speaking, threshing often signifies a faith test given by God. Sifting, on the other hand, often signifies a process of separating trash from true at the hands of Satan. Spiritual sifting is an all out attempt of the enemy to destroy you and cause you to quit. Satan intends to accuse you until you believe yourself to be all trash (chaff). God permits sifting to rid you of the ugliness of self and leave only usable, authentic seed to make you more like His Son — the Bread of Life. The outcome of a season of sifting is left to the free-will faith of the sifted one.

Many people are uncomfortable with the subject of evil or the enemy. Studying Satan should never become the sole focus or primary objective in our walk with Christ, as he can cause us to fall while our eyes are not on Jesus. However, it is important to be aware of the warnings of Christ concerning the enemy so that we can stand when under attack. It is easy to disregard the notion of evil and its power in the world. If fact, it would be nice to pretend as if it were not real. However, if we believe God's Word to be true, we have to believe there are dark and evil forces at work against us. Ephesians 6:12 states, *"For our struggle is not against flesh and blood, but against the rulers, against the authorities, against the powers of this dark world and against the spiritual forces of evil in the heavenly realms."*

It may be hard for us to imagine how God could allow Satan access to one of His children. If He loves us, why would He let us be sifted at the hands of the enemy? It is a valid question and God can handle our asking. In fact, I asked Him the same question in my own season of sifting at the hands of the enemy. Before I share my story, I want us to look into the Scriptures for truth regarding this very concept. In Luke chapter 22, we see Jesus speak of sifting to His disciples just before He is betrayed into the hands of the enemy and crucified. We are going to peek in at a moment at the Passover table in the upper room to see what we can learn.

Jesus said, "Simon, Simon, Satan has asked to sift you as wheat. But I have prayed for you, Simon, that your faith may not fail. And when you have turned back, strengthen your brothers." But he replied, "Lord, I am ready to go with you to prison and to death." Jesus answered, "I tell you, Peter, before the rooster crows today, you will deny three times that you know me." (Luke 22:31-34)

These four verses are rich with instruction, prophesy, and truth we can apply to our 21st century circumstances. Look closely. In the two verses just before Jesus tells Simon Satan asked to sift him as wheat, Jesus conferred on His disciples a kingdom, telling them they will eat and drink at His table in His kingdom and sit on thrones. Then immediately afterward, we see Jesus address Peter by the name he was known by before Jesus called him to follow. Jesus tells Simon-Peter Satan has asked to sift him as wheat. The original language signifies He was not only addressing Peter, but was addressing all of His disciples and thus including you and me. Peter intends to dispute Jesus, saying he is ready. He is ready to go to any lengths to follow his best friend and teacher. Jesus knows Peter is not ready for such commitment and predicts Peter's three time denial before the sunrise. However, a season of sifting will do wonders to help prove Him completely true. I think we are often like Simon Peter. We believe we are ready for the kingdom. We desire to sit on thrones at Christ's table. We want what He has to offer but Jesus knows we are not qualified to receive. A season of sifting will reveal the truth. Are we trash or are we true?

There are three points from Luke 22:31-32 we need to focus upon as we learn about the concept of sifting in our growth from a child of God to the bride of Christ.

1. Satan must receive permission to obtain access to one of God's children.
2. Faith is critical to a victory over evil.
3. Sifting produces fruit for your own good and yields strength for others.

First let us look closely at the first point: **Satan must ask permission to sift one of God's children.** In Job chapter 1, we see a conversation between God and Satan. God grants Satan access to everything God's servant Job has. But God restricts him from laying a finger on

Job himself. Clearly God gives Satan permission to sift Job, but He also gives conditions to which even Satan must comply. I think it is interesting to note here that even Satan must obey God's commands. But know also that Satan will exploit the access he is given for his evil advantage and our detriment.

In James 1:13-14, we see another way in which Satan is given access to one of God's own. *"When tempted, no one should say, "God is tempting me." For God cannot be tempted by evil, nor does He tempt anyone; but each one is tempted when, by his own evil desire, he is dragged away and enticed."* These Scriptures tell us that it is possible to be dragged away and enticed by evil when we are not directly under the shadow of God's protection because of our own evil desires. When we have wandered from God, Satan has access simply because we are away from God's protective covering.

Does that mean we are at risk of losing our salvation? No. Romans 8:38 assures us as God's children. It says nothing—not even demons—will be able to separate us from the love of God that is in Christ Jesus our Lord. John 10:29 tell us no one can snatch out of the Father's hand [s]he who follows Christ. Hebrews 13:5 and Matthew 28:20 say the LORD is with us always, wherever we go.

If you have believed in your heart and confessed with your mouth that Jesus Christ is Lord, your eternity is secure. *But* it is possible to suffer loss—fellowship with God, rewards, blessings, abundance. (1 Corinthians 3:11-15) A superficial and selfish person's work will be burned while [s]he will be saved only as one escaping the flames. Paul even teaches of turning a believing brother in Christ over to Satan for the destruction of the sinful nature so that the spirit may be saved. (1 Corinthians 5:5)

Obviously there is value and glory at stake in the process of sifting for both God and evil. God intends sifting to destroy the sinful nature and render one more faithful and true that she can more effectively cause Kingdom gain and receive Kingdom blessings. Satan intends the sifting to destroy God's child's resolve rendering her useless for further Kingdom gain and thus forfeiting Kingdom blessings. In the doing, Satan hurts God as he hurts one of His own. The stakes are high with both eternal and present consequences. The struggle is the essence of spiritual war over the sons and daughters of man.

At the risk of appearing to have lost my mind, I want to share a few scary recurring nightmares I've had. It may sound strange, but looking back, it seems too prophetic to be coincidence. I had these nightmares on a regular basis when Mycah was very young (before her cancer diagnosis), while living far from the fold of my First Love. The setting was often different but the theme was always the same: A man with evil intentions lurks outside an open door. Upon noticing him, I close the door and turn a number of locks, latches and dead bolts to secure my safety. I grasp the door knob to ensure it is completely locked, testing it for my peace of mind. The door opens, proving the locks are not functioning. I close the door again, turn the locks, and test the door's security to find the door still opens and the locks are useless. The commotion makes the evil one pursue with greater intensity. I fidget with the locks unsuccessfully and then rush to lean on the door with my full strength when, just as the door begins to close, evil arrives at the threshold. Inevitably I always woke at that point, breathless and cold but perspiring, terrified as the nightmare seemed very real.

The other dream occurred less often but was much more disturbing. I hesitate to mention it here because it is horrific. However I feel it is important to share as it relates to this chapter's subject. In this nightmare, an evil man breaks into our home, takes toddler Mycah from her bed and then comes into the room where I am. He clutches her in his hands as she cries and reaches for me. I beg him to give her to me but instead he uses her little body as a weapon. He holds her by the ankles and swings her body like a club, beating me. His actions leave her lifeless and me dead inside.

I am aware of the disturbing nature of these dreams and shudder to think of them again. To write them down is especially brutal. It is now my belief these dreams were, in some way, a warning of an approaching season of sifting at the hands of the enemy. Evil would attempt and succeed in gaining access to my home. My own efforts would prove futile and evil would use someone I love as life itself to hurt me. It is not my intention to evoke fear, but to testify to my experience and strengthen my sisters.

As it came to pass, Mycah became very sick with malignant blood cancer at the age of four. A cancer entered her body and took up residence, destroying life as it rapidly consumed her healthy bone marrow. Her physical illness could have been a representation of my spiritual illness. In the very deepest marrow of my soul, a cancerous fear had taken hold, destroying the life God intended in sin. I am not blaming Satan for Mycah's cancer or my sins, but I do believe he intended to exploit them and use them to accuse me of being nothing but trash. So as the circumstances were allowed to come to us through the sovereign fingers of God, Satan planned to destroy Mycah, me, and our entire family, rendering us useless to the Kingdom of Glory. Contrarily, God hoped to strengthen us for a calling powerfully useful to His Kingdom. A season of sifting had begun—a war with eternal and present consequences raged in unseen battlefields disguised in ordinary life.

There is a second point from Luke 22: 31-34 we will focus on for truth regarding sifting. Jesus told Peter Satan had asked to sift him and all the others as wheat. Then Jesus says He has prayed for Peter's faith to not fail. This teaches us that **faith is critical to a victory over evil**.

Jesus predicts Peter would deny knowing Him three times before the rooster crowed that very day. Luke 22:54-62 gives the account. Peter indeed denies knowing Christ three times to save himself from persecution. Verses 60 and 61 break my heart. When accused of being with Jesus for a third time, *"Peter replied, 'Man I don't know what you're talking about!' Just as he was speaking, the rooster crowed. The Lord turned and looked straight at Peter. . ."* Not only did Peter disown Christ three times to save his own skin, but he looked right into the eyes of Jesus, fully aware of his faithlessness. Verse 62 tells us Peter went outside and wept bitterly.

At the Passover table, Peter said he was ready to follow Jesus unto death. That very night he denied knowing Jesus three times to avoid it and Jesus looked right at him as the third denial fell from Peter's lips. Jesus would soon be crucified and laid behind a stone. Peter must have been destroyed at the thought of his last encounter with Jesus. I assume Satan jumped at the opportunity to accuse Peter of being a worthless failure. In the days to come, a sifting at the hands of Satan caused Peter to go back to his former life of a common fisherman. (John 21:3) It appeared as if Satan had won. Simon Peter was no longer a powerhouse for God's kingdom, but returned to that from which he came. Sister, if you've had a life-changing Jesus experience, never buy into Satan's lies. He will try to tell you the whole thing was false or that you're a failure so that you will return to your old life. Don't you fall for it. You were meant for glory.

In the following verses of John chapter 21, we see Jesus appear after His death and resurrection to His disciples and reinstate Peter as a faithful apostle. Jesus gives Peter three opportunities to proclaim his love for Him and in doing so Jesus redeems each of Peter's three denials through faith. Little did Peter know at the time, Jesus had just returned from defeating death and hell rendering Satan's accusations null and void. Jesus came from hell holding victory over the enemy in His nail-scarred hands for Peter — and for everyone else whose faith remains in Him.

About a year into Mycah's season of fighting leukemia and my season of spiritual sifting, she awoke in the middle of the night after having a terrifying dream. As she told me about her nightmare, I immediately was shaken as fear stirred and tossed in the currents of my mind. I couldn't believe her words, but I wrote them just as she described the details in my journal:

"A crocodile monster who didn't walk – he floated – came into our house. He went down the hall and into you and Daddy's bedroom and looked at you sleeping but he did not touch you or attack you. He passed by. Then he went into my room and put me into a net and wrapped me in it. I screamed a little. Then you (meaning Mommy) came in the room and took his hands off the net and untied me. Then the crocodile dragon floated away and disappeared."

Revelation 12 refers to the enemy as "the great dragon — that ancient serpent." My five year old child described him as a crocodile monster. At the risk of sounding insane, I believe her dream meant evil had gained access to our home, our lives. My recurring nightmares had come to my reality.

Mycah was my most treasured possession. I believed I could protect her. In turn, I foolishly thought I could protect my own heart from being hurt again the way it was hurt when my daddy died suddenly in a plane crash many years before. Satan knew my greatest fear was losing my daughter. So he passed on the opportunity to hurt me or my husband and chose to target Mycah. Knowing that by destroying her, he would destroy me and my marriage as well. He is cunning with the access He is given and certainly no match for mortals.

I came face to face with the reality that I might lose her one night in an ambulance. I begged God, "not Mycah! LORD, take anything — just not Mycah!" God allowed me to take a good, long look at my worst fear. Satan was betting that I would be destroyed in a mess of doubt, anger, and disillusionment. He was betting that I would trust in my own ability to protect her — he had every reason to believe I would continue down the path I had taken for so long — and in so doing, would lose her. He told me some very believable lies while I felt so afraid in those first weeks after the night in the ambulance. He went about the deception and the accusation that left me struck down in unspeakable pain. *"It's your fault. You've messed up too bad. You never deserved her. You aren't good enough. How could a God who is supposed to love you, allow this to happen. . .again? God can't be trusted. He will surely turn His back on a failure like you. Do what you think is right because God won't save her."*

Yes, his attempts to steal, kill, and destroy were in full swing. However, Christ had another purpose for us. He meant to use the mess I had made for His glory. You see, His specialty is turning any affliction, any circumstance of suffering, any curse into a blessing. (Deuteronomy 23:5) What's more, I believe He takes extreme pleasure in using Satan to accomplish His Kingdom's gain. All along Satan wanted to burn me in his flames, but he ended up fanning the flames of a love and passion for Christ. Flames that forged a weapon fit for work to refute the tongue that accuses. (Isaiah 54:16-17)

I wonder what the powers of darkness thought when they saw me look to the Word for the first time with eyes hungry for the Truth? I wonder what happened in the heavenly realms when Chris and I knelt together in prayer and offered Mycah to Jesus? I would love to know what happened in hell when I cried out to my Redeemer and laid down my fear so He could exchange it for His peace. The enemy must have known the moment I fell in love with Christ and gave my whole heart over to Him, would be the moment he would be hurled down from our home.

Admittedly, I was troubled by Mycah's dream. But upon further examination of it with the help of Jesus, I was able to understand it more fully. It was a dream of victory! I was able to take the hands of the evil one off of her. I know that I am certainly no match for Satan on my own, but as a servant of the LORD, no weapon forged against me will prevail. (Isaiah 54:17) James 4:7 says it this way: *"Submit yourselves, then, to God. Resist the devil, and he will flee from you."* Mycah said in her dream he floated away and disappeared.

Because of faith in Jesus, what Satan intended to destroy is now a reflection of God's glory. I once asked why God would allow one of His children to be turned over to the hand of Satan for a season of sifting. If He loves us, why would He allow it? God allowed me, through my own circumstances in a personal season of sifting, to understand. In allowing Satan to sift His children, God achieves the ultimate retribution over the enemy. Satan becomes a tool in which God uses for His glory. It is how God turns evil into workers for His harvest. Paul said it like this, *"We. . .speak a message of wisdom among the mature, but not the wisdom of this age or of the rulers of this age, who are coming to nothing. No, we speak of God's secret wisdom, a wisdom that has been hidden and that God destined for our glory before time began. None of the rulers of this age understood it, for if they had, they would not have crucified the Lord of glory."* (1 Corinthians 2:6-8) God turned the tables on Satan's plot. Just when that serpent thought he won, Christ's death became the key to life. Can you even begin to imagine how angry Satan becomes, how much regret he experiences upon realizing that God used his sick intentions to bring ultimate glory and gain for heaven's Kingdom?

I get great satisfaction in knowing Satan regrets the day he dared to touch my child. Christ went into the fires of hell to pursue and defeat the accuser once and for all. It only takes faith in Jesus to join Him in victory over that ancient snake. If we will comply in faith, God makes Satan regret the day he dared to touch His children. We can taste righteous anger and share in His triumphant victory in our reality.

If you are in a season of sifting, don't you dare believe the father of lies. (John 8:44) He will accuse you of being all trash. Don't buy it. You are of great value to God. He sent His only Son to buy you with His blood. The fact that Satan has asked to sift you should bring you great hope. Wake up and see. He fears what you could be if you dare to put your full faith in the One who defeated him. Make him regret the day he dared to touch you. Allow Jesus to turn you, in your circumstance, into Satan's worst nightmare.

The last point we are going to focus on from Luke 22 is this: **Sifting produces fruit for your own good and yields strength for others.** Sifting allows the chaff to be blown away and the true seed to be left as an abundant harvest. That is our goal. We want an abundant harvest for the glory of God. We want Him to bear fruit in and through our spiritually mature lives. When you survive a season of sifting, not only do you taste the sweet victory over the enemy, but you are left with useful seed to plant in others, feeding them on God's glory. Now the sinful nature has been separated from your spirit and you are closer to becoming conformed to the likeness of Jesus—the Bread of Life.

Peter experiences the fruit of his personal season of sifting. In John 21 we see Jesus give Peter the task of caring for His sheep. He commands him to "Feed my lambs." Remember in Luke 22: 32, Christ tells Peter when he turns back, to strengthen his brothers. A season of sifting is useful to bear fruit in your own life, but it also allows you to strengthen others with the seed of your faith. Indeed Peter realizes this truth in his reality. Instead of a chicken shaking in fear at the sound of a rooster, he becomes the rock on which Jesus builds his church, winning many lives for Christ, performing miracles through the Holy Spirit—even boldly following Christ into prison and death.

The fact that I am now writing a book testifying to the truth of Scripture proves Jesus' statements to Peter and His other followers. I count it a miracle. I was living according to my own flesh. Biding time in a prison of fear, until circumstance brought a season of sifting I thought I would never survive. My only daughter was my life and to lose her would be my death. Satan intended to prove me all trash. God used the situation to bring Himself glory. In faith, I dared to believe Jesus for my every move and He didn't disappoint. On the other side of the sifting, I find myself in a position to open my mouth and speak of things my mind never conceived I would ever see or hear. I can now share the abundant harvest to strengthen my sisters. He is faithful to every stroke of His Word. Glory!

There was a day just before Mycah was finished with all of her cancer treatments when God allowed us to realize just how victorious we were through His Son. I had had an especially difficult week. The days had been long and frustrating and I was at the end of myself. I must have looked like a homeless wreck of a woman, but I ran my legs up to the church as fast as they would take me and plopped my tear-stained mess into a chair in my Wednesday night ladies Bible study group. Afterward, I cried and shared with a few of my sisters about some of my frustrations. They prayed for me and then one of my dear sisters insisted on blessing my family with groceries that very night. I came home overflowing with the daily bread that the Lord provided through her and my tears refused to dry at the thought of the tender mercies. I got out of the car, my hands full of bags, and started toward the garage to go inside. I stopped suddenly at the sight that turned my insides-out. A snake was slithering into the garage — into my HOME. A serpent! Here I am with arms full of blessings and a dang snake is in my way. Sometimes the LORD speaks subtly and sometimes He speaks LITERALLY.

He was giving me a chance to redeem the nightmares of evil entering my home. I shouted out in pure instinct, "CHRIS!" Of course my man was inside caring for our daughter and had no idea I was outside in crisis. Now before you get mad at me for not killing the snake myself, remember to look at the situation with your spiritual eyes. When we are under threat from evil, we have to call out to our

"Head," the Provider, the Eternal Bridegroom. So this spiritual lesson being played out on the soil of earth's reality, made me call out for my earthly bridegroom. I didn't know it at the time, but it wasn't that I was too scared to kill the snake myself. I was just being spiritually discerning (wink). Just then my bridegroom hero, Chris, came through the door of the house into the garage. Mycah, in her pajamas, followed closely. I breathlessly said, "There's a snake!"

He grabbed the aluminum Louisville slugger by the garage door and made his way over to the serpent. I heard my voice suddenly turn deep and sinister say, "KILL. IT." Within a second, its head was smashed flat and it was no longer a threat.

Before drifting to sleep that night, I read Psalm 91:13 aloud. Psalm 91 was the anthem of the season of leukemia for me. From the very beginning, it is the Scriptures the LORD used to capture my hard heart and turn it toward Him. Verse 13: *"You will tread upon the lion and the cobra; you will trample the great lion and **the serpent**."* (emphasis added)

Indeed.

I told Chris I was going to look up the Hebrew meaning of the word "trample" in that Scripture. He replied that he thought there should be a photo of an aluminum Louisville slugger on the page of the concordance.

Indeed. Sweet victory in Jesus.

If you are in the throes of a hellish sifting, put your faith in Jesus. He has gone ahead of you into the depths of the fire. He has been there, defeated that. All you have to do is follow Him in faith. God may allow you to be sifted at the enemy's hand, but Jesus won't let go of yours as you press on through the flames. He will hold your hand every step of the way and lead you to the other side. When you get there, extend your hand back to strengthen another who is still feeling the heat. In doing so, God allows you to play a part in revealing Satan to be the fool he is. It is the ultimate vengeance. Get you some, sister.

I won't say sifting is easy. In fact, I will tell you it is terrifying, dangerous, and kingdom glory is at stake. Nothing apart from your free-will faith in Jesus leads to beautiful victory. But know this: the winds of hell burn only the chaff; the breath of Jesus delivers life to pure seed. If you are spent from a season of sifting, let Him come so close you sense His heart beating for yours. Let him gently exhale abundant life over your limp body, awakening your eyes to see what they have never seen and your ears to hear what they've never heard.

"Awake, north wind! Rise up, south wind! Blow on my garden and spread its fragrance all around." (Song of Songs 4:16 NLT)

The nightmare of sifting has brought forth the clarity of all your dreams coming true in the One who led you in a death-defying adventure through hell. He is the Lover of your soul and He breathes promises of eternity over you. His desire is to bring forth abundance through your sifting. The produce of your proven trust in Christ is His treasure. This is no ordinary harvest. No, this seed will be set apart for a wedding feast.

"Let us rejoice and be glad and give him glory! For the wedding of the Lamb has come, and his bride has made herself ready." (Revelation 19:7)

You were bought at a price. . . (2 Corinthians 7:23a)

Chapter 6

His Extravagant Purchase

I have a black journal with a gold cross on the cover. My sister-in-law brought me the brand new blank journal the second day of our week-long admission to Children's Medical Center. It was a hellish week of waiting to discover the cause and remedy to Mycah's high fever and low blood counts—when I first learned of things no one wants know: like an oncologist's first name, the color, pattern, and number of tiles on floors inside the operating room, the staggering contrast of cool, sterile sheets against feverish little girl skin, and the deep end of panic that swallows hope's promise. The black journal with a gold cross on the cover initially served as a place to record doctor's instructions, medicine doses, and questions I wanted to ask the oncologist when he made his rounds the next day. It quickly turned into a record of raw pain and the deepest spiritual questions of my soul.

On the other side of that nightmare season of sifting, I often look back through the pages of the black journal with a gold cross on the cover. I see my heart, mind and soul were completely consumed with the tragedy and tasks at hand. All I saw was my child's disease and my desperate desire for her healing. Everything God told me in those days I looked at through the limited lens of a mother broken, grieved for her baby. But on one page, I find the faintest fine lines, curves, and dots. Words scripted by this mother's hand who barely believed what she'd heard whispered into the dark: *"This is about so much more than leukemia."*

God made that bold promise to me way back when all I could see was the quicksand trap that feeds on fear of which I wrote in heavy-handed scribbles of frantic. My belief in seeing His bold promise fulfilled was as thin as the pencil lines forming the words of His still small voice whispered into the small curve of my faith. He must have known I needed a physical sign of His promise — evidence of Himself to touch with my hands. One month after our week of anguish at a children's hospital, He assigned hard proof on an ordinary October afternoon. I documented the story in the black journal with a gold cross on the cover. *"Come and listen, all you who fear God; let me tell you what he has done for me."* (Psalm 66:16)

October 25, 2007.

To look at the weather, it is an easy, light, shiny fall day. But to me, it's one long night hovering over the bare hard stones of my heart. Today Mycah and I loaded into the car for a drive. We've been home-bound because of Mycah's risk of infection (her immune system is very weak from chemotherapy) for an entire month. I had to get out of the house and remember the world is still turning because He is still holding it in His hands. If I don't see signs of life, I know mine will surely snuff out. There was very little conversation. When talking was necessary, I commented on the trees, birds, and wind blowing. One might think I was teaching my daughter, but really I was warning off the buzzards hovering too close, ready to pick at my cold soul. Mycah, quiet and oppressed from the medicines, finally commented meekly from the backseat that she wished we had a tree in our backyard. We've lived in this house a year and we don't have a single tree on our half acre property. More regret. I told her that maybe someday we would plant a tree together and watch it grow through the years as she grew up. Secretly, I wondered if I spoke wishful lies in light of the difficult circumstances and life threatening diagnosis she is under.

Later in the afternoon, a man rang our doorbell. Normally I do not answer the door to men I don't know when Chris is not at home. I'm not sure why I opened the door for him. Perhaps he was a serial killer and secretly I wished someone might put me out of my misery. As it turned out, he was not a serial killer but a door-to-door tree salesman. He said he was selling the trees he had on his trailer and would give us a great deal on one or an even better deal on several. He even offered his service and expertise to plant them for us. The reality of a tree salesman on my porch on the exact day my sick child hoped for a tree was too strange to disregard. So I asked him to come back after 5:30 pm when my husband would be home and could talk with him.

The tree man indeed returned and spoke with Chris and me about his trees later this evening. Mycah even ventured outside for a few moments to admire the trees on his trailer. The kind salesman inquired of Mycah, her illness obvious. We briefly shared the bare details of her diagnosis with him and, for some reason, the day's spoken desire of her heart – a tree in the backyard. Unsure of most things these days, we put him off and delayed giving him a commitment to purchase trees.

As providence would have it, an axel broke on his trailer as he tried to leave. So rather than drive back home with it broken, he left it parked in front of our house. He'll return tomorrow and possibly plant a tree or two for us.

October 26, 2007.

Overnight, Chris and I discussed spending money on trees. Ultimately we both felt that under the circumstances, no matter how good the deal, we should not spend money on things that are not absolutely necessary given the uncertainty of what Mycah's cancer diagnosis might do to us financially. Chris called the tree salesman early this morning to let him know of our decision. When he came later today to fix his trailer, he knocked once again on my door. He wanted me to know he was leaving and thanked us for providing his trailer safe keeping through the night. Then he said, "And ma'am, I left your girl a little tree in your driveway. I want her to have her tree. But you'll have to plant it. I gotta be going." Tears immediately stung my eyes and I couldn't keep from wrapping my arms around his sweaty neck and thanking him for bringing a message of God's goodness to us.

Looking back on those journal entries now, I clearly see. The sorrow of the difficult season *was* about so much more than leukemia. Abundance from the threshing and sifting season was promised and intended all along. He even confirmed the covenant with a sign as beautiful as the rainbow after a flood. At the time, I thought the tree was free. God soon taught me it had an extravagant price tag.

In the previous chapters, we have been diligently attending the tasks of bringing forth a harvest. From preparing the field of our hearts, planting seed in faith, cultivating our patience in the waiting, to passing a threshing test and enduring a good sifting at the hands of the enemy, we've been hard at work cooperating with God for our spiritual maturity. Welcome to the harvest, sister! *"The LORD will indeed give what is good, and our land will yield its harvest."* (Psalm 85:12) He is so faithful to yield a harvest in His children. Certainly, now you can celebrate at the sight of pure seed in heaps upon the threshing floor of your heart. It is not by accident, nor through luck that you've arrived here. A blessed harvest is God's intention for His children and it brings Him much glory, but it is extremely hard on mere flesh of dust. Many fall away before they ever experience glorious seed of promise-plenty caress human fingers. If you've made it this far, you can know you've been walking in obedience to God's Word, doing what He commands even when the circumstances look impossible. He's pleased to show you that His ways always work and are never unproductive.

It might be tempting to assume that this is the end of the story. Perhaps we are complete and mature Christians and now we can go forth feeding those around us from the abundant harvest and spiritual bread we've worked so hard to yield according to God's ways. While that may be true, I am just about the burst to tell you. So I will just announce: NOW IT GETS GOOD! Please stay tuned. You've done a lot of difficult and tiring work to step your pretty but weary feet on this threshing floor among the fruit of an abundant harvest. God wants to redeem every tear you've shed to get here.

That's heavy. I know. Let's look deeper so you'll be thoroughly convinced through His perfect and timeless Word. We are on a quest for our First Love, all the while growing into a complete woman of the Word. If your desire is a deep, personal, and intimate relationship with Jesus, the Word made man, it is critical to stop and rest on the rock-solid truth of Mount Moriah. There was a recent time when I was completely unaware of Mount Moriah. I knew very little of the events that occurred there. I never once considered it was of any consequence to me personally. I am certainly not a Bible scholar or historian and I've never even been to Israel. However, the LORD showed me I had much to learn about His holy mountain and then He took me on a personal journey of discovery to the very place. I want to share with you some of the valuable seed I gleaned while working the harvest on my heart's threshing floor.

You'll recall from our study in chapter four, King David's multiple choice threshing test on Mount Moriah. Do you remember how the location was described in the Scripture when God commanded the angel of the LORD whose hand was raised to destroy, *"Enough! Withdraw your hand"? The angel of the LORD was then standing at **the threshing floor of Araunah the Jebusite."* (1 Chron. 15b emphasis added)

The Scriptures are repetitive in mentioning this particular location and its function as a threshing floor. It comes to pass that the angel of the LORD gets word to David to go up and build an altar to the LORD on the threshing floor of Araunah the Jebusite. Verse 20 of 1 Chronicles 21 picks up the account and we see David acting in obedience to purchase the threshing floor.

1 Chronicles 21:20-26

[20] *While Araunah was threshing wheat, he turned and saw the angel; his four sons who were with him hid themselves.* [21] *Then David approached, and when Araunah looked and saw him, he left the threshing floor and bowed down before David with his face to the ground.*

[22] *David said to him, "Let me have the site of your threshing floor so I can build an altar to the LORD, that the plague on the people may be stopped. Sell it to me at the full price."*

[23] *Araunah said to David, "Take it! Let my lord the king do whatever pleases him. Look, I will give the oxen for the burnt offerings, the threshing sledges for the wood, and the wheat for the grain offering. I will give all this."*

[24] *But King David replied to Araunah, "No, I insist on paying the full price. I will not take for the LORD what is yours, or sacrifice a burnt offering that costs me nothing."*

[25] *So David paid Araunah six hundred shekels of gold for the site.* [26] *David built an altar to the LORD there and sacrificed burnt offerings and fellowship offerings. He called on the LORD, and the LORD answered him with fire from heaven on the altar of burnt offering.*

Before King David interrupted his harvest duty, I wonder if Aranauh the Jebusite was ever aware of the importance of his threshing floor. Was he, in some unexplainable way, drawn there in his spiritual need and contemplation year after year? I wonder, while about his work, if he sensed the rocks of Mount Moriah crying out praises to God. Had he ever experience the awesomeness of the place? Did he see visions of the gate of heaven resting upon the land he cultivated with his bare hands? Could he have ever imagined in his wildest dreams that his threshing floor was the house of God?

Obviously, this particular threshing floor on Mount Moriah held great significance to God. In fact, we learn the location becomes the place of God's temple, His Holy dwelling. *"Then Solomon began to build the **temple** of the Lord in Jerusalem on Mount Moriah, where the Lord had appeared to his father David. It was on the **threshing floor** of Araunah the Jebusite, the place provided by David."* (2 Chronicles 3:1 emphasis added) We will study more about the temple and its significance to us spiritually in the next chapter. But for now, we need to digest a few key truths for our current purpose. This threshing floor location on Mount Moriah had been set apart by God as His house or temple many generations before David actually purchased it from Aranauh the Jebusite so that the temple of the LORD could be built there by his son, Solomon.

Let this truth sink in regarding your personal place of threshing: The threshing floor of your heart is highly significant in your personal testimony, as well as highly valuable to God. Your threshing experience is exactly the place God wants to put His glory and reveal Himself holy in your pain. You see, God created everything in all heaven and earth. And all things belong to Him. (Colossians 1:16) Everything except the one thing He prizes above all other created things. He chose to give you free-will custody over the heart He created in you. You can choose to offer your heart to whomever or whatever you please. God sent His Son so that He might live in your heart and secure your soul for eternity. But there is more.

Just as we have free will over our heart, we each have our own personal threshing floor. It is the place we experience our own unique fairy-tale shattering experience. We were created for "happily ever after" paradise as it was in the Eden garden. Because of sin, fallen humanity — each and all — will endure an event that breaks our ideal of perfection we realize deep-down we were made to know. A trial, tragedy, loss, wrong, temptation, persecution, or suffering comes to each of us at some point. Your personal threshing floor is where you are crushed, beaten, tested, shaken, tossed, sifted, and sorted. We live in a broken and fallen world, and none of us escapes the human experience of choosing for ourselves how to handle our personal sites of threshing. As much as we try to ignore them or cover them, the wounds inflicted as a result of personal threshing call out for attention. I wonder if you've lain awake at night and mourned for dreams lost, if you've suffered alone because of a pain you can't quite describe or make another fully understand. Sister, be encouraged. God knows about your secret place. To be sure, He hates sin, but He loves you. He knows about your heart's hidden stony place, how it hurts you, and most likely caused you to sin out of brokenness. . .and it is precious to Him. He is obsessed with His will to bring healing for you.

Before we go a word further, please hear and understand this: God does not take your threshing floor experience lightly. He doesn't expect you to just get over it, move on, forget and deny it entirely. Nor does He want it to dictate your choices, make you a perpetual, life-long wounded victim, or one who can only focus, live and speak out of hurt, shame, sorrow, or bitterness. An unredeemed threshing floor will always debilitate a heart from growing up in Him and can never fully display His rich abundant blessing in a life.

My heart sustained a deep and brutal wound when I was eleven years old. One summer day a small airplane carrying my daddy and four others fell out of the sky. My heart was broken and I wonder to this day what might have been had it not suffered such a devastating wound. It didn't matter, I decided. Life has a way of happening and for reasons unknown, I faced living without my daddy at precisely the moment I needed him to be the man in my life. Instead of allowing God to heal the wound, I hid it away and attempted to arrange for my own happiness and security. Fear dictated my decisions and actions for many years and I built a prison wall around my heart and shackled myself in a faithless captivity. But like a band-aid over a deep wound, it did little to bring healing. And on dark nights, the pain bled from a still fresh but very old scar. The deep hard wound was bleeding the red life right out of me. I knew somewhere in the depths and tangles of my spirit, my Heavenly Father loved me too much to let me bleed forever. On tearful nights I heard His whispers. He was calling, *"I want your heart, but I will not take what is yours."* A fresh season of sifting and threshing 20 years later would test my faith and sift the waste from my life. God showed me that He sent His Son to take the place of my daughter. By His wounds she would be healed. Little did I know, the season of leukemia would also cause me to grow and mature into the woman God intended me to be; a fit bride for His Son. But in order to completely qualify me for royal union, all of my heart must be pure and whole. The woman had matured in many ways, but the eleven year old girl was still broken.

Somehow I thought the present tragedy of Mycah's leukemia would cause me to get over that old wound and move on. When I was a kid, I remember having an injury on my finger. It was tiny but painful. I went to my older brother for sympathy. He kicked me in the shin and said, "There. Now I bet you forget about that pain in your finger!" I thought God had done the same. Perhaps a new pain would cause me to forget the old one. I've never been more wrong about Him. His will is to heal. He had a personal promise for the thirty-something year old child.

I remember the day with complete clarity. It was early spring and the bluebonnets and Texas wildflowers were beginning to stretch their vibrant heads toward the sun in a mosaic of God-green and rainbow. Our little family was on a Sunday afternoon outing. Mycah's cancer treatment entered into the maintenance phase and the world seemed to be exhaling in relief with us. Her hair was beginning to grow back as fresh and soft as the fur of new-born spring bunnies. Everything new.

Chris and I lifted our voices in our own private Sabbath worship service, Mycah kept time with the nod of her sweet head in the backseat. We are all the worst of the American Idol rejects, but on this day, it felt as if the heavenlies accompanied us and we sounded divine harmonizing with the radio's loud angelic chorus. I looked out into the sunny meadows as we drove past when suddenly and unexpectedly, I heard God's voice with my heart's ears. It was not how He had spoken to me in the past year and a half since I'd been willing to listen. This was new. I think it was because His message was 'new'. He told me, "Angie, it's spring. I am making all things new and I'm coming back for you."

What?

Not knowing what exactly to make of it, I sat still and listened a little longer, trying to hear His voice again amidst the sound of Mycah and Chris's chaos, I mean chorus of praise. Nothing. It wasn't until that evening, when I was all alone with Him, that He revealed the full meaning of His words whispered to me using Luke 8:40-53.

Here is the record of Jesus approached by the synagogue ruler who begged Jesus to come to his house to heal his little girl, who was dying. On the way, people pressed on Him from all sides, but He noticed the touch of a hand on His cloak and knew suddenly healing power had gone out from Him. He asked, "Who touched me?" Everyone denied it and His disciples wondered how He could know as many people in the crowd were touching Him. Then a woman, knowing she could go unnoticed, confessed and told why she touched Him. She had been bleeding for many years and no one could heal her. He said to her, *"Daughter, your faith has healed you. Go in peace."* (Luke 8:48) Then Jesus went on with the synagogue ruler to his house. Everyone thought his little girl already dead. But Jesus said to her, *"My child, get up!"* (Luke 8:54) And she did. He healed them both!

The LORD spoke into my heart, "Angie, my ability to heal is limitless. I can heal a little girl and I can heal a woman that's been bleeding for many years. You, my daughter, need both. You are a grown woman who's been bleeding for many years. And yet the place in your heart that is still an 11 year old broken child, all but dead inside, needs healing too. I haven't forgotten the girl. I'm coming back for her. (from Isaiah 54:7) I am making all things new.

Will you let Me redeem that portion of your heart too? It is especially precious to Me. I desire your healing so much I will pay with My only begotten Son's life for even it. Only My Grace is sufficient payment for something so valuable to Me."

Nothing could have prepared me to hear those tender words that addressed a need in me no one else could fully know or understand. Recalling them now bring fast tears to my eyes. He wanted to buy each and every broken piece of my heart and even heal a 20 year old wound. Like Aranauh the Jebusite, who offered not only the threshing floor, but the threshing sledge, and the oxen for free, I quickly offered everything. Take it LORD, take it all. It is yours. You are my King, and I want you to have it.

"*. . .my own vineyard is mine to give.*" (Song of Songs 8:12)

But He said, "I will not take what belongs to you. I want to purchase it at full price." He knew I would never be able to move on in my own strength, so He came back and got me. He took me once again to Mount Moriah. This time, we went to a place near but overshadowing the threshing floor. It is a portion of the mount now known as Galgotha. There the Son of Man, my Savior, paid the full price for even that old, bleeding and broken part of my heart. This time Mount Moriah claimed the True and Perfect sacrifice for *my* secret place of brokenness. His actions on Calvary spoke in clarity of fine jewels, "Even this. I want to pay for even this. Especially this."

We are going to bite into three delicious precepts from the new harvest of God's work in our lives regarding the purchase of the threshing floor and see how they relate to our own places of broken-ness, or our personal threshing floors.

1. The particular payment

2. The personal promise

3. The 'Presence' portion

First let's chew on the precept of "The particular payment." Take a look at 1 Chronicles 21:25. These Scriptures say David paid Araunah *six hundred shekels of gold* for the site. 2 Samuel 24:22 says David bought the threshing floor and the oxen and *paid fifty shekels of silver* for them. Some Bible critics have sighted the difference in the price David paid Araunah for his land as a critical discrepancy, saying the Scriptures contradict themselves and thus conclude the entire Bible is unreliable and false. The original language clears up the misunderstanding and the concept it reveals is beautiful for our study of the price paid for our threshing floors. We don't want to overlook these details. Every stroke of God's Word has essential meaning. David paid six hundred shekels of gold for the entire site, meaning all of the land surrounding the threshing floor. He then gave another separate and particular payment (50 shekels of silver) in addition for the threshing floor and its contents (oxen, threshing sledges, and the grain). He paid two separate amounts to obtain not only the land, but *particularly and especially* the threshing floor. I really want you to grasp this. Perhaps you've given your heart and life over to the Lord in general for your eternal salvation. I am proposing He is offering a separate and additional payment for especially that secret place of brokenness — your threshing floor. The beauty of "The particular payment" is that your threshing floor is of upmost value and importance to God and He will pay especially for it. It is sacred ground and the foundation of a glorious temple romance. No higher price has ever been paid. Christ's death is an extravagant price tag. It is sufficient payment. Hebrews 9:26 says, *"But now he has appeared ONCE for ALL at the end of the ages to do away with sin by the sacrifice of himself."* (emphasis added) His one sacrifice paid not only for your heart's salvation in eternity, but also, for the threshing floor God values and wants to use for His glory in your present days on this earth.

Now let's take a second bite of abundance and chew on the precept of "The personal promise." There are well over 3000 promises made by God in the Bible. God invented the concept of covenant, He cannot lie (Hebrews 16:8), so everything He does is based on covenant. We can see that throughout both the Old and New Testaments (Covenants) as well as in the present age. To believe He intends to pass you by on your threshing floor brimming with harvest, without offering you a personal promise, is to not know Him at all. God confirmed the personal covenants or promises He established with both Abraham (Genesis 22:15-18) and David (1 Chronicles 22:8-10) after their testing upon the threshing floor at Mount Moriah. I am convinced there is a personal covenant for you and me on the other side of a fruitful threshing floor experience. Isaiah 54:10 speaks of a covenant of peace. *"Though the mountains be shaken and the hills be removed, yet my unfailing love for you will not be shaken nor my covenant of peace be removed," says the LORD who has compassion on you."* You can be assured your personal covenant will bring peace to you while bringing glory and gain for God's kingdom plan at large.

I want you to begin to see the importance of God's nature to establish and fulfill His covenants. But know also that a covenant often requires a commitment from you as well. A personal covenant established on the threshing floor requires a separate and additional payment, and likely a separate and additional responsibility. God will pay even and especially for the threshing place of your wounded heart. He won't take what is yours. He will pay extravagantly for it with His Son's blood. But then it belongs to Him and will be used for His holy presence and glory. Full surrender for payment rendered is your side of the covenant. And full surrender for the payment is displayed in full obedience to how He uses the threshing floor for His presence and glory — a temple in you. Your very own Bethel — house of God. As it is written: *"Love the Lord your God with **all** your heart. . ."* (Matthew 22:37 emphasis added) He won't ask you to forget your threshing floor, deny it, and move on. Instead, He will purify it with His holiness and reveal it sacred. It will be the display of His presence and glory in your past pain.

Now let's swallow the precept of "The Presence portion." Eternal salvation and daily provision as God's children is, in itself, unmerited favor we cannot afford. However we see God confirmed *abundant* promises to both Abraham and David on the other side of their threshing floor tests when they exhibited trust and the character of Christ — spiritual maturity. To Abraham, God covenanted, *"I will surely bless you and make your descendants as numerous as the stars in the sky and as the sand on the seashore. Your descendants will take possession of the cities of their enemies, and through your offspring all nations on earth will be blessed, because you have obeyed me."* (Genesis 22:17-18) To David, God promised, *". . .you will have a son who will be a man of peace and rest, and I will give him rest from all his enemies on every side. His name will be Solomon, and I will grant Israel peace and quiet during his reign. He is the one who will build a house for my Name. He will be my son, and I will be his father. And I will establish the throne of his kingdom over Israel forever."* (1 Chronicles 22:9-10) These were big promises — promises of lavish abundance.

Let me give you some more truth from the Word of God for you to consider regarding abundance. When the "children of Israel," as they are called in the King James Version, were wandering in the desert following their deliverance from slavery in Egypt, God provided for their physical need of hunger with manna. *"Each one is to gather as much as he needs. Take an omer for each person you have in your tent."* (Exodus 16:16) The last verse of Exodus chapter 16 tells us an omer is one tenth of an ephah. Now I don't know what an omer or an ephah really look like in our present age of cups, liters, and pints, but it isn't really necessary. Stay with me. When God commanded Moses on the tabernacle articles, He commanded the bread of the Presence (Exodus 25:30), that was to be before Him at all times, to be made with two tenths of an ephah (Leviticus 24:5) of fine flour. So the provision portion for the children of Israel was one tenth of an ephah of manna that was given by God. The portion for the bread of the Presence, placed before God in His dwelling, called for a double portion of flour from the harvest. God always provides for His children. But I believe the Scriptures tell us that there is a double portion (abundance) for those willing to come into His Presence — into His dwelling place. A heart's belief in Jesus for salvation makes a *child* of God who is qualified to freely receive a portion of God's provision. Our threshing floors bought by God become the temple of His glorious presence in our lives and give the foundation for abundance

127

and the gateway to communion with Christ as His *bride* (more on that to come).

Isaiah chapter 61 is the prophet's rendering of the heart of Christ for His church. In fact, Jesus read the scroll of Isaiah 61 in the synagogue as recorded in Luke 4:18-21 saying, *"Today this scripture is fulfilled in your hearing."* (Luke 4:21) Isaiah 61:7 says, *"Instead of their shame my people will receive a **double portion**, and instead of disgrace they will rejoice in their inheritance; and so they will inherit a **double portion** in their land, and everlasting joy will be theirs."* (emphasis added) So while manna was graciously provided to "the children of Israel," Christ speaks of a double portion for the Church, His bride. (see Isaiah 61:10) This new covenant is unique and personally selected for you in this time and place to go beyond eternal salvation and daily provision granted to God's children and into the depths of unfathomed abundance as Christ's bride. Abundance is the evidence of your divine love story.

After two years of walking with the LORD, enduring the sorrow of the threshing of Mycah's cancer and selling the threshing place of my daddy's plane crash, God gave me the opportunity to touch the evidence of His plan in the pain. He brought me full circle one day when I went back to the hometown in which I grew-up to attend a relative's funeral. My mother and I needed to waste some time, so we got a soda from the local hangout of my youth and went for a drive. We drove past the home where our picturesque young family of five resided in the years before my dad's death. The house was vacant and for sale. We pulled into the driveway and took a tour around the outside of the house, peeking in windows and remembering sunny childhood days of endless play. From our assessment, we learned my bedroom was no longer painted pink, the swing set and wooden rocking horse my Pawpaw made no longer stood cemented in the ground. But so much about the house matched my memory that I couldn't help but feel deep regret at the realization that this location was the place I last believed in fairy tales and happy endings.

Mom and I walked to the little outdoor building that once housed my dad's tools and garden equipment. As I pushed the door open and crossed the threshold, sun spilled onto the dusty cement floor. I looked down and saw year's numbers and my name written in stone hard concrete. Underneath were the small handprints of the child of 1985. Bending down, I dusted the area with my woman hands and tried the small imprints on for size. I considered the writing of my nine year old hand. Then I realized my Daddy's voice. "Angie, child of mine, this story was written before time began. I've been here all along, weaving the tears, pain, and sorrow in grace, peace, and love. Child broken, meet woman healed. This stony foundation is the setting of your 'once upon a time' love story. All the sorrow of the threshing floor was for the sake of a better 'happily ever after'."

Sister, what about you? Perhaps you've believed God for salvation, perhaps He has access to your heart in general. But does He own that deepest, darkest, broken place too? Have you allowed Him to pay full price for even your threshing floor. . .especially your threshing floor? He won't take what is yours. He insists on paying full price.

We are a heart-sick people. Hurt, disappointment, depression, disillusionment, discouragement, these things are of epidemic proportions. We are living in troubled times and we are walking around with bleeding wounds many years and sometimes even decades and lifetimes old. Often, it is not because we are not children of God. We love Him, serve Him, and believe Him. Many of us are attending, working, and even serving in church for crying out loud. We walk around crying and begging for healing, letting go of everything at the cross. And we wonder why we still carry such burdens with dry bones of defeat. I am suggesting it might not be so much that we do not realize His payment in full for our eternity, but that we fail to let Him purchase our threshing floor so He can put His glory on it and reveal it sacred. But this is the day to understand. An offer of expensive grace, an extravagant price, is upon your threshing floor. Will you sell it to the One who knows it is sacred ground, the One who set it apart for His house before time began? If we sell it to Him, the threshing floor is no longer the location of fairy-tales broken, but abundant life and Kingdom glory restored for all to see.

You've done a lot of difficult and tiring work of obedience to get here, but stand up straight, sister. Dust off your dirty hands. Smooth your soiled skirts. You started this journey as a child, but through perseverance and submission, God has qualified you as a spiritually mature woman. And it just so happens, you were chosen for this before the creation of the world. (Jeremiah 1:4) The Most High God is looking for a fitting bride for His Son, Jesus, and now that you've planted your pretty but weary feet on this threshing floor among the fruit of an abundant harvest, God wants to redeem every tear you've shed to get here. The unfading beauty of your gentle and quiet spirit is of great worth in God's sight (1 Peter 3:4) and has caught the eye of the Son. In fact, He is enthralled with you. He wants to purchase the threshing floor of your heart so He can put His Holy presence in this place. And it gets better. He wants to enter into an eternal personal covenant with you. In fact, don't look now, but I think He is offering a bride price for your heart. You've got a deal to make.

"In your unfailing love you will lead the people you have redeemed. In your strength you will guide them to your holy dwelling." (Exodus 15:13)

And in His temple everything says, "Glory!" (Psalm 29:9b NASB)

Chapter 7

Beautiful House of Glory

When was the last time you were certain of your beauty? As a girl did you envision your future self as a leading lady in one adventure-filled, epic love story? Youth is innately convinced of royal standing; certain enough to imagine futures of fairy tales. As girls we fantasized our "happily ever-afters," complete with all the details of a Hollywood movie or a royal wedding televised for millions of viewers—thinking of the exact words spoken and the subtle intonation of how they are whispered, shouted, or halted in unforeseen surprise. We dreamt of our handsome hero and how we'd fight side-by-side to defeat the foe of our love. Might you describe yourself, in your current season of life and circumstance, as a barefoot temptress, as bold and fierce as you are beautiful—the object of a mighty king's desire? I really believe the Author of Life (Acts 3:15) wrote the penchant for just that sort of romance in the hearts of women. Yes, we are creatures built with a critical need to be the beautiful bride heroine in a personal, mysterious, and dangerous adventure. But the daily drudge of life can be as brutal on a heroine as a wet blanket on a fire. Still, deep inside, you know. You remember the royal princess inside, don't you?

A good demonstration can be taken from the musical, *Mamma Mia!*[6] Perhaps you've seen it. It is a movie adapted from the Broadway production of the same name based on the music of the 1970s music group, ABBA.[7]

ABBA was a staple on my mom's gigantic record player (which was more like a piece of furniture than a music machine) in my house growing up. I think she probably bounced me to sleep as a baby to the beat of the tambourine. I knew the lyrics to "Fernando" at the age of three and by four I requested ABBA on a regular basis to practice my queen's dance routine in the living room. When the opportunity arose a few years ago, how could I not take a chance to see Hollywood's movie version of the music of my youth with my own "Mamma Mia"? We had a blast watching while singing along in her living room. We even let Mycah stay up and watch with us, ensuring the heritage of our family's dancing queen for the next generation.

My hands-down favorite part of the movie is the scene set to the song, "Dancing Queen". If you haven't seen the movie, I will try to describe the magic of it for you. The middle-aged mother (played by Meryl Streep) is in need of some cheering up. Her two best friends, who are visiting to attend the wedding of Meryl Streep's character's daughter, break into song. With ridiculously over-the-top wardrobe changes, they begin to dance. Before long, the best friends have coaxed their grumpy girlfriend into jumping on the bed, singing at the top of their voices. They are once again transformed, if only in their memory, to the seventeen-year-old Dancing Queens of their youth. When the music consumes their senses like a devouring fire, and dance they must, the three women take to the streets with their parade of remembered royal splendor. The trio pass woman after woman in the courtyard and along the village streets busy in the daily drudge of hanging laundry on lines, serving food to hungry family, hefting heavy loads. The music takes all captive and before long each female in town—young, old, rich, poor, thin, or plump feel young and sweet. Each one is convinced of her noble duty to dance as the queen she recalls she once was. . .and perhaps, just maybe, she still is.

I am convinced women have a dancing queen somewhere inside. God set it in our hearts before creation. *"I will be a Father to you, and you will be my sons and daughters, says the Lord Almighty."* (2 Corinthians 6:18 emphasis added) We are the King's daughters, as well as, His Son's bride—royalty. *"Then maidens will dance and be glad. . ."* (Jeremiah 31:13a emphasis added) Dancing Queens. Whether we allow her to come out or not is another thing. But I know every woman has a memory of donning a dancing dress, or feather boa, perhaps your mom's high heels, glittery jewels of any kind, while twirling and jumping around, having the time of your life. Remember? How long has it been since you were in the mood for dance? How long since you've had the chance? How long since you were convinced you were made for joyous glory of unfathomed value?

I hope you will let the Word of your Father King presented in this chapter renew your belief in epic love stories and especially your vital role in the eternal one He is writing in you as the bride of His Son. In the previous chapter, we studied David's particular payment for the stony threshing floor of Araunah the Jebusite. I presented that perhaps God desires to pay a particular payment for the threshing floor of your heart. The price paid is higher than any payment rendered in all of history — the crucifixion of Christ Himself, the Chief Cornerstone. We've studied a number of critical events that all occurred in one highly significant and eternally important locale — Mount Moriah.

Abraham's Moriah moment told of the ram in the thicket, characterizing Jesus as aggressive and protective as a substitute sacrifice. David's threshing floor testing and subsequent purchase on Mt. Moriah reflects the desire of God to pay particularly and especially to redeem the threshing floor of your heart so He can put the temple of His glory in that place. As we will see, David's son, Solomon takes it a step further and gives a multitude of meaning in the temple's construction and architecture pointing us to Christ. To state it plainly: Mount Moriah pointed to Jesus, even as He was crucified nearby at Galgotha. The events and concepts in that physical location have much to teach us about our Bridegroom. To know Jesus, His true character, His actions, thoughts, and desires is a bold endeavor. Something only a truly brave heroine would risk. If we dare to seek to know Him, really know Him, we should understand the adventure could be perilous. Our Savior is not weak. His ways are not always easy, or safe for that matter. But He is good and everything He creates is good. I am begging us all to remember the time we were sure of our birthright of bravery as princesses of Love and war. I pray you and I will dare to believe what we've learned about our Bridegroom from Mount Moriah. Dare you persist to learn what the sacred mount's temple of glory means for His beloved bride?

Just to review briefly: King David bought Araunah's stony threshing floor with a particular payment. *"Then David said, 'The house of the LORD God is to be here. . ."*(1 Chronicles 22:1) David had it in his heart to build a house, the footstool of his God in that exact spot. However, God told David he would not build a house for His Name, but instead, David's son, Solomon would be the one to build His house (see 1 Chronicles Chapter 28). *"Then Solomon began to build the temple of the LORD in Jerusalem on Mount Moriah, where the LORD had appeared to his father David. It was on the threshing floor of Araunah the Jebusite, the place provided by David."* (2 Chronicles 3:1)

You may be thinking to yourself, "What is so special about the threshing floor on Mount Moriah as the location of the temple and what does it have to do with me?" Sleeping beauty, awake and realize how awesome is this place! This is none other than the house of God. This is the gate of heaven—in you. It is time we realize our personal threshing floor redeemed by God for the extravagant price of His Son's lifeless body on a cross is the exact location of a holy dwelling for the risen Christ in us. If you've received and accepted the particular payment for your threshing floor, clear the way for construction. This is the site of abundant, rich, holy glory!

In this chapter, we are going to support that claim with the sturdy proof of God's Word. I pray we will have in our hearts a desire for a temple of the LORD upon this sacred location. The focus of this chapter is to construct a temple model in our understanding of God's plan for the threshing floor. In keeping with Solomon's example, we will lay a foundation, build the structure, and then pray for the Spirit of the LORD to fill the temple. Thankfully, Jesus is a carpenter. May the words on this page and the impact I pray it translates in your life be under the supervision and direction of His plan.

Laying the Foundation:

As any carpenter will tell you, a building is garbage without a solid foundation. Jesus said so Himself in Matthew Chapter 7. A wise man (or woman) builds his house on the rock. I don't believe for a single moment that the fact we just so happen to be standing on a rocky, level threshing floor is any coincidence. Begin right here—on this threshing floor of your heart—to lay the ground work of a solid foundation. Solomon laid a foundation sixty cubits long and twenty cubits wide (1 Chronicles 3:3) for the temple with quality, dressed stone. We will lay a foundation with history and rock solid fact straight from Scripture:

- David had in writing from the hand of the LORD understanding and details of the plans for the temple. (1 Chronicles 28:19) He gave the plans for the portico, the buildings, storerooms, and upper parts, inner rooms, the place of the courts of the temple of the LORD and all the surrounding rooms for the treasuries of the temple to his son, Solomon (1 Chronicles 28:11), but the plans were God's.
- The plans included how the leaders of Israel and the priests and Levites were to be divided to perform and supervise the work of the temple of the LORD and the division of the priests for ministering at the temple and in the service of the temple.
- The temple was built by over 180,000 laborers including craftsmen, and artists.
- Construction took seven years. (1 Kings 6:38)

- The temple was built with fine stone, marble, cedar, pines, gold (almost everything was overlaid in gold), silver, bronze, the finest linen (2 Chronicles 3:14), even the nails were gold and weighed one and a quarter pounds each. (2 Chronicles 3:9) The wick trimmers, tongs, bowls and dishes were made of solid gold.
- David provided 100,000 talents of gold (3,750 tons), a million talents of silver (375,000 tons), and quantities of bronze and iron too great to be weighed. (1 Chronicles 22:14)
- The stones were dressed at the quarry so that not even the sound of a chisel or hammer was heard at the site of the building of the temple. (1 Kings 6:7)

These are just a very few details written in the Word of God about the temple of the LORD Solomon built. The temple is a topic that can be researched in great depth. Everything about the temple, the ministrations within its walls, the Feasts of the LORD that occurred there, and the regulations regarding the priests and their duties is rich in meaning. Everything is a reflection of God's holiness, authority, and His plan of judgment, sacrifice, and atonement. The temple of the Old Testament was a symbol abounding with meaning of the New Covenant to come in Jesus Christ. We could spend a lifetime uncovering the treasures contained in the temple's design and plan. However, I really think the purpose of our particular study is best served if we focus on a few key truths at this point.

First of all, I want you to take note that Solomon's father, David is the one who received the specific plans for the temple from God. David then gave the plans and understanding he received to his son,

Solomon. The son, Solomon, carried out the plans of his father, David. David and Solomon were a fore-shadow or symbol of what was to come in Christ. Jesus made no secret of the fact that He was sent by His Father in heaven and He was only and all about carrying out His Father's plans (John 5:19, John 6:44, John 8:16 to name a few). Keep that truth in mind because it will become even more relevant in the coming chapters.

Secondly, we can't talk about Solomon's temple without talking about riches. We need to comprehend that the temple was spectacular, its value and worth all but immeasurable. With upmost reverence and care, Solomon executed the temple's precise plans of intricate detail. The temple was a big deal. Capital B big and Capital D deal! It was to be the House of Yahweh God, His holy footstool for His throne in heaven. The closest one could get to an invisible God this side of heaven, the temple's ground was sacred, the Presence powerful. A place to worship, pray, and meet with God in holy fear and awe, its structure was the small scale representation of the temple in heaven, (Hebrews 8:5 and 9:23) which means it is a reflection of God Himself.

God never needed a temple to hear prayers, but instead He allowed its construction to meet the limitations and needs of His people. It symbolized the hearing and seeing of God toward them. It was a place of refuge, where believers sought grace while fearing the manifest presence of God. The Old Covenant was kept within its walls, but the covenant and even the walls themselves were just a fore-shadowing of a better covenant—the New Covenant through Christ.

I find great encouragement in the lavish glory God chose to display in His temple upon the threshing floor. 1 Corinthians 3:16-17 says, *"Don't you know that you yourselves are God's temple and that God's*

*Spirit lives in you? If anyone destroys God's temple, God will destroy him; for God's temple is sacred, and **you are that temple**.*" (emphasis added) Ephesians 2:21 tells us that in Christ the whole building is joined together and rises to become a holy temple in the Lord. *"And in Him **you too are being built together to become a dwelling in which God lives by His Spirit**.*" (emphasis added) If I am the New Covenant's temple of the Living God, I love to learn how God acted toward His temple of old, because He is the same yesterday, today and tomorrow. His attitudes and actions toward the temple of the Old Covenant will give us insight to His attitudes and actions toward His temple of the New Covenant. For starters, we see the temple had worth the likes unheard of then and now.

Maybe my attitude needed adjustment. For most of my life, I took pride in an "it'll do" attitude. I am usually not one to lust over expensive clothes, jewelry, cars, or houses. I reasoned somewhere along the way, desire usually winds up in disappointment, so I settled into a life of "it'll do." However, once I discovered the truths in Scripture that I am the temple of God and the house of His Holy presence, I dove head-long into the depths of misguided revelation.

I shared in the previous chapter I believe God told me He was coming back for me. He was making all things new again. I felt Him bringing spring again to the hurt places of my 11 year old girl's heart. An offer of full payment for my threshing floor was extended and I accepted. He wanted to place the temple and presence of His glory on my threshing floor. His track record in building temples is an impressive one. I could hardly stand it. He was coming for me with glory and riches and soon they would be manifest within me. I couldn't wait to look like Solomon's temple.

Jeremiah 31:12-14 tells what will happen when the Lord comes back, *"then maidens will **dance and be glad**. . . ."* I coupled that with my new knowledge of the temple's extravagant wealth and reasoned, "If He's coming back for me I am going to need a fancy dancing dress."

At the time, Mycah, Chris, and I were set to volunteer at a hoity-toity fund-raising event for children with life threatening medical conditions. This particular event was one in which the attendees dress-up. Like tuxedos, evening dresses, and jewels kind of dress-up. I was so excited and figured it to be the perfect opportunity to buy me that dancing dress. About a week before the event's date, I took Mycah shopping. We were on a mission for my new look. I failed to recall the last time I bought an evening dress. But I knew it preceded baby Mycah's arrival in our family. I needed the works—dress, shoes, and jewelry. It felt as if I hit the fashion lottery that evening.

But I have to tell you. The whole fancy fashion quest is out of character for me. Remember, I am the "it'll do" girl. My style is to borrow someone else's dress or pull something from the long-forgotten, dark and dusty depths of my closet and attempt to salvage some type of make-do ensemble. That said, the revelation of the temple's extravagant beauty put me in the mood to sparkle. It felt destined when I found a flowing dress the color of tropical oceans. Next I discovered a fabulous pair of strappy silver heels. I reasoned it made more sense for them to be overlaid in pure gold since even the nails in the temple were solid gold. But the salesman said I looked fabulous in the pair I tried-on and contemplated in the reflection of the shiny floor mirror. He wouldn't exaggerate, would he? Then I secured the perfect costume jewelry after only a few minutes of spinning the plastic display thingy. I felt like a million talents of gold as I

142

walked in majestic strides, holding the bags of my imperial shopping excursion. Finally, for a moment, I allowed myself to desire to display the value God said I have in His Word.

When I got home, I tried it all on and hurried to show Chris. His response underwhelmed—not at all what I conjured in my head. I expected a cartoon reaction. His eyes should have popped out of his head while his jaw hit the floor and his heart beat wildly in and out of his chest. I heard "a-WOO-ga" sound effects in my mind. But in reality I got nothing. He half-hearted looked my way and said I looked "good." Good? I heard only the air leaking quickly from my inflated, but ever so fragile ego.

When I got hurt and pouty, I stomped away to tattle-tell to God— He would be on my side. Instead of finding Him bent low to catch me in my dramatic fall-to-the-floor fit, He sat silent and offered no affirmation of my cause. I whined, "LORD, You said I am your temple. Your Word says You make all things new. You said it is spring. If the color of THIS dress isn't spring, then I don't know what is. LORD, what is wrong?"

After my pouting paused a moment, I only felt Him ask one gentle thing. "Angie, why are you arranging for your beauty?"

Well, that did it. My feelings hurt. I decided to take it back. I didn't want any of it now anyway.

The next day I schlumped into the department store, Mycah in tow. In pitiful protest, I put my hair in a pony tail, wore my six year old work-out pants and a t-shirt I got free for donating blood. Convinced I just wasn't 'that' girl, I called myself stupid to desire in the first place. Hadn't I learned? Desire equals disappointment.

I felt as if the sales people either pitied me or laughed at me as I went to three different departments to return all my counterfeit beauty. "Oh, you are returning the shoes? Are they the wrong size?" they mocked. "No." is all I managed between lips bitten closed, fighting back hot, angry tears. On the way out of the store, I tried my best to conceal my sobs from Mycah. She found me out and asked why I was crying. To even have to come up with an answer for her made me loathe myself all the more. Not so mad about returning trinkets of splendor, never mine to begin with, I hated being the girl mourning a stupid dress, phony silver shoes, and fake diamonds. Instead of a royal ball, I attended a pity party.

Chris asked me why I took it all back and I didn't know how to answer him. Over the next few days, I nursed my wounded ego by seeking the Word of the LORD. Even when I don't like His answers or if the meaning of His questions allude me, I know His ways are worth finding. First the LORD ruled out some issues. He revealed it not an issue of fiscal responsibility. He holds all the riches of heaven and earth and can bestow them at His discretion and He certainly is not stingy with it. He told me He is gloriously wasteful and lavish toward all He loves. I knew that already. I had, after all, just learned about His extravagant temple. I wondered why I couldn't have some of that sort of lavishness. I believe He also addressed the question of fashion. The dress was neither too modest nor too un-modest. Lastly, He disclosed it not an issue of punishment.

I continued to search for the answer to my questions, all the while wondering how to be authentically glorious in Him while displaying the lavish riches of His kingdom. How can I display temple riches and the extravagant beauty of His holy presence in me? I wanted to look like God said I am. He said He is enthralled with my beauty. (Psalm 45:11) He said He gave me a crown of beauty instead of ashes, and a garment of praise instead of a spirit of despair. He said he clothed me with garments of salvation and arrayed me in a robe of righteousness as a bride adorns herself with jewels. (Isaiah 61:3,10) I wasn't asking for the garments of one of Solomon's wives, I just wanted one dress and some sparkly heels. Solomon covered almost everything in his temple with solid gold, for crying out loud. I wanted only faux diamonds. It'd do.

A few days later, I believe the LORD spoke to me. "Stop arranging for your beauty. Trust Me." I read in John Eldredge's book, The Journey of Desire, "*You did not bring this spring, dear Child, you do not have to arrange for the summer to follow. It comes from thy Father's will, and it will come.*"[8]

More worried about being un-glorious than un-glamorous, terrified I might have a ram-shackle instead of a temple for God's presence in me, I wanted to learn more. I had come too far with God to give up on the promises of the New Covenant. How could I display His glory for the splendor of His Name?

He answered. His way is to give generously when His children ask for wisdom. Solomon asked for a discerning heart and God was so pleased with his request that He gave him both wisdom and riches. (1 Kings 3:9-13) I will tell you the rest of the story and about the example He gave me, but you are going to have to read on. His answer is best saved for later.

For now, let the foundation settle upon your understanding. Solomon built the temple to house God's glory. It was extravagant in value, covered in abundant riches, and held glorious meaning in every intentional detail.

Building the Structure:

If we want a temple for the LORD's presence upon the threshing floor of our heart, we need to address the building's structure. Having the location and foundation secure, we need to put stone on top of Chief Cornerstone and let the construction begin. Solomon said to God at the temple dedication, *"O LORD, God of Israel, there is no God like you in heaven or on earth — you who keep your covenant of love with your servants who continue wholeheartedly in your way. You have kept your promise to your servant David my father; with your mouth you have promised and with your hand you have fulfilled it — as it is today."* (2 Chronicles 6:14-15) God indeed made a promise with His mouth and in fact fulfilled it with His hand. The temple structure was completed after many years of labor according to the intricate plans set forth by God and revealed to David and Solomon. You can be sure God plans to fulfill His personal promises to His children even today, and you can be assured every detail has been thoroughly planned and executed according to His will. Let's continue to build upon the foundation of history and facts with the structure of God's temple. Our God is a God of intentional structure and design. Let me show you an example that will be precious to us as we continue in our quest to be His fruitful bride.

Based on the structure God showed Moses of the mobile tabernacle (Exodus 24:9), also known as the Tent of Meeting, (used to house the ark of the covenant from the time of the exodus from

Egypt to the conquering of the promised land) God also ordained the structure of the temple. His sanctuary or dwelling place had a Holy Place and also a Most Holy Place. The two were separated by a curtain. (Exodus 26:33) As part of the ministry of the temple, the high priest was allowed to enter the Most Holy Place one time a year after following special instructions to consecrate himself in order to make atonement for the people. Remember, it is a bold endeavor to come near a holy God. Apart from this one time a year, no one entered the Most Holy Place. The original language offers insight into this structure set forth by God. When you look at the Hebrew concordance for the Scripture regarding the Holy Place and the Most Holy Place, (as in Exodus 26:33) you will find that the Holy Place is termed with one word *'qodesh'* translated "holy". The Most Holy Place is termed with the exact same word *'qodesh'* two times.[9] So literally, the Holy Place was "Holy" and the Most Holy Place (often known as the "Holy of Holies") was 'Holy Holy." Think double portion of Holy.

In the previous chapter, we considered the "Presence" portion based on the provision of manna provided to the children of Israel, as well as, the double portion set forth for the Bread of the Presence within the dwelling place of God. I wonder if there is a connection here whereby God is teaching us His structure for relationship. Make no mistake. Yahweh God is completely holy, set apart, sacred, and pure. His dwelling place is untouchable and any who enter must be consecrated. We should not flippantly speak of entering His fellowship, but realize to do so means we must be holy as He is holy. (1 Peter 1:16) There is only One Way to be holy. It is through the blood of the perfect holy sacrifice of Jesus Christ. No one comes to the Father but through Him. When Jesus breathed His last breath on the cross, the curtain separating the Holy Place from the Most Holy Place was torn in two from top to bottom. (Matthew 27:51) In Christ, we become holy and may enter into a relationship with God Himself.

We know a heart is holy through belief and profession of Jesus Christ as LORD. I'd like for you to consider that perhaps a personal threshing floor, sold to God for the particular and sufficient price of Christ's death is holy holy and the location of an even deeper, double-portion relationship with God. We've seen that Mount Moriah was the location of the temple. Could it be that the threshing floor was the foundation of the Most Holy Place? There is some architectural and historical evidence to support that it is likely, but I am not skilled to understand or debate such a claim. However, I do know my personal threshing floor experience has certainly served as a gateway to an intimate relationship with the LORD and a foundation for rich revelation of His Word. It is not my intention to write a doctrine based on this assumption. Instead I am asking you to inquire of the LORD for wisdom regarding your threshing floor. Perhaps He brought you to the threshing floor just to establish His manifest, double-portion holiness on it. If your heart is holy, perhaps a redeemed threshing floor is two times holy. The threshing floor just might be the foundation of the holiest place of God's presence this side of heaven—in you.

We were made for relationship with the God of heaven and earth. We were created to crave intimacy, fellowship, and communion with our Creator. How can mortal flesh bear that kind of Holy Love? Perhaps only through the structure of His design. We know it though, don't we? You know you were made for more than what your earthly eyes see when nothing of this world satisfies the longing and loneliness within your soul. We are creatures with a need for righteous fantasy fulfilled in the truth of our reality. Most often our need for intimate adventurous love is twisted and cheapened into indulgence in romance novels, movies, cheap affairs of the mind or flesh *or*, on the other extreme, pushed back, strangled, chained, and buried in neglect and denial under the guise of religious rules. Both are equally detrimental in their loss and murderous affect on a heroine's heart. Only a powerfully personal and intimate relationship with Jesus Christ can fulfill the desire for perfect love within a soul. I am suggesting the threshing floor provides the foundation for a holy holy temple romance and the gateway to receive His glorious, beautiful Presence abundantly evident in you.

"O afflicted one, storm-tossed, and not comforted, Behold, I will set your stones in antimony, And your foundations I will lay in sapphires. "Moreover, I will make your battlements of rubies, And your gates of crystal, And your entire wall of precious stones." (Isaiah 54:11,12 NASB)

Ask for the Glory of the LORD to fill the temple:

Now that we have the concept of the structure of relationship with the LORD built upon the foundation of the threshing floor with the chief Cornerstone in His rightful position, it is time to dedicate the temple and call upon the Name so that it might be filled with the glory of the LORD. Look at 2 Chronicles, chapter 6. Here we find a prayer of Solomon asking the LORD, the God of Israel, to hear the cry and the prayer he was praying in His presence. *"May your eyes be open toward this temple day and night, this place of which you said you would put your Name there."* (v. 20) Solomon earnestly asks the LORD God

149

to come to His resting place, inviting His might to dwell in the sanctuary. Chapter 7 of 2 Chronicles says when Solomon finished praying, fire came down from heaven and consumed the burnt offering and the sacrifices, and the glory of the LORD filled the temple. (v. 1) The LORD appeared to Solomon at night after he succeeded in carrying out all he had in mind to do in the temple of the LORD and said, "Now my eyes will be open and my ears attentive to the prayers offered in this place. *I have chosen and consecrated this temple so that my Name may be there forever. My eyes and my heart will always be there.*" (v. 15)

Consider God's Word regarding the temple of the Old Covenant in light of the New Covenant temple Paul speaks of in 1 Corinthians 3:17: "*. . .for God's temple is sacred, and you are that temple.*" His temple is chosen and consecrated, sacred and holy. In Christ, you are that temple. I love God's confirmation of His presence there. He makes everything glorious. Jesus was the presence of God on Earth and the gateway of access to the Father. In Him, we have access as well. He specializes in transforming threshing floors to temples of His glory. Without God's Holy Presence, the temple was just an expensive building; without His Holy Presence, we are just walking dead. If you've secured the location of the foundation of your threshing floor, considered the place holy holy in its construction, call upon the LORD to set His Name on it. Ask for His eyes and ears to be attentive to your prayers in that place. Call down His glory to reveal your threshing floor as hallowed ground and the foundation of a temple of immeasurable worth where you can come into the presence of God through Christ.

Being in the presence of God makes one radiant. Just ask Moses. (Exodus 34:29) Nothing short of an intimate relationship with the LORD in the Holy of Holies of your heart will radiate such glory. That type of beauty can never be bottled, traded, purchased, or put-on. If you've ever had the high honor of experiencing someone radiant from an authentic relationship with God, their beauty pierces deep into your memory. It is captivating glory to behold. But it is easily missed because God often hides glory in ordinary—like an inside secret only for those blessed to have it revealed by His good pleasure. I will never forget the first time God pulled back the veil of my human eyes to let me glimpse the true and glorious beauty of His bride. Ever since, the experience serves as a reminder of the beauty God esteems in His princess daughters and gives me an authentic example of the glory He can reveal through a faithful servant who loves Him.

Ms. Lynn is a sweet volunteer we met at Children's Medical Center of Dallas's Center for Cancer and Blood Disorders. Our little family spent hours in the waiting room in several month's worth of clinic days. I often saw Ms. Lynn (who was old enough to be Mycah's grandmother) on her knees helping a child put a puzzle together. I watched her inviting quiet and scared children to a game of Candy Land. I witnessed the powerful moment she knelt before my own child and placed both of her hands on Mycah's knees, locked sure eyes on Mycah's fearful ones, and with divine passion and certain enunciation said, "You are so special to God and He has an important plan for your life." I saw her, time after time, elbow deep in the mess and ordinary tragedy that is the pediatric cancer world. Ms. Lynn quickly became one of Mycah's most favorite clinic friends and a bright spot of light in a very dark, scary place.

It came to pass our family had the opportunity to attend a fancy fund raising event for our Children's Hospital. This one was a luncheon, a few weeks before our scheduled formal evening event for the other children's charity. It seems once your child becomes a part of the critically ill children's community, there are many opportunities to help with fund raisers. At any rate, this event didn't require formal attire, but the attendees were no less opulent. As a patient of the cancer clinic, Mycah was asked to be a featured model and artist in a fashion show and auction to raise funds for pediatric cancer research. On the day of the event, the Jennifer Stroud Foundation hosted a lovely breakfast for the parents of the children models, who were swept away for dressing and primping. I previously heard of the Jennifer Stroud foundation and read it was established in memory of a sweet little girl who died of leukemia. Her parents desired to honor their daughter's life by helping with childhood cancer research and providing assistance to families with children fighting leukemia. My heart went out to the family of Jennifer Stroud and I admired their willingness to use their resources to help others after they experienced a profound loss themselves. We enjoyed the breakfast; the generous food and lavish setting spoke of my Savior's servant heart and a five loaves and two fishes type of miracle.

Later, I stood in the silent auction area with Chris waiting for the beginning of the fashion show. Among the crowd of Dallas social elite, decked out in luxury, I saw Ms. Lynn—the sweet volunteer lady from clinic. She looked so different in a dusty pink skirt suit and high heels. Normally, I saw her in blue jeans and a blue volunteer smock. Glancing at her name tag, (just to be sure I hadn't mistaken her identity) I saw it had the logo for the Jennifer Stroud Foundation on it, as did the one I was given at breakfast. Then I read her name. Lynn Stroud. Like a stone fits into a structure with a sharp clank, the pieces of my understanding came together.

The volunteer lady Mycah adores.

The one always wearing the blue smock at clinic.

The one joyfully serving in humility in the waiting room.

She is the mother of precious Jennifer Stroud—

the little girl who has gone to be with Jesus.

The family whose foundation just sponsored an

elaborate feast for hundreds of people.

When the final stone shifted secure, a beautiful mother who experienced the loss of her sweet little girl years ago displayed God-glory so lavish Solomon's temple appeared a cheap imitation. A volunteer lady transfigured in my spirit's eyes into the royal bride beauty of a mother on bended knee, serving my daughter as she battles the same disease that stole her daughter's life.

Jaw Dropping.

Brave and fierce.

Breathlessly Stunning.

I clumsily made my way over to her, practically tripping over Chris. I said, "Ms. Lynn! You're Lynn *Stroud*? Jennifer Stroud's mom? You never mentioned that when we chatted on so many occasions in the waiting room. I am so sorry. I didn't know. . . You. . . Your daughter. . ."

Somehow I think my tear-toned rambling began to make sense to her and we connected in the way only moms of precious children with cancer can. "But you serve so humbly. . ." I said before I could stop myself. She simply replied, "It's my joy," obviously uncomfortable with personal praise. There is a rich temple of God's radiant glory upon the threshing floor of that mother's heart. The love she has for her King is evident in the ways she dances for Him. No doubt about it. Lynn Stroud is a true and authentic dancing queen.

When I wondered how I could display God's glory in this new covenant temple, He showed me the selfless, humble love and service of a mother whose baby girl died. An ocean blue cocktail dress, some sparkly heals, and fake jewels could never display the glory of my Redeemer's love. Not even Solomon's temple can hold a candle to the radiant beauty of Jesus Messiah. As proven by a last-nameless volunteer at my child's cancer clinic, one who gives the LORD full possession of her threshing floor enters into double-portion Presence in spirit and truth and her temple beauty is spectacularly enthralling.

It is an all consuming desire to sit at the foot of the mercy seat and bask in His glory. One can't leave that place and not shine as a star in the heavens. I want that sort of beauty. There is none more beautiful than Jesus. In eternal covenant union, we, who with unveiled faces all reflect the Lord's glory, are being transformed into his likeness with ever-increasing glory, which comes from the Lord, who is the Spirit. (2 Corinthians 3:18) Jesus said while praying to His Father, *"I have given them the glory that you gave me. . ."* (John 17:22a) In overcoming zeal and passion, He ripped the curtain in two with nail scarred hands to lead His bride into the Holy of Holies of His presence. *"He turned my wailing into dancing and removed my sackcloth and clothed me with joy."* (Psalm 30:11)

Are you up for some truth or dare? Truth: The King is enthralled by your beauty. (Psalm 45:11) Dare: See yourself as Jesus sees you. If you dare to take a look at yourself in the reflection of Christ's eyes, it will change everything. But to see yourself in the reflection of His eyes, you have to be really close to Him. That's a heavy holy move. Brave and fierce.

Dare you believe He is wooing your heart toward His glory? Dare you not? Dare you live as one gloriously radiant as His chosen and consecrated temple? Can you believe you are the heroine in His epic Love story? Nothing is more beautiful than a woman set ablaze by the consuming fire that is our God. (Hebrews 12:29) Your dancing dress will be given to you by the Lamb. (Revelation 19:8) No need to arrange for your own beauty.

He says, *"I take great delight in you. . .I rejoice over you with singing."* (Zephaniah 3:17)

If He's singing, sisters, let's dance. Dance to the remembered song of royal glory sure. Dance certain again of the wedding coming. The King announces the betrothal of His Son, called Faithful and True to His radiant beloved. Don't you see? To reflect the riches of His temple glorious, you, my dear, are as fierce and brave as you are blameless and beautiful.

"One thing I ask of the LORD, this is what I seek: that I may dwell in the house of the LORD all the days of my life, to gaze upon the beauty of the LORD and to seek Him in His temple." (Psalm 27:4)

"I will betroth you to Me forever; Yes, I will betroth you to Me in righteousness and justice, In lovingkindness and mercy; I will betroth you to Me in faithfulness, and you shall know the LORD.

(Hosea 2:19-20 NKJV)

Chapter 8

Betrothal of the Virgin Bride

From the moment she was born, I knew someday it would happen. Chris and I have to face the facts. She is beautiful after all. Those deep blue eyes framed by dark, long curly lashes speak of a beauty beyond the limits of this earth. We've become accustom to her allure drawing others toward a youth and wisdom that normally contradict but somehow are complete in her. Mycah's soulful giggles and philosophical musings reach into even the grumpiest old, crusty hearts, leaving them hypnotized in her unique magic and hanging on her every word. We witnessed it many times. Complete strangers are taken by her and liken her essence to that of an angel. It seems as if she has a secret, like she's seen something of God and radiates an intangible glory. Perhaps it is because of all she endured in her first seven years of innocent life. Cancer couldn't steal her soul and somehow the battle revealed a prize inside that one is unable to fully comprehend or describe.

Yes, I realize I am her mother and may be a bit skewed in my opinion of my only child. But I experience her in the difficult and trying moments too. She still spills her grape juice on the sofa and tries to hide it with a pillow instead of telling me. She sings the same chorus about ice cream and cake over and over until I feel like stabbing myself in the eye with an ice pick, and she interrupts my most juicy telephone conversations with questions like, "Mom, where is the sticky tape? I am making a new outfit for the cat." However, I knew someday I would hear the words. I just never dreamed they would come so suddenly. She is only in kindergarten for mercy sakes.

"Mom, I think a boy in my class wants to marry me."

She said it reluctantly from the backseat of the car. Aware the words might prick my heart, she delivered them as gently as her sweet lips could form the sounds, as if knowing they might leave a permanent scar.

I admit. Her words surprised me. Mycah is not one to wonder about the things of boys and girls yet. She is much more interested in kittens and horses, toads and sand boxes. Even though her beauty is something you have to experience to understand, it is not something she is aware of or attends to with any intention. She is particular about having long hair, but that has more to do with enduring the chains of chemo's bald consequences for almost two years than presenting a beauty for others to notice or enjoy. She feels God gave her curls as evidence of freedom from her cancer and most often refuses pony tails and ribbons. Taming her locks is like braiding the flowing mane of a wild mustang in her little wise mind. It just isn't right. So it did surprise me to hear her speak of kindergarten puppy love.

Initially, I wanted to laugh (mostly to keep from crying). I pictured her daddy's face if he had been there to hear the words tip-toe from her lips. We might need to redirect the car and rush him to the ER for chest pains. However, I pulled myself together to seek further information like a wise and loving mother should. Do not confuse loving interest for meddling or flat out prying. It is a fine line, but mothers should know how to walk it like trained tight-rope circus queens. It was time for my first performance without a net. I expected a few more years before maintaining that balance, but here I stood, no-hands over an ominous abyss of consequences. Freaking out meant she might not trust me again with such sensitive information. Backing out meant she'd miss a valuable lesson of wise motherly council. I took a breath and looked straight ahead. Here goes:

"What do you think about that, Mycah? Marriage is an important decision."

I expected to have a wise-beyond-her-years back and forth delving into the Holy covenant of matrimony, offering brilliant illustrations from my own experience and ending with a crescendo hug and mother-daughter tissue moment. I wondered how this heavenly creature with unseen awareness of God might respond.

"He is cute and everything. Sometimes he smiles at me. And the other day, his friends told me he likes me. But I think it's kinda creepy. Can I have some marshmallows when we get home?"

Glad marshmallows took the place of a heart to heart on marriage and its intricate, complicated, and beautiful web of potential joyous mess, I drove on. She really does possess wisdom beyond comprehension. Marshmallows trump six-year-old boys and puppy love. But I wondered how long it might be before the child-like understanding is traded for the opportunity to experience an adventure of true love. God wrote on our souls with His pen of desire. Our hearts long for an eternal and perfect romance. But there is no reason to arouse or awaken love before it so desires. (Song of Songs 2:7)

Just as a six-year-old is as mature and ready to understand that committed love and marshmallows have little reason to be discussed in the same breath, a babe in Christ is not ready to understand Holy betrothal. I can say that because I know it personally. I came to know Christ as my Lord and Savior at the age of seven. I knew I'd be in heaven and not hell at the end of my life and that truth satisfied me. But I stayed in about that same age of awareness until 31 years of age. Upon asking Jesus to be my Lord and Savior, He sent His Holy Spirit to live in me, making me a member of His forever family as His adopted child. He provided for me, watched over me, and never left me — even when I strayed from His loving cover, living in rebellion to the covenant I accepted. Always, because of my profession of His Son as my Savior, I belonged to Him. But our God's bigger plan includes the wedding of His beloved Son, and a spiritually immature child of God does not make a fitting bride. Praise Him, He had more in mind for my life—a plan in which His provision went beyond necessity and reached into His storehouses of abundance. *"When I was a child, I talked like a child, I thought like a child, I reasoned like a child. When I became a [wo]man, I put childish ways behind me."* (1 Corinthians 13:11)

To grow from a child of God to the bride of Christ means learning to prepare the field of your heart, plant and cultivate the seed of His Word, reap a harvest through perseverance, and endure with long-suffering seasons of threshing and sifting to allow Him to make your heart pure, pleasing and submissive. The threshing floor is a pivotal piece of property as we have seen in previous chapters. How you handle the threshing floor of your heart influences intimacy with the LORD not only in the age to come, but also in the days at hand. Through the purifying work of Christ upon the threshing floor of your heart, you've gleaned a gentle, quiet spirit and an unfading beauty that is of great worth in God's sight (from 1 Peter 3:4). Sister, you are growing up. Your Father has seen to the details of your healing and holiness. His righteousness not only allows the threshing floor of your heart to become the sacred ground of a rich, beautiful temple of His glory, it restores the threshing floor of your heart to perfect Holy purity—virginal purity. In that place, you are as you were meant to be from the beginning.

Isaiah 62: 4 says, *"No longer will they call you Deserted, or name your land Desolate. But you will be called Hephzibah (my delight is in her), and your land Beulah (married or owned one), for the LORD will take delight in you, and your land will be married."* Did you ever dream the lines and curves of God's Love story would dance across your very heart? I can't wait to help place the veil upon your silky tresses and turn the mirror of His Word so you can see yourself as a bride beautifully dressed for your Husband. *"In that day,"* declares the LORD, *"you will call me 'my husband'; you will no longer call me 'my master'.* (Hosea 2:16)

There will be a wedding, but not just any old wedding—a Jewish Wedding. Jesus was born a Jew and the Jewish wedding customs were designed and given by God to display His redemptive plan for His people. Understand this: Jesus followed the Jewish wedding custom in obtaining you as His bride. *"Let us rejoice and be glad and give him glory! For the wedding of the Lamb has come, and his bride has made herself ready."* (Revelation 19:7)

Sometimes we miss abounding meaning in Scripture because we are not familiar with Hebrew (Jewish) background, culture, and customs. But this truth is way too important to miss. God has made it my purpose to help you understand. Jesus was born from Jewish parents from the line of King David. Christ's family tree can be traced back to Abraham. He alone is The Branch who connected the Old Testament with the New Testament in complete perfection. If our heart's desire is to be the bride of Christ, we must understand the Biblical roots of the Jewish betrothal and wedding tradition. We must look into the Jewish marriage customs of Biblical times to glean a greater awareness of a holy bride's destiny as the betrothed of the LORD. Believe it or not, the intricate details of these customs are rich with meaning for those of us in this present generation. It serves us well in our personal relationship with the LORD to dig into the Scriptures dealing with the ancient Hebrew customs and search out the heritage of our faith. As a young Jewish bride undoubtedly gathered any information she could uncover about her future husband, we must seek out our eternal Bridegroom with equal curiosity and anticipation. Let's get started with some basics:

An ancient Jewish marriage had two distinct parts. The first step was the betrothal or "Kidushin." The second step was the wedding ceremony or "Huppah." The betrothal ceremony occurred first and the wedding ceremony happened about one to two years later. In this chapter, we will be looking specifically at the betrothal portion of the Jewish wedding. In the coming chapters we will look with greater detail into the period of time between betrothal and the wedding and then the wedding itself. Keep this in mind: just as weddings today are often carried out in all manner of circumstance, the pattern for marriage is set by a God of order for His purpose. Humans often twist and skew His intended pattern. The Jewish humans of Biblical times undoubtedly did on occasions, as well.[10] However, the traditional ancient custom was consistent with the following pattern:

The ancient Jewish betrothal was very similar to our modern tradition of engagement except that the betrothal was entirely legally binding and could only be broken by an orthodox divorce. (Matthew 1:19) The man and woman were considered bound to one another from the period of the betrothal until the wedding in every way except that they did not physically live together. The "home taking" was reserved for the wedding ceremony when the couple began to live together as a man and wife, consummating the union. Until that time, they were afforded no physical contact. Often times their union was arranged by the father of the groom. The bride might not have met or even seen her husband to be (as in Isaac and Rebekah in Genesis 24). She knew only that she'd spend the rest of her life with him if she said yes to the marriage.

Now let's dig a little deeper. When a young man found the woman he wished to marry, or when his father decided upon a suitable wife, an offer of betrothal was extended. The young man went to the house of the young woman by himself to arrange the marriage between himself and the woman's father. He must carry three items: (1) A large sum of money and/or many items of extreme value. Often the man brought with him all of the wedding garments and jewelry for the bride to wear as well as gold, livestock, deeds to property, or other items of worth in order to pay the "mohar" or bride price. The sum intended to show the worth of the prospective bride to the groom. (Genesis 34:12, Exodus 22:16,17, 1 Samuel 18:25) (2) A betrothal contract or "ketubah" with his promises to the bride written on it. The contract was entirely in favor of the bride and detailed her unalienable rights and guaranteed the groom's return. The groom promised to work for her, provide food, clothing, and necessities for her in honor and in truth. (3) A skin of wine. [11]

If the woman's father approved of the bride price and the terms of the betrothal contract, his daughter was called in and advised of the offer of betrothal. She had the right to accept or reject the suitor's contract of marriage. (Genesis 24:57) At this time, the gifts were presented to the woman as symbols of love, commitment, and loyalty. A cup of wine, called the cup of the covenant, was extended in the right hand (the hand signifying power and authority in the Jewish understanding) of the groom. He first sipped from the cup and then offered it to his intended. If the young woman sipped from the cup, she was accepting the offer of betrothal and the promise was sealed and binding. If she did not sip from the cup, she was stating her denial to the offer of marriage. If she accepted by sipping from the covenant cup, the contract was signed in the presence of two witnesses (necessary in the Jewish law to validate contracts or testimony) and given to the bride and her father as a guarantee of the bridegroom's return. His return was of upmost importance. If he did not return, she was legally bound, but had no one to care for her or give her a hope or future family.

Following the signing of the marital contract, the bride had a water immersion, or "mikvah." This was symbolic of a ritual cleansing in which she indicated she was leaving an old way of life and taking on a new life with her spouse. Next the bridegroom prepared to leave in order to go and prepare a room onto his father's house (the bridal chamber) and make arrangements for the coming marriage. A period of one to two years was customary for making the necessary preparations. Before departing, he made a pledge to his bride. "I go to prepare a place for you; if I go, I will return again unto you." He then left to begin building a place for his bride. Sometime within the next two years, the father of the groom must okay his son's preparations and declare the bridal chamber and all other preparations suitable and complete. At that time, he sent his son to get his bride. During the groom's absence, the bride was set apart for her groom alone and began to prepare herself for his unknown time of return. She had to be ready at a moment's notice because the groom often came in the middle of the night.[12]

I am sure you can begin to see the ways in which these ancient customs are mirrored in Jesus' actions. What does all of this have to do with your personal journey from a child of God to the mature and complete bride of Christ? Let's tie the old Jewish wedding customs to the actions of Jesus and the New Covenant. I pray your eyes will be opened to see His love in a new light. I pray you will understand His offer of an adventure in true love.

First of all, the marriage is often arranged by the father of the groom. The Word of God is, in essence, the story of a loving Father seeking a perfect bride for His Son, Jesus. The Bride must be totally devoted, pure of heart, in love only with Him, submitted and flawless in His sight. God's standards are very high because He esteems His Son above all others. He is King of kings and a fitting bride must be of royal status. God searches the heart and mind (Psalm 7:9) of all mankind and He chooses a bride according to the plan of His will for the glory of His Son. (Ephesians 1:11) Just as in the beginning, God made Eve from man. Adam gave his bone and flesh for His bride. God presented Eve to Adam as a suitable helper. Jesus gave His life for His bride and God presents those He has chosen (Ephesians 1:4, John 6:44) to His Son for eternal union. The bride price (mohar) He paid in full was extravagant beyond any other before or since. Jesus paid for His bride with His life. It was the only way in which flawed humanity could ever be pure and fitting for a Holy God. You have the choice to accept His offer or reject it. If you choose to accept Jesus as your eternal covenant bridegroom, you have every promise and right written within the flawless Scripture as your betrothal contract (ketubah). Within the Scripture, Jesus promises to provide for all your needs. Second Corinthians 1:20-22 says, *"For no matter how many promises God has made, they are "Yes" in Christ. And so through him the "Amen" is spoken by us to the glory of God. . .He set his seal of ownership on us, and put his Spirit in our hearts as a deposit guaranteeing what is to come."* When we accept the offer, Jesus gives us the Word of God as our binding contract and the gift of the Holy Spirit as a guarantee of what is to come.

Just before His betrayal and death, Jesus partook of the cup of the covenant with His disciples in the upper room. Luke 22:20 gives the account. *". . .he took the cup, saying, "This cup is the new covenant in my blood, which is poured out for you."* Then Mark 14:23 tells the response of the disciples to His offer. *"Then he took the cup, gave thanks and offered it to them, and they all drank from it."*

Next we see Jesus wash the feet of His disciples demonstrating His willingness to lay aside His authority to serve and honor his bride. This symbolized their "mikvah" or spiritual cleansing. Then we see Jesus proclaim His intention before departing as He comforts His disciples by speaking the words of the Jewish wedding rite. *"Do not let your hearts be troubled. Trust in God; trust also in me. In my Father's house are many* rooms; if it were not so, I would have told you. I am going there to prepare a place for you. And if I go and prepare a place for you, I will come back and take you to be with me that you also may be where I am." (John 14:1-3)

Is this beginning to make sense to you, sister? Jesus then was crucified, resurrected, and ascended to sit at the right hand of His Father in heaven. He has gone to prepare a place for you and every promise and statement He offered to His disciples, He has made to you. He is coming back for His bride. *"No one knows about that day or hour, not even the angels in heaven, nor the Son, but only the Father. Be on guard! Be alert! You do not know when that time will come."* (Mark 13:32-33)

As individuals who have accepted Christ's mohar offer, we have to know He is with the Father to prepare a place so that we might be with Him where He is. We do not see Him, but we have every promise in Scripture to meet our needs. We have the Holy Spirit and the fruit of the Spirit as gifts to guarantee His return. In fact, we have the Holy Spirit as a messenger or interceder until that day. A bride and groom were not allowed to have physical contact, but sometimes a messenger acted as an avenue for the couple to communicate and trade information. For the bride of Christ, the Holy Spirit serves as the messenger. Jesus said, *"But when he, the Spirit of truth, comes, he will guide you into all truth. He will not speak on his own; he will speak only what he hears, and he will tell you what is yet to come. He will bring glory to me by taking from what is mine and making it known to you. All that belongs to the Father is mine. That is why I said the Spirit will take from what is mine and make it known to you."* (John 16:13-15)

Jesus has attended to every detail, tradition, and law in obtaining you as His bride. You are of great worth to Him. God has chosen you for His Son because you are of royal status and if you've accepted the cleansing of your soul through the blood of Jesus, you are a pure and flawless virgin fit for the King. I wonder if you realize that fact as your eyes and ears perceive the words He has divinely orchestrated you to see and hear in this very moment. You. Yes, you are a royal bride if you choose to sip from His cup and accept His righteousness as your own. Do you recognize your Kinsman-Redeemer? If not, I hope you'll come again with me to that pivotal piece of property. Come again to the threshing floor.

Yes, I know. The threshing floor is not always a pleasant place. Not only is it the place where you experience the difficult, sweaty, and painful tasks of threshing and sifting. It is the place of God's glory and manifest presence. . .and let's be honest, sometimes that is an intimidating and frightening place to be. And more than that, it is where Jesus Messiah opened the door for intimacy with an offer of betrothal. I know that can be a daunting and almost awkward meeting. We wonder if we are ready to reveal ourselves in that type of intimate relationship. It can be scary because truth and purity are pre-requisites to an eternal covenant union. Are you really capable and willing to go that far?

Sister, I've been there. And if you are like me, the proposition seems tempting. To be swept away in the adventure of true Love allures some hidden empty space in your soul. You hear the whispers of an eternal romance deep inside and want to risk everything to realize a new and *life*-filled reality. But you also wonder if the leap of faith will leave you fallen into a pit of broken dreams. How can your dirty soul really be pure enough to accept the extended hand of the perfect King? I want so badly to tell you, but it is not for me to tell. It is for Him to show you. But you have to come to the threshing floor.

Meet my friend, Ruth. She has much to teach us regarding marriage proposals and threshing floors.

Ruth was born and raised in the country of Moab. As a young woman, she married a foreign man (a Jew) from Bethlehem who lived in her village. He had come there with his family to escape the famine in his home land. I imagine that something about this strange family and their religious customs drew her ever closer to the God they worshipped. Her mother-in-law, Naomi especially caused Ruth to wonder about this Jehovah. He seemed so different than the gods of her family. It came to pass that her husband's father died. She comforted her mother-in-law in her loss and shuttered at the thought of losing her husband someday. Soon the thought turned to a reality when Ruth's husband died too. In fact, both of Naomi's sons died and suddenly Naomi found herself alone in the foreign land of Moab without her husband or two sons. When Naomi learned that the LORD had provided for her people in Bethlehem and the famine was over, she prepared to return home. Her two daughters-in-law set out with her on the road back to her home.

Naomi told her daughters-in-law to turn back and return to their own mother's homes, she was too old to offer them any more sons to become their husbands according to the laws of her faith. In her bitterness, she turned them back so that they might find other husbands in their own country of Moab. One of them surely listened and set back to her home. But Ruth would have none of it. She insisted on going with Naomi saying, *"Don't urge me to leave you or turn back from you. Where you go I will go, and where you stay I will stay. Your people will be my people and your God my God. Where you die I will die, and there I will be buried. May the LORD deal with me, be it ever so severely, if anything*

169

but death separates you and me." (Ruth 1:16-18) The oath convinced Naomi of Ruth's determination so she stopped urging her to go back.

Naomi and Ruth finally made it back to Bethlehem but Naomi felt bitter and rejected by God in all of her losses. The pair was highly vulnerable as they had no way to make a living and no man to care for their needs. However, the barley harvest was beginning and Ruth determined to go to the fields and pick-up the leftover grain behind anyone in whose eyes she found favor. It just so happened, Boaz, a relative of her dead husband, was a wealthy land owner, honorable and respected in the community. Ruth found herself gleaning grain behind the harvesters in his field.

"Just then Boaz arrived from Bethlehem and greeted the harvesters, "The LORD be with you!" (Ruth 2:4) Boaz noticed the new young woman in his field and inquired of her identity. When he learned she was the young Moabitess who returned with Naomi, he instructed the foreman to allow the young foreign woman to work in his field free from harassment. He invited her to harvest in his field, to take rests in his shelters and to drink from his water jars. Ruth was overwhelmed with gratitude and wondered why she – a foreigner—had found favor in his eyes. He replied, *"I've been told all about what you have done for your mother-in-law since the death of your husband. . .May you be richly rewarded by the LORD, the God of Israel, under whose wings you have come to take refuge."* (Ruth 2:11-12)

Boaz arranged for her to eat with his harvesters, and instructed the men to allow her to gather among the sheaves, not to embarrass her, and even pull some stalks for her from the bundles for her to pick up. Ruth worked hard and harvested a good amount of barley for herself and Naomi. At the day's end, Ruth returned to Naomi and told her mother-in-law where she gleaned the grain and all about how Boaz provided for her. Ruth continued to work in Boaz's field by day, returning to live with her mother-in-law, until both the barley and wheat harvest were finished.

One day, Naomi decided to initiate a plan for herself and Ruth. She instructed Ruth in a most scandalous plot. *"Is not Boaz, with whose servant girls you have been, a kinsman of ours? Tonight he will be winnowing barley on the threshing floor. Wash and perfume yourself, and put on your best clothes. Then go down to the threshing floor, but don't let him know you are there until he has finished eating and drinking. When he lies down, note the place where he is lying. Then go and uncover his feet and lie down. He will tell you what to do."* (Ruth 3:2-4)

Ruth followed her mother-in-law's instructions and did everything she told her to do. *"When Boaz had finished eating and drinking and was in good spirits, he went over to lie down at the far end of the grain pile. Ruth approached quietly, uncovered his feet and lay down. In the middle of the night something startled the man, and he turned and discovered a woman lying at his feet.*

"Who are you?" he asked.

"I am your servant Ruth," she said. "Spread the corner of your garment over me, since you are a kinsman-redeemer." (Ruth 3:7-9)

Hold up. We can't go any further until we pull out some of the very juicy bits of this story and bite down to taste some sweet and delicious drama. This is better than any reality dating game. We could do a whole other study just on the book of Ruth and its rich feast of spiritual truths. However, for our purposes now, we will have to try to focus on certain aspects and come back for seconds later. First thing we should understand is the definition of a kinsman-redeemer.

A kinsman-redeemer is a male relative who, according to various Jewish laws, had the privilege or responsibility to act for a relative who was in trouble, danger, or need of vindication.[13] Ruth and Naomi were in need of someone to buy the family land in order to ensure the name of Naomi's sons would remain in the historical records. To do so, meant Naomi needed an heir for her deceased husband and sons. (see Leviticus 25:25 and Deuteronomy 25:5-10)

Another detail we must fully grasp is that, in those days, women did not go to the threshing floor while the men were harvesting— especially unmarried or widowed women. To do so would be seen as an act of promiscuity and inappropriate boldness. (Ruth 3:14) And lastly, we need to understand that when Ruth asked Boaz to spread the corner of his garment over her, she was essentially proposing marriage to him. (Ezekiel 16:8) A bridegroom spread his garment over his bride as part of the wedding ceremony signifying she belonged to him and was under his authority. So we need to realize the bold action and risk Ruth was taking in this threshing floor moment.

She was risking her reputation as a woman of nobility. A reputation she had worked hard to establish as a foreigner in a new land of religious zealots.

She was asking for Boaz to marry her.

She was asking for Boaz to father an heir for another man so that Naomi's sons might continue their family heritage, giving up claim to his property for his own name through his heirs.

Sister was risking rejection, her fragile moral status, her future ability to provide for herself, as well as, her mother-in-law, and her life.

Okay, now that we understand the full weight of Ruth's actions, let's get back to the rest of the drama and see how this turns out. Since

I have a feeling our God is a sucker for a good love story, I bet we won't be disappointed.

"The LORD bless you, my daughter," he replied. "This kindness is greater than that which you showed earlier: You have not run after the younger men, whether rich or poor. And now, my daughter, don't be afraid. I will do for you all you ask. All my fellow townsmen know that you are a woman of noble character. Although it is true that I am near of kin, there is a kinsman-redeemer nearer than I. Stay here for the night, and in the morning if he wants to redeem, good; let him redeem. But if he is not willing, as surely as the LORD lives I will do it. Lie here until morning." (Ruth 3:10-13)

So Ruth did as Boaz asked and lay at his feet until morning. But she had to leave before the sun revealed her identity. Before going, Boaz poured out six measures of barley and put it in her shawl. Then he went into town to settle the legal and business matters of buying Naomi's property and taking Ruth to be his wife. He did not rest until the matter was settled that day. Ruth became the wife of Boaz and bore a son to be the heir for Naomi's dead sons. They named him Obed. In the flawless treasures of this story, we see Obed is the father of Jesse and Jesse is the father of David. . .yes, that David. The Messiah Jesus came from the blood line of King David as a result of his covenant with God.

I love that Ruth's story is our story in so many ways. I love that her loyalty and obedience in difficult circumstances afforded her name to be forever written in Holy Scripture. She has an entire book of the Bible named for and about her life and story. Obviously, God esteemed even a foreign widow who risked the threshing floor in order to experience divine covering. If He did it for her, He will esteem us for boldness, loyalty, and obedience in our circumstances, as well. Take note that this story was set amongst the abundance of the barley and wheat harvest. Ruth had been through a difficult, threshing season of losing her husband and moving to a foreign land, leaving her family to live in a land she had never known to scrape an existence among the poor by gleaning leftover stalks of harvested grain. Because of her loyal acts of kindness to Naomi, Boaz, who points to the character of Jesus, allowed her to work among his fields and provided for her basic needs while she toiled. It is not until after her bold actions on the threshing floor that she is given an abundance of grain (six measures poured in her shawl) for which she *did not* work. It seems a small "mohar" from such an established land owner as Boaz, but we see how much He is actually promising her in his actions to come. So much of Ruth and Boaz's story is relatable to our study on threshing floor trials, threshing floor abundance, and threshing floor betrothal. However, let's settle on three big ones that we might harvest great truth for ourselves.

1. Abundance is the promise, but you must go down to the threshing floor to get it.

Naomi advised Ruth of a very wise and carefully pondered plan of action. She felt confident the timing and circumstances leant themselves to an amiable outcome. Boaz was a man of power and authority, as well as, wealth and prosperity. Much was to be gained if he agreed to be a kinsman-redeemer for Ruth; but much to be lost if he refused. The only way for her to know for sure? Go *to the threshing floor*. Perhaps you've found yourself in a similar circumstance. Often it is in the trying times of life when the option to "go there" with Jesus is most risky. As we've learned, the threshing floor is not always a pleasant and glorious place. It is a place of hard work, often painful and exhausting labor.

There use to be moments when I longed for a dynamic and adventurous experience in this life. Somewhere in the depths of conscience and incoherent tangles of my mind, I would hear the whispers of my First Love, "Come to the threshing floor." When I felt the call to come out of my comfort zone and step into the realm of the unknown deep, I quickly faded in fear. If a life of adventure meant experiencing something difficult or painful, I soon found satisfaction in the shallow end of faith. In fact, I actually prayed God would spare me the experience of feeling a free fall, exposed, and overwhelmed. It seems too ironic to be coincidence that I use to pray I might never see the inside of Children's Medical Center in Dallas. I told God how thankful I would be if I went my whole life without ever stepping foot in the building. It always seemed the saddest and scariest of places to me when we drove passed its immense tower in downtown Dallas. I couldn't think of anything more devastating than facing a serious or chronic illness in my only child and it never occurred to me to go there to help or comfort another facing that reality. Funny how our worse case scenarios are often how God calls us to the threshing floor so we come face to face with His Son, the Kinsman-Redeemer.

I wonder if you are like me. Do you avoid the threshing floor at all costs? Do you pray even, that you won't have to "go there"? Perhaps there is a way to fall madly for Jesus and skip the pain and discomfort of "going there" with Him. Do you wish there is another way? Have you ever considered. . .what if the threshing floor is the place where a pure bride and perfect bridegroom meet and recognize one another? We've seen how the threshing floor is a place where God wants to build a temple for His presence and glory. It is the location and foundation of the temple inside you. Why in the world do we avoid it as if it were not acceptable? Is anything worth missing out on the abundance to be found here? Why won't we "go there" with Jesus?

2. If you are brave enough to "go there," you must then trust enough to be vulnerable when you get there.

Sometimes we find ourselves flat on our hind ends upon the threshing floor. He called to us to wash and perfume ourselves and go on our own, but when we refuse, we might just find that life's circumstances have landed us on the cold hard stones and we don't know quite how it happened. For me, that was the case. My four year-old daughter was healthy and vibrant one week and listless and pale the next. I looked up and found myself literally sleeping on the cold, hard floor of the very place I hoped and prayed never to set my foot. I was on the threshing floor facing the tangible reality of my worst fears. Time ticked, offer extended and the question hung. Would I lay down at His feet in submitted faith or walk away in rebellious doubt?

When Ruth went down to the threshing floor, she had to lay everything out and expose her every need to the one who might be able to cover her. Not only was she asking for Boaz to buy her dead husband's land, she was asking him to marry her and proposing he give her a son to carry on another man's name, giving-up his name in the historical record. She was in serious need and she went to his feet, exposed herself, poured out her heart, shed her every pretense, and laid bare every bit of her vulnerable life to his will.

If the threshing floor isn't intimidating enough, now we see that we must not only be bold enough to "go there" but we must be vulnerable enough to lay bare our every weakness, pour out our heart, confess our need, and expose our soul in complete truth. If there is a bride price being offered, why can we not just accept it, drink of the cup and move into the appointed position of eternal bride to the Most High? That's what I wanted to do. The last thing I desired was to strip down spiritually and expose the ugly truth of myself to Christ Himself. But God let me know the high priority He placed on His Son's bride. She must be of royal status, a pure and flawless virgin. I knew if the criteria were flawless virginity and pure perfection, I was out of luck. He had the wrong girl.

Coming to the threshing floor is the beginning of opening ourselves for intimacy. Once there, nothing short of absolute truth can enable Christ to redeem the pain and exchange it for a temple of His glory. His blood is capable of washing even the messiest stains, transforming sackcloth into glorious, white linen. But for Him to be able to cleanse the crimson stains, we have to take off our rags so He can exchange them for the gift of garments of salvation. Intimacy requires truth, and truth requires complete spiritual nudity. One of the hardest things I have ever done was to hand over my stained clothing to allow Jesus to shine His love upon the deepest, most painful and hideous places of my bare-naked soul. Being that spiritually vulnerable required more trust than I ever mustered for any other reason before or since. And make no mistake, it is absolutely precious to Him—a kindness even greater than that which you showed earlier.

Sister, what are you still wearing? Have you stripped off every shred of your old self and poured out the deepest secrets of your heart to Him? He can handle it. I promise you. I know only because I experienced it myself. It does not matter how sinful, stained, twisted, sick, or broken. You can be made new again, as white and pure as fresh fallen snow. You do not possess the one soul beyond His reach to restore. On the authority of His Word, I promise you He can and will forgive and restore every bit of your heart if you present yourself to Him as a willing and accepting bride. He is pleased to purify you in His love. His desire is for you to trust Him. . .with everything. But by holding on to the rags of sin, you forfeit the covering of His garment. It takes trust. More trust than you have mustered for any other encounter of your life. Will you risk full honest exposure to wear His divine and glorious covering? Boldness and vulnerability normally contradict one another, but in Christ we can and must be completely both.

3. The truth leaves you spiritually naked, but Jesus will cover you with His garment.

When Ruth went to the threshing floor and made herself completely vulnerable, Boaz was touched and surprised to realize her identity and intention. In complete honesty and openness, she says to him, "*I am your servant Ruth. . . Spread the corner of your garment over me, since you are a kinsman-redeemer.*"(Ruth 3:9) The request for covering is an intimate proposal. It symbolized marriage and the fact that she would be his. We see a beautiful picture of this in Ezekiel 16:8 when God takes Israel as His own, "*I spread the corner of my garment over you and covered your nakedness. I gave you my solemn oath and entered into a covenant with you, declares the Sovereign LORD, and you became mine."* And Psalm 91:4, *"He will cover you with his feathers, and under his wings you will find refuge."* Christ offers His garment as a garment of salvation. Because of His perfection, we are made perfect and pure. . .a fitting bride of royal status for the King of kings. Like Ruth, we have to say in all tenderness and honesty while laying flat at His feet, "I am your servant. Spread the corner of your garment over me." With all that is within me, I know He lives to hear those words fall from your lips. In fact, I experienced His warm glory cover my bare shoulders before I finished breathing the request.

The threshing floor can be the setting of a glorious betrothal ceremony. Don't take my word for it. Take it straight from the mouth of Jesus. John's gospel gives the details of Christ's last moments in human flesh. As Jesus hung on the cross, He said, *"I am thirsty."* A jar *of wine vinegar was there, so they soaked a sponge in it, put the sponge on a stalk of the hyssop plant, and lifted it to Jesus' lips. When he had received the drink, Jesus said, "It is finished." With that, he bowed his head and gave up his spirit."* (John 19:28b-30)

"It is finished." We think of this statement as Christ's last words and the announcement of His completion of the Father's will and fulfillment of the work of the cross. And it is. However, for those who look for abundance, the flawless poetry of God's Word offers a play on words. The Aramaic word (which Christ spoke on the cross) for "finished" is "kelal", meaning to complete, finish, and make perfect.[14] We know Jesus' death on the cross made us perfect and complete as He finished the task given Him by God the Father. While Jesus spoke the Aramaic word, "kelal", the Hebrew word for bride is "kallah", translated bride or spouse.[15] It comes from the Hebrew word (kalal), to complete![16] Jesus used His last breath to send a message to His bride. He paid the mohar (bride price) to complete and fulfill the Jewish law stating how He must obtain Her. You are so valuable to Jesus; He paid your mohar with His perfect life, with His very blood. The cross was for you. With His last breath, He spoke your name.

The mohar is offered. The betrothal contract is His Holy Bible and every promise is yes in Christ and entirely for your good. He extends the cup of the covenant and awaits your response.

"Arise, come, my darling; my beautiful one, and come with me." (Song of Songs 2:13)

It is risky. Straight-up righteous scandal. Do you hear the call of His song arousing love according to His desire? Will you arise, beautiful one and go to the threshing floor? Heed His betrothal offer and grab two handfuls of the dirty rags hanging as death around your ankles. Cast them aside that you might sprint to the threshing floor, take the cup in His right hand and drink deeply the cleansing offer of promise and redemption. What are you waiting for? Don't miss this. Do not keep Him waiting one more second.

It is almost a rags-to-riches fairy tale cliché. Except God is the first and last poet and this verse was written for you before *"In the beginning. . ."* Receive the garments of a pure and royal bride. Let His words wrap your bare soul in warm, white down.

Beloved, shed the grave clothes you wear like a mask.

"Don't be afraid—I will do all you ask."

Here is my glory cover, it makes all things new.

My offer is forever. . .but what about you?

Mine is a perfect adventure an eternity long.

Now it's your time to respond to My song.

Breathe the two words I died just to hear.

Whisper, Beloved, "I do" in Mine ear.

"Because you are my help, I sing in the shadow of your wings (kanaph). My soul clings to you; your right hand upholds me. (Psalm 63:7-8)

". . .at your right hand is the royal bride in gold of Ophir." (Psalm 45:9b)

Chapter 9

Preparing A Place

I blame it on my mom, really. She had me watching the musical, *"Seven Brides for Seven Brothers"* since I was in diapers. So I guess it seems natural that, as a very young girl, I pretended and dreamed about my wedding day just about every day. Wedding was one of my most favorite things to play. A pillow case for a veil and a cheerleader pompom for a bouquet is all I needed to envision myself as a beautiful bride with all eyes on me. John from *C.H.I.P.S.* or Michael J. Fox from *Back to the Future* were intermittently exchanged as the groom at my discretion. I practiced the right-together, left-together wedding walk until perfected without even having to whisper, "left-together, right-together" to myself. Instead, I hummed the tune of *"Here Comes the Bride."* For me, there was nothing more beautiful than a bride dressed in white.

But somewhere between the time my daddy's plane smashed into the ground and the moment I rationalized my beauty went up in flames with it, I lost the desire to dream in veiled flowery melodies.

Unaware, it slipped away quietly, like the lift mysteriously escapes a helium balloon left overnight.

When I met Chris, my Mr. Right, at the ripe old age of 17, the picture I once dreamed faded and was long forgotten in the depths of my heart's hope chest. The dream lost was not a reflection of my groom's quality though. I believed him magnificent in every way. Best friends turned googley-eyed love birds—more romantic than wise—we went together like a horse and carriage. So we decided to let our love tie us together in marriage.

On Tuesday, July fifteenth nineteen hundred and ninety-seven
in Ocho Rios, Jamaica
Angela Gay Grunden and Christopher Paul Nichols
gave themselves to each other in marriage
becoming Mr. and Mrs. Christopher Paul Nichols.

That's what it says on our wedding announcement. We sent out wedding announcements instead of invitations. We believed our circumstance especially difficult in which to plan and organize an ideal wedding. First of all, neither of us had the funds at age 19 and 20 to afford a big wedding. And second, we both had complicated issues and family backgrounds making a traditional and picturesque church wedding sort of out of the question. Chris was adopted into a large family and his mother and father divorced when he was very young, thus two large and complicated family units with adopted, step and biological family bundled, often dysfunctionally, together.

In comparison, my family was relatively small. My dad had been dead for almost ten years at the time, and for that reason, I believed my perfect wedding was tainted from the beginning because the father of the bride was absent. His blue eyes were supposed to spill tears upon the vision of his baby girl, grown up and dressed up radiant. I was supposed to wipe them away while reassuring him I would always be his baby girl. He was supposed to give Chris a private speech, offering his blessing for our union, but also scare him to death with a warning never to hurt me. He was supposed to choke back sobs as he gave me away at the altar and then take his seat and my beautiful mother's hand into his. If he couldn't walk me down that aisle, I reasoned I didn't want to walk an aisle at all.

For better or worse, Chris and I — two broken kids trying to mend our pieces together — came to the decision that it was, after all, our wedding and opted to skip the whole ceremonial scene and took off alone for Jamaica. It's not like we stole away secretly to elope. Our family and friends knew the particulars. They just weren't invited.

Chris and I had a fabulous time. In fact, the memories of our wedding and ensuing honeymoon are never far from my mind. When I smell the perfume I wore that afternoon or look at the photos from our magical day, I am instantly there again — barefoot on the beach, hand in hand, with my best friend.

Don't get the idea I am trying to say our wedding or, more importantly, our marriage is perfect and we've been living only days of happily ever after. We've run into some traumatic circumstances and also caused some very difficult seasons. We even foolishly allowed ourselves to teeter on the edge of divorce a few times, more out of laziness than anything that fits Biblical criteria for issuing one. But God has been so very faithful to help us see His plan in each other's eyes. No, our wedding was not what I had dreamed as a young girl.

185

We did not say our vows in a church, in front of scores of family and friends, with all eyes on me. And without going into detail about things that are not anyone's business except mine, Chris's and God's, we were in violation of a few key laws regarding ideal holy matrimony. But we prayed like mad on the day of our wedding for God to help us build a strong and lasting marriage. Nothing is too hard for Him. Thank God I can sit here today and speak this testimony in full confidence that God prefers perfect holy unions, but can redeem even the messiest hitches for His glory. I know because I watch Him do it for me every day.

But this is not a study or even a chapter about earthly marriage. This is a book about growing from a child of God to the bride of Christ. It is about growing up in faith and owning the position of the betrothed of the LORD. However, it is impossible to study the concept of our relationship with Christ as His bride without thinking also of our personal experiences and earthly knowledge of marriage. In fact, I am convinced God meant it that way all along. God instituted marriage for that very reason. He created man and woman and ordained their union so that we might understand His relationship with His people in a more tangible way. God, throughout all of history, placed circumstances and real-life touchable experiences in the lives of His people in order to teach them about Himself, so that we might know Him more.

As previously discussed, the ancient Hebrew customs are the heritage of our faith as followers of Christ. Jesus was born a Jew and lived as a Jew. He taught his followers spiritual lessons using illustrations from the Hebrew culture of His time. It is easy to miss out on some of the delicious richness of His lessons when we do not understand the context from which He spoke. I want to savor every morsel of His Word. You and I may or may not be Jewish by birth, but we've been adopted as children into the family of God through Jesus (Ephesians 1:5) if we have accepted Him as our Savior. Let's make it a priority to become more fully aware of the heritage of our faith. There is an abundance of true seed within the ancient traditions and law if we will persevere in the harvest that we might partake more fully of the Bread of Life. When we seek to understand the precepts of God's Word and ask Him to help marry them with the real circumstances He allows in our lives, we begin to walk in a new realization of His active presence throughout history and right into our everyday personal existence.

We discussed the significance of the betrothal in the last chapter. In this chapter, we will look closely at the time between the betrothal and the wedding and then take a peek at the "hometaking" itself — much more on that to come in another chapter. First we will look at the bridegroom and bride separately to reveal what each did in the meantime between the betrothal, or "Kidushin" and the wedding ceremony, or "Nisuin." Then we will look at the wedding "Huppa", also called the "hometaking." Finally, we will learn how the Old Testament Feasts of the LORD teach us about the big-picture of God's redemptive plan and eternal heavenly marriage. They hold abundant meaning for, not only the kingdom calendar, but also our individual lives.

As you will recall, we last left off as the bridegroom departed the bride's home to prepare a place (the bridal chamber) for the bride in his father's house following the betrothal establishing the marriage covenant. The bridegroom had to complete a number of tasks in order to prepare to bring his bride unto himself. First, he had to prepare the bridal chamber. It would be attached to or within his father's house and must be a fitting and lovely place for his new wife. He must also prepare a home for himself and his new bride to reside together after the wedding celebrations concluded. All of the bridegroom's preparations were overseen by his father. As you might imagine, a young man, anxious to bring his beautiful bride home, might throw together a ramshackle bridal chamber with four walls and a bed then run to fetch his lady. But a wise and understanding father knows one should not expect to woo a woman's heart, mind, body, and soul without going to great effort on her behalf. He may send his son back time and time again to add or adjust certain arrangements in order to teach him valuable lessons of excellent matrimony. Careful attention might be given to observe or ascertain her favorite colors, favorite flowers, her family background, loves, and dislikes. Great thought and effort went into each detail. Once the father deemed the arrangements complete, he gave his son permission to go retrieve his bride. No one knew when the day or hour would come — not even the son himself.[17]

The bride, once her bridegroom left her to go prepare for their new life together, had several responsibilities as well. Set apart for her bridegroom alone, she must remain committed to him until his return. She wore a veil as a symbol of her devoted status. (Genesis 24:65)[18] She set about the tasks of assembling her trousseau, or all the wedding garments and clothing she needed to begin a life as a pure wife. The groom sometimes provided the bride with all of her wedding garments, but if so, they most likely needed adjustments and alterations to satisfy the bride's figure and desires. She also used this time to make blankets, linens, coverings for her marriage bed, and other items for her new home. A bride often saved many years to be able to purchase special perfumes, cosmetics, and jewelry for her wedding celebration. So she gathered and learned to use these items before her bridegroom returned for her. [19]

While about her tasks, she was assisted by other female family members or friends. They spent time talking over the things of married life and instructing the young bride in the ways of a wife of noble character. She also made arrangements for her close unmarried friends or family members to act as bridesmaids. They stayed close by to assist her in preparations and to light the way into the bride's home when the bridegroom and his friends unexpectedly arrived in the night. As time passed, she began to prepare for the unknown night and hour by having all of her belongings packed and ready to go. She might sleep in her wedding garments as to not delay her bridegroom when he arrived suddenly and without advanced notice. Upon her bedside table, she placed her veil, her oil lamp and extra oil to be ready and accessible.[20]

This was a time of preparation for both the bride and bridegroom. Each completed their tasks with ever increasing anticipation of the coming union. Call me sentimental, but the thought of it makes me get a sweet squishy feeling inside. The one I get when I watch old romantic movies. I love to imagine a blushing bride surrounded in the loving advice of her women family, anticipating the coming joyous occasion of her wedding. It makes me giggle to think of a young husband-to-be, probably anxious and nervous, attending to every detail of the bridal chamber. As the days passed, I imagine the anticipation rose to new heights for both bride and bridegroom, as well as, for their families and friends.

At the appointed time, the father of the bridegroom gave his consent for his son to go to his bride. It most often happened during the night. The groomsmen ran ahead of the groom sounding the shofar (ram's horn) like a trumpet and shouting to announce the bridegroom's imminent arrival. At once, the bridesmaids trimmed and readied their oil lamps and took their positions to guide the groom and his companions into the home of the bride. The father of the bride "turned his head" while the bridegroom came like a thief in the night to steal his daughter. The bride rushed and hurried to gather her personal belongings, put on her veil, and prepared her lamp. In ancient times, the bride was placed into a carriage lifted by poles and carried to the ceremony. The word, Nisuin (for the wedding ceremony) means to "lift up" or carry.[21] While all of the bridal party organized, prepared, and gathered to make their way to the ceremony, family members and other special invited guests (hearing the commotion of the trumpets and yelling) made their way to the father of the groom's home. They arrived to a banquet the father prepared while his son was away collecting his bride.[22]

When the wedding party arrived, the bridegroom and his veiled bride entered into the carefully prepared and lovely bridal chamber (huppah)—alone. You will remember that the legal union between the two was established during the betrothal. There was really no need for a ceremony of vows like we have in our modern wedding ceremony. The covenant was previously agreed upon, signed, and binding. All that was left to do then was consummate the union. The word "huppah" means "covering" in the Hebrew language. It is still customary for the Jewish wedding ceremony to take place under a canopy of some type. Often it is the bridegroom's prayer shall (tallit) or a fabric covering tied to poles that cover the bride and groom symbolizing they are no longer two, but have become one. It is reminiscent of the story of Ruth and Boaz when Ruth asks Boaz to cover her with his garment.[22]

When the bride and bridegroom entered the private quarters of the wedding chamber, they were alone for the first time. Within the private inner chamber, their union became complete. The bride's veil was removed, he covered her with his body, and the man and his wife became one flesh. (Genesis 2:24)

Women are very into details. Before you worry that this book is suddenly going to turn racy, I am talking wedding details here. . .not intimate details—that's for chapter 11 (wink). But women do care about details. It is why we take great time and care to choose the right shoes to go with the perfect outfit and sought-after accessories. It is why when given the chance, we pay careful attention to just the right flowers, colors, clothing, food, and accompaniment for our own weddings. Women love to think over the symbolism and significance of each aspect of the occasion. So we should be highly impressed at the attention to detail and significant symbolism of the messages and meanings God instituted through the Hebrew wedding customs. We will highlight and savor just a few here. But it is an amazing subject to research more fully on your own. I am certain the LORD has treasures for you, His unique bride, lying beneath the surface of these traditions. He invites you to uncover them as He reveals more of Himself to you through His Word.

First of all, take a look with your heart's eyes at the care and detail the bridegroom gave toward the bridal chamber. I am a romantic at heart, just as I am sure you are too—even if you won't admit to it. God wrote the beginning of an epic personal love story in our DNA from everlasting to everlasting. It is who we are to seek out the complete and ever-after conclusion. For this very reason, I love to ponder the sweetness of his effort. The bridegroom certainly tried to gather just the right furnishings, setting a mood to overwhelm his new bride's every sense with beautiful sights, scents, textures, sounds and tastes. If he came to know her favorite flowers were Rose of Sharon, he might have carved their likeness into the doorframes. If he discovered through a messenger or mutual friend she favored the scent of cinnamon, he might place clusters of cinnamon branches around the room. If his father taught the young man well, he probably took great care in the smallest details, knowing their first moments alone together should overwhelm her with tender emotion. Girls, we know pleasure is heightened by true relationship. Think of the sweetness of this custom. Even though a bride and bridegroom had no physical contact before their huppa, a relationship and the evidence of his care most certainly showed in his preparations. He spent a great deal of time to arrange the room in such a way as to let her know he was eager to understand her, know her, and please her with the desires of her heart.

Psalm 37:4 says when you delight yourself in the LORD, He will give you the desires of your heart. Not only does He know your desires so that He can give them to you, He is the One who put them in your heart from the beginning. When He said He goes to prepare a place for you in His Father's house (John 14:2-3), you can bet your inner room will be filled with the furnishings and details that speak to the desires of your unique heart. Until the day He comes to take you there, I believe He works to prepare the inner chamber of your heart, your personal Holy of Holies, as a place where He can be at one with you in spirit. He regularly writes His Word upon the walls of my heart, reminds me of His faithfulness with memories of His loving work in my life as if hanging framed photos of us together, and cleans out the dirty sin and lies I've believed that threaten to ruin our sanctuary.

He is surely giving great thought to every act of His hand on your behalf. Jesus is incurably in love with you (Jeremiah 31:3) and is anxiously awaiting His Father's signal to come for His bride. (Matthew 24:36)

As for the bride's responsibility during her betrothal, she had to be devoted and single-heartedly pure toward her betrothed. She must stay true to him alone, setting herself apart in thought, word, and deed for only her bridegroom. In fact, one of the reasons for a two year period between the betrothal and "huppa" was to ensure the bride's faithfulness to her bridegroom and verify her virginity at the time of her acceptance of his betrothal offer. If not, there would likely be evidence (a pregnancy) during that time to reveal the truth. Likewise, it is our responsibility to love the LORD with all our heart, soul, mind, and strength. Paul warns the early Church in 2 Corinthians 11:2, "*I promised you to one husband, to Christ, so that I might present you as a pure virgin to him. But I am afraid that just as Eve was deceived by the serpent's cunning, your minds may somehow be led astray from your sincere and pure devotion to Christ*". It is of upmost importance to guard our minds and hearts against the enemy's accusations and our own

193

flesh so we might remain true to Christ alone. And as a bride works diligently to prepare items for her new home and gather the treasures of her trousseau, we too must give careful daily attention to lay up treasure for ourselves as a firm foundation for the coming age to take hold of the life that is truly life. (1 Timothy 6:19) We must give care to the wedding attire He gave us. Revelation 19:8 says fine linen stands for righteous acts. So we must be diligent in demonstrating righteousness toward others. And we must be always ready and alert for His coming. Our lamps need to be full of oil and the wicks trimmed so they are efficient in burning a steady and constant light. In other words, The Holy Spirit should be abundant in our lives, and we must maintain a life that shines the light of Christ within. (See Matthew 25:1-13)

As the bridegroom came unexpectedly for his bride, 2 Peter 3:10 says the day of the LORD will come like a thief in the night. 1 Thessalonians 4:16-17 says, *"For the Lord Himself will come down from heaven, with a loud command, and with the voice of the archangel and with the trumpet call of God, and the dead in Christ will rise first. After that, we who are still alive and are left will be caught up together with them in the clouds to meet the Lord in the air. And so we will be with the Lord forever."* At the appointed time, Christ will return for His bride and He will fulfill each prophesy of His second coming just as He fulfilled every prophecy of His first coming.

God is blow-your-mind consistent. Psalm 90:2 says, from ever-lasting to everlasting He is God. He penned the story of glorious redemption before the mountains were born and before He brought forth the earth and the world. He ordained every stroke of His Word, weaving history, prophesy, truth and revelation into an eternal and flawless tapestry. We would be sorely remiss if we did not take a look into God's historical and prophetic calendar to glean true seed in our quest toward spiritual maturity. Especially since the appointed Feasts of the LORD relate to Israel's agricultural seasons of planting and harvesting and depict the entire redemptive career of Jesus Messiah, our Bridegroom.[23]

The Old Testament, in Leviticus 23, records the LORD's instructions to His people about the seven holidays or "the feasts of the LORD." *"These are the LORD's appointed feasts, the sacred assemblies you are to proclaim at their appointed times."* (Leviticus 23:4) The seven feasts of the LORD occurred each year as instructed by God according to the Hebrew calendar. God implemented His feasts to teach the people about Himself and the big picture of His plan.

"The Hebrew word translated "feasts" means *appointed times.* The idea is that the sequence and timing of each of the feasts have been carefully orchestrated by God Himself. "Each feast is part of a comprehensive whole. Collectively, they tell a story. These feasts are also called, "holy convocations," that is, they are intended to be times of meeting between God and man for "holy purposes."[24]

Four of the seven holidays occur in the spring of the year.[25] The first four feasts — the Spring Feasts — Passover, Unleavened Bread, Firstfruits, and the Feasts of Weeks (also known as Shavuot), have been fulfilled in the events of Jesus' first coming. Passover is the first feast. The Jewish people celebrated Passover when God led them out of Egypt. At that time, a lamb was sacrificed and the blood was applied to each door post. When it was done in faith and obedience to God's command, that home was "passed over" and the life of the first born was spared. All subsequent observances of the Passover feast over the centuries have been memorials of that one and only first Passover event. In precisely the same way, there was only one occasion when Jesus' flesh was pierced and His blood spilled on the cross of Calvary for the sin of the world. And it was not coincidence, but rather appointed, that Jesus was crucified on the Jewish date of Passover. Christ is the once and for all Passover sacrifice.

The Feast of Unleavened Bread began the day after Passover and lasted for seven days. When God instituted this particular feast during the Old Testament, He instructed His people to eat only bread made without yeast. In the Bible, leaven symbolizes evil or sin. (Matthew 16:6, Mark 8:15) The Feast of Unleavened Bread in its fulfillment in Christ, proclaims that Jesus' physical body did not experience the ravages of death and decay while in the grave because He was without sin (leavening).

The Feasts of Firstfruits occurred next on the second day of the seven-day Feast of Unleavened Bread. The Jewish people were to bring a sheaf of their barley harvest and other offerings to the temple and present the firstfruits of their crops to God. In its fulfillment in Christ, the Feast of Firstfruits proclaims that death could not hold her Foe. Jesus rose from the grave on the third day, the actual day of the Feast of Firstfruits. First Corinthians 15:20 says it this way, *"But Christ has indeed been raised from the dead, the firstfruits of those who have fallen asleep."*

The Feast of Weeks (Shavuot) was the last of the spring feasts. At the time of its institution, God told His people to count seven weeks from Firstfruits and then the "day after," or fifty days, the Feast of Weeks was to be observed. (Leviticus 23:16) The Feast of Weeks is also called, "Pentecost" meaning "fiftieth." (Acts 2:1) The Feast of Weeks was fulfilled in Jesus as well. Christ rose from the dead on Firstfruits and then He spent forty days with His disciples in post-resurrection ministry. (Acts 1:3) He promised them the Holy Spirit who would come to help in His absence. (John 14:16-17) Also, He told them to wait in Jerusalem until the Counselor (the Holy Spirit) came. They waited only ten days (do the math and that is 50 days all together). The Spirit of God descended on the first-century believers on the day of Pentecost (fiftieth day) or the exact day on the Jewish calendar of the Feast of Weeks. At this time, Jesus made both Jew and Gentile at peace with God through His flesh. (Ephesians 2:14-15)[26]

Before you get bogged down and confused as to what all this has to do with you, stay with me. I am praying like mad the LORD will open your eyes to see yourself here. The Jewish people celebrated the Feasts of the LORD each year for centuries without fully comprehending the true significance (their future fulfillment in Christ) of the traditional laws in keeping the feasts. Then each major event of Jesus' first coming occurred on the precise date of the appropriate Jewish holiday. I think we would be wise to believe that each of the three major events to be associated with His second coming (Christ returning for His Bride) will also fall on the appropriate Jewish holiday. Those three feasts (the fall feasts) are–the Feast of Trumpets (Rosh Hashanah), the Day of Atonement (Yom Kippur), and the Feast of Tabernacles (Sukkot). The Feast of Trumpets points to the Rapture of the Church when Jesus comes for His Bride and will judge the wicked. The Day of Atonement points to the salvation of Israel and the wedding of the Lamb, and the Feast of Tabernacles points to the establishment of the Messianic Kingdom.[27]

We can research and look to the words of prophesy in Scripture to learn about the things to come. In fact, Jesus says when the Spirit of truth comes *"he will guide you into all truth. . . .and will tell you what is yet to come."* (John 16:14) It is our pleasure and responsibility to seek God in His Word and learn about the coming of His kingdom. However, no one knows the future fully and no man can say exactly how and when the events of Christ's second coming will play out. To hash out the coming events in great detail is not the focus of this study.

What is helpful for our purposes is to look at the Feast of Trumpets (Jesus coming for His Bride) and the Day of Atonement (the wedding of the Lamb) and see what delicious truths we can taste in these two yet-to-be-fulfilled Feasts of the LORD (We will be looking at the Feast of Tabernacles in the final chapter). Now that we have some foundational understanding of the feasts and God's kingdom calendar, we will see their significance related to the Hebrew wedding tradition and thus our quest to grow into spiritually mature women complete and fit for eternal holy union.

Something to remember: the first four Feasts of the LORD were fulfilled by Jesus in His first coming. The Old Covenant was established by the law (Moses and the Ten Commandments). People of the Old Covenant came to know God's character through keeping the laws He gave them, as well as, the laws regarding the Feasts. God put tangible tasks to complete in their personal lives in order to teach them about His plan.

For example (still talking about Old Covenant here), for Passover, the law stated each man must take a lamb without defect for his family and care for it until it is a year old and then slaughter it at twilight on Passover. (Exodus 12:3-6) These lambs were surely beloved pets by that time and the children of the family most likely held, hand-fed and romped with the baby sheep. To slaughter the precious thing was surely a sacrifice and a tangible painful experience for the family. At The Feast of Unleavened Bread, it was customary for the family to intentionally spread bread crumbs around the house in hard to clean areas. In doing so, when it was time to remove the yeast from the houses (Exodus 12:15) the people had to work extra diligently to obey, even going so far as to scald the cooking utensils and folds of their clothing to rid the yeast from their homes. They had to put their hands to the work and experience the law in their personal circumstance. At the Feast of Firstfruits, each man had to bring to the priest a sheaf of the first grain (probably barley) he harvested. His family must not eat any bread or roast the new grain until the day he took the offering to God. (Leviticus 23:9-14) If a family was short on bread and anxious to eat again of the fruit of a hard worked harvest, they must wait, according to the law, to do so. At the feast of Weeks, the people brought two loaves of bread made with the finest flour from the wheat harvest. The two loaves represented the Jews and Gentiles as God was showing them, through touchable items, His plan to provide for and reconcile both through His Son.

The Old Covenant was established through the law. The New Covenant was established through the Spirit. Second Corinthians 3:5-8 says of the New Covenant, it is not of the letter (law) but of the Spirit; for the letter kills, but the Spirit gives life. Okay. This is big so hold on here. I am suggesting just as the four spring Feasts fulfilled by Jesus in the first coming of Christ were experienced by the people through the law (under the Old Covenant), the remaining three Feasts, yet to be fulfilled in the second coming of Christ, can be experienced in our present day circumstances through the Spirit (under the New Covenant).

What I am saying is, the remaining three feasts on God's Kingdom calendar will come to completion and will be fulfilled when Christ returns. But until then, God's people can more fully know God's character when we experience the truths represented by the feasts in our personal circumstances through the Spirit. So yes, someday on the Feasts of Trumpets, Jesus will return with a shout and trumpet blast (1 Corinthians 15:51-52) to retrieve His Bride, the Church. And there will be a Day of Atonement when the wedding of the Lamb is come. (Revelation 19:70) But until then, believers may experience God's intended plan of these feasts in their personal relationship with Christ through the Holy Spirit.

The Feasts of Trumpets for Israel (Jewish) was literally a very dark day. It occurs at the New Moon when the moon is in its darkest phase. In its fulfillment, it will be a day of judgment to bring about repentance and awareness for God's chosen nation (Israel), still living under the Old Covenant, to enter into the New Covenant and recognize Jesus as their Messiah. However, for the bride of Christ, or the Church living under the New Covenant, the Feasts of Trumpets speaks of the Hebrew wedding custom when the Bridegroom comes with shouts and trumpet blasts to retrieve His bride. Same day of the calendar, but it has a much different meaning and outcome for the two groups.[28] I am suggesting individually, we too, may have a personal Feast of Trumpets in our tangible life experiences.

Let me give you an example from my personal testimony while living in rebellion to the New Covenant I accepted as a child. I will never forget the night of September 14, 2007. Mycah was still fighting a low-grade fever she had for about a week. It was a Friday night (just after dark) and our family doctor's office was closed for the weekend. Mycah complained of being tired, and her legs were hurting off and on. While bathing her that night, she told me her ear hurt. I believed I finally had an answer to the persistent fever and thought she had an ear infection that could be easily healed with a course of antibiotics. Instead of waiting until Monday, I told Chris I wanted to load her up and go to the urgent care clinic, about a fifteen minute drive from our home. The urgent care doctor concurred she may be developing an infection of some type and agreed to give me my wish. He wrote a prescription for an antibiotic and Chris and I immediately drove to an all-night pharmacy to have it filled. We talked and laughed and even picked up a midnight snack in a drive-thru as we waited for the pharmacy to complete our order while Mycah slept in the backseat. Life was moving along nicely and I was confident in my ability to solve the issue of Mycah's illness. However, I still remember a deep-seeded feeling of decay that seemed to persist in buried fears.

About four days later, Mycah's fever worsened to the point that Chris and I bundled her up in the dark hours of the night and headed toward the emergency room of the closest small town hospital to our home. Immediately, the doctor confirmed my fears when he told us something was wrong with her bone marrow as all of her blood counts were extremely low. Then four days later, we received the blow. Mycah was officially diagnosed with leukemia, a malignant cancer of the blood. I didn't know it at the time, and in fact, only recently discovered, the date of our first visit to the urgent care center was during *Rosh Hashanah*, the Jewish Feast of Trumpets—a very dark day indeed. Mycah was officially diagnosed on the date of *Yom*

Kippur (the Jewish High Holiday, The Day of Atonement). In the Old Testament, the Day of Atonement was the one time a year the high priest entered the Holy of Holies in the temple and made blood sacrifices for the people to atone for their sins. The Feasts of the LORD are called "holy convocations"; that is they are intended to be times of meeting between God and man for "holy purposes."[24] God had a holy purpose in these dates for me. He put tangible circumstances in my life that I might more fully know Him.

Matthew 24:36-39 says, *"No one knows about that day or hour, not even the angels in heaven, nor the Son, but only the Father. As it was in the days of Noah, so it will be at the coming of the Son of Man. For in the days before the flood, people were eating and drinking, marrying and giving in marriage, up to the day Noah entered the ark; and they knew nothing about what would happen until the flood came and took them all away. That is how it will be at the coming of the Son of Man."* And it was with me. The night of my personal Feast of Trumpets, Chris and I were eating fast food, drinking sodas, laughing and joking. We had no idea of what was to come. God used the meaning of the Feast of Trumpets to call for my repentance on the darkest day in my history.

On my personal Day of Atonement—which was also the literal Day of Atonement according to the Jewish calendar, Mycah was diagnosed with a cancer of her blood. In fact, her red blood cell count was 2.4 when we took her into the ER. Normal is about 14. In other words, she had no blood and was in a critical condition. Leviticus 17:11 says, *"For the life of the flesh is in the blood, and I have given it to you upon the altar to make atonement for your souls; for it is the blood that makes atonement for the soul."* It felt as if Mycah's life and blood were being called for. God said in His law, *"The first offspring of every womb. . .belongs to me."* (Exodus 13:2) Blood is absolutely necessary for the atonement of sin. Would I repent and trust in the blood of Jesus as my atonement cover, or persist in rebellion to the New Covenant I once accepted and pay with the blood of my first born child? We will either live by accepting the New Covenant or experience death according to the Old Covenant. There is no remission of sin without blood. (Hebrews 9:22)

Girl, God is no joke. He means business. He is slow to anger and abounds in love (Psalm 86:15), but He will call His children to repentance. Romans 2:5 says it like this, *"But because of your stubbornness and your unrepentant heart, you are storing up wrath against yourself for the day of God's wrath, when his righteous judgment will be revealed."* The Feast of Trumpets and the Day of Atonement for me was a time when God was calling my actions into judgment. In my affliction, I sought repentance and reconciliation through Christ's atoning sacrifice.

You know the rest of the story. I fell to my knees and crumbled in a heap before the Almighty, rent my heart in a desperate plea for my daughter's life. I came to the threshing floor and gave everything up to Jesus. He relented from sending calamity. (Joel 2:13) He is from everlasting to everlasting God. What He used to teach the nation of Israel in ancient days, He will use to teach a thirty-one year old Texas mother in the 21st century. The revelation must always result in an awareness of and faith in Jesus Messiah. When I became fully aware of Jesus and recognized Him and what He did to pay for my sin and heal my wounded heart, I fell for Him right there on the threshing floor. And I am hopelessly in love for all eternity.

My family was going about the business and busyness of life. Eating, drinking, moving, and breathing all the while, I was living in rebellion to the covenant of Christ I accepted as a child. On the actual Feast of Trumpets in 2007, the LORD called me to judgment upon the threshing floor. Nine days later, on the actually Jewish date of the Day of Atonement, Mycah was diagnosed with blood cancer. God was calling me to repentance and renewed commitment to the New Covenant of Jesus. It was the appointed time, both literally and within my personal circumstance to meet with the LORD for "holy purposes."

I finally surrendered more than just my eternity to Him on October 8 that same year. It was that very night when I could not take another breath on my own, when the fears and failures of Mycah's cancer hurt too much for me to take one more step further. It was the night I laid her and all else at the cross, broke my white knuckled grip on my own ways, and gave Him my entire life along with my eternity — when I wanted Him more than I wanted anything else — even more than the health of my baby girl. It was a personal Day of Atonement for me, a day of true repentance, a day when Jesus offered His blood to cover my sins. God put tangible circumstances in my life that I might know Him more. It is interesting to note at this point that the Hebrew word for "atonement" translates to include the meaning "cover." Jesus is the atonement cover for our sins. But He is also the eternal Bridegroom destined to marry His flawless bride and become "at one" with her in a heavenly marriage. The word "huppa," the Hebrew word used to label the consummation of a marriage, also translates "cover." Atonement and His eternal marriage are the two motivations in the life of Jesus Messiah.

Now I refer to October 8 as my anniversary with Jesus. . .the date of my betrothal, if you will. It was the day I took the cup of His

New Covenant and drank deeply, accepting all the benefits and all the responsibilities that came with it. Because the Hebrew calendar is based on both the lunar phases as well as the solar seasonal year, the dates for LORD's Feasts are not the same each year; as Christmas is always December 25 and Independence Day is always July 4. The Feasts of the LORD fall on different dates each year. I was surprised to realize that my one year anniversary of living for Christ, October 8, the following year (2008), was the Jewish feast of the Day of Atonement. This year, the Day of Atonement was not about judgment for me. I repented and now lived according to His New Covenant of grace. This time, it was about "At-one-ment," being of one mind and heart with Christ. His Feasts are a romantic pursuit of His bride. He used them to make me aware of the law that kills so He might reveal to me how His blood provided a New Covenant of grace and life. From judgment and atonement covering according to the law, He can bring a wedding announcement and eternal consummation of one-ment covering through the Spirit. We would be well served to praise Him for the mercy to bring the revelation while there is yet time.

On the two year anniversary of my personal Day of Atonement, our family was in Florida. Mycah had the opportunity to participate in a seaside family retreat for children with cancer. Literally, the week before we left, God put me in front of the research that taught about the Jewish wedding traditions for the very first time. Until then, I never knew anything about it really. I never knew there were two parts—betrothal and "huppa" or "covering" and how the two events were normally one to *two years* apart. You might imagine the shock I felt at the knowledge and understanding He revealed to me. I was on-the-floor astonished at His divine arrangements of all these things in my personal little life. It was the second anniversary of my "Day of Atonement" — literally and spiritually. Are you seeing this? When I was living in rebellion to His New Covenant, He called me to judgment under the Old Covenant — sin required death and a blood sacrifice. However, now that I was fully living under the New Covenant covering of Christ's blood sacrifice, it was a time of one-ment — or a union. It was as if the LORD was telling me that the time had come to realize our anniversary as more than a day of atonement for sin, but that He wanted me to realize it was a literal day of at one-ment with Him as His bride. What I had experienced literally through the law would now (two years later) be made into something new I would experience through the Spirit. It was my wedding day! First Corinthians 6:17 says that [she] who unites [herself] with the Lord is *one* with Him in spirit just as two become one flesh. Much like my wedding to Chris, Jesus was going to whisk me away to a beach, this time in Florida! He knows I love beach weddings. And this time, I was fully aware of the presence of the Father of the bride. He would walk me down the aisle of covenant commitment and place my hand into His Son's nail-scarred one.

A few days before we left for Florida, I felt the Lord leaning on my heart in ways I'd never experienced before. He told me to arise early on the morning of October 8 and meet Him in the sand for a private showing of His glorious sunrise. Mornings are, by far, not my cup o' tea and I could not recall one time sitting alone to watch a sunrise in my entire life. It would be a virginal experience, if you will. And I was determined to not miss this for anything. Jesus and I had come a long way and we both waited a very long time for this day. I had been His and His alone for two years. I was finally living as a devoted bride, set apart for Him. He spent the two years preparing a place in my heart — my personal Holy of Holies — cleaning out the darkest corners, illuminating long forgotten desires, giving special attention to my uniqueness in the treasures He began to place there.

We arrived in Florida on a sunny afternoon. The next morning was the big day. I told no one about my private wedding plans. The evening before, we went down to dinner with all the people attending and volunteering at the family retreat. It was getting dark and I fretted that I did not know what time the sunrise was in the morning. I wondered how I would know what time to be on the beach. I stood half-way listening to the conversation of the group, when, as if on cue, like an archangel making divine announcement, I heard one of the volunteer men say, "Yeah, at 6:30 am that sun is going to start its rise and if the shades on your windows aren't closed, you'll be up with it." There was the information I needed heralded from an unsuspecting groomsman. He might as well have held a shofar to his lips. I could have sworn I heard holy trumpets announcing my Bridegroom's imminent arrival.

Do you hear the sound of trumpets in the distance? Sister, if you have allowed Him to purchase the threshing floor of your heart He will build a temple of His glory right on top. It might take a while, but if you remain devoted to Him, there will be a Day of Atonement for you. He will rip the veil and invite you into the Holy of Holies where you will be one with Him. It is an intimate, secret and sacred place. He paid special attention to your uniqueness so that when you go there for the first time you will feel comfortable and safe, overcome with tender emotions.

Jesus got my attention through ancient dates appointed on His Kingdom calendar, the blood of my first born, and the atonement covering I experienced within my personal Holy of Holies. He spent two years, literally, preparing a place within my heart. Then He came back for the devoted, mature and flawless bride He died to purchase. What kind of God do we serve? He arranged this marriage and wrote it in the DNA of His chosen one.

I don't think I slept at all that night. I woke up every hour thinking the sun was to rise at any moment, dreaming I was missing it. I had my clothing ready, and watched the clock tick off the minutes. At 6:00 am I bounded from the bed, left Chris and Mycah sound asleep, and stole away to meet my eternal Bridegroom. I was on my knees before the first rays of dawn lifted up the night's veil. And when the Son rose on that morning, He rose to cover me in His warm love. Within the sacred chamber of my heart, the place He spent two years preparing for me — upon the Holy of Holies within the temple built upon my threshing floor, I experienced, for the first time, a new kind of one-ment in Christ as His bride. It was truly my personal day of at-one-ment, my personal wedding day. And until I see Him face to face, I continue to meet with Him privately, intimately within the Holy of Holies inside my heart, through the Spirit.

Just as every single bride throughout all of history has a unique wedding story, your spiritual betrothal and ensuing wedding with the Lord will be unique and personal. It is not my intention to present my experience as a canned process for you. God is far too creative for that. Instead, I pray it will be sort of a siren call — like a sweet scent on the air that will lead you to desire and pursue one-ment with Christ. Ask God to open your eyes to see what He is using to speak to you.

Look closely in His Word, in the timing and spiritual parallels of your daily circumstances. Prepare and be ready when He comes for you. He is anxiously waiting the appointed time. And His Father has been overseeing this plan since before the creation. We can experience the treasures of abundant life as the bride of the King of kings in our temporal, earthly circumstances through His Spirit until we see Him face to face. The threshing floor. . .Christ can turn it into your bridal chamber. He is a carpenter by trade, Savior by birth, Rescuer in death, Conqueror in resurrection, and Lover of your soul.

All glorious is the princess within her chamber. . . (Psalm 45:13a)

The threshing floors will be filled with grain,
The vats will overflow with new wine and oil.
Then you will know. . .
That I am the LORD your God,
And that there is no other. . . (Joel 2:24, 27)

Chapter 10

The Wedding Feast—Something New From Something Old

W hile in the process of writing the last chapters of this book, I decided to re-decorate our dining room. I wonder what I was thinking! Perhaps, a distraction would be the remedy to some serious writer's block I've had lately. And I just love food, so the dining room seemed a good place to find needed sustenance (or a reasonably justifiable hiding place). Turns out it was—sustenance in abundance, that is.

It all started when our family was on vacation in South Carolina. I found the cutest wooden serving dish in the shape of a little fish while shopping with my mom and sister-in-law. It called to me from amongst a myriad of fine house wares in a charming old town, main street boutique. It was an odd choice, but I liked it because it reminded me of the story of the two fishes and five loaves from the Bible. I knew I wanted the little fish for my dining room to teach Mycah about the Biblical miracle and for it to serve as a reminder for our family to pray for two fishes and five loaves kind of miracles. Well, long story stretched too long, I ended up collecting several items and decided to give the dining room a Biblical food theme.

You'll have to pardon me for a moment just while I laugh at myself. If someone had told me three years ago, I'd decorate my dining room in a Biblical theme of any sort I would have choked on my plate full of sinful life. But God has a way of capturing one's soul. And once you get a taste of Him, it's worse than any chocolate addiction. You just cannot get enough. An authentic and powerful relationship with the Living God through His Son has nothing to do with knick knacks and religion. No, a living, breathing, and affective relationship is the only thing that keeps this girl craving more of Him.

So for several months I determined to collect items for my new project. And let me tell you, I went from cute boutiques in South Carolina, to wheat fields in Oklahoma, to a Texas Judaica (historical materials relating to Judaism) store, to Hobby Lobby—you can't be creative without making a few purchases at Hobby Lobby, let's just be real—gathering items for my design vision. Much of what I gathered pertains to the very concepts I've researched and come to love while writing this book.

- Wheat and barley stalks (in cute vases)
- Wheat seed and wheat flour (in little glass jars)
- Unleavened bread (if you've been paying attention at all in the first chapters, you will understand the significance of these).
- Wine

- Salt from the Dead Sea (in a glass jar) and Candles — because Jesus commanded us to be salt and light of the earth (Matthew 5:13 & 14)

- Honey — The Promised land was characterized as a land flowing with milk and honey and to represent Psalm 119:103, *"How sweet are your words to my taste, sweeter than honey to my mouth."*

- A Kiddush cup — I went on pilgrimage to a Texas Judaica store an hour from my home to get it and it is my favorite thing in the whole room I think. Remember a Kiddush cup is the cup used in traditional Jewish dinners, holidays, and betrothal ceremonies. My Kiddush cup has a Hebrew engraving on the base. It has the traditional blessing said over wine and is translated: *Blessed are You, the Lord our God, King of the Universe, Creator of the fruit of the vine. (Amen)*

- Photos of Mycah in my mom's wheat field and several Scriptures pertaining to food printed and framed

One Saturday, my little family worked together to put my vision onto the actual walls. Chris had the job of hanging a little ledge around the room to serve as a display for all the items. His tasks included anything requiring power tools, levels, or ladders. Mycah helped wash and dry the glass jars and put all the ingredients into their display containers. I organized, assisted and bossed everyone around. The evening seemed pretty normal to me. Our family has worked on projects together many times. But looking back on the whole scene, pondering all these things in my heart, I can't deny that God must have highly favored this particular endeavor.

I recall telling Mycah about the components of the design. As we placed unleavened bread pieces into a glass container, I told her again that unleavened bread, in the Bible, is a symbol of Jesus — there was no sin (yeast) in Him and His body was broken so we could be saved from our sins. And with each item we placed in the room, we discussed its meaning and significance to both physical and spiritual nutrition. Now don't get the idea these were all Normal Rockwell painting sort of moments. It went on amongst my husband's power-tool profanity (completely innocent and accidental whispers of course), short and rude remarks between husband and wife typical during home improvement projects, and hasty discipline when little hands and fingers were placed on forbidden objects.

But somewhere in all the chaos God must have stooped low to pour upon us the Holy Spirit in generous servings. And like His water to wine miracle in Cana, the timing couldn't be sweeter.

At some point in the afternoon, Mycah asked to taste the unleavened bread. So I consented, more out of distraction than anything else. Then she asked for grape juice. I served her while quickly rushing to hand Chris the masking tape while he balanced on a ladder too short for the job. In passing, I remember telling her how in Jesus' day people sometimes dipped the bread into their wine. She proceeded to try it with her grape juice and commented, as I sped back by with the hammer, that she liked it. I think I might have responded, I don't exactly know.

When the room was complete, the p.m. of the day had almost turned to a.m. Worn out and beat down, I climbed the rungs of Mycah's bunk bed to complete the day's last task of tucking her in tight. My eyes were beginning to give in to the urge to close, when Mycah started asking questions about heaven.

Again.

Heaven has been the subject of many pillow talks. It started after she was first diagnosed with leukemia. As morbid as it may sound, I wanted to be sure she wasn't afraid of heaven. A good mother tries to prepare her children for the things they might soon encounter. Like when they go to school for the first time or a new social event. Since she was in a fight for her life, I felt it both heartbreaking and necessary to prepare her for heaven, just in case. . .

We looked into Scripture together for descriptions of heaven and fantasized about what wonderful things we will do and see there. She was never aware of my intentions to speak of these things or the full weight of her cancer diagnosis. She just enjoyed the conversation. And I prayed like mad she was listening, pondering, and falling in love with a God who would invite us to such eternal happiness. While I prayed she would live to have the chance to choose Him for herself someday, I also came to a place where it was well with my soul if God allowed, in His sovereignty, to call her to heaven before. I am completely confident that we can and should cry out to God to heal our children from disease or injury. He is certainly capable. But often when I am tearfully desperate, begging Him for what I believe is best for an endangered child, wonder what I might not be able to see. I mean, what are we really asking for? We cannot have a clue. He can see things we cannot. I finally determined and surrendered that God alone knows what is best and He can see eternity. Maybe He is protecting them and us from unseen evil or pains too brutal for us to take. If Mycah's eternity was at stake, or if He knew something of her future I could not, I wanted the Lord to ensure she'd be protected in heaven with Him. Even if that meant He brought her home before

I was ready. I hate to hear when a child dies. I hate it, but in many ways, I am happy (please do not ever mistake that for envy) for parents whose children are waiting for them in heaven. They can know their little one is complete, whole, healthy, and living an abundant, eternal life with Jesus. Their precious souls escaped a moment's more of the desolate trouble of this world, protected by an all-knowing God. Trying to reconcile the horrible pain of a child's death with the relief of a child's health restored is too much for finite human minds. God alone knows. His ways are good and He loves mercy.

In the days when Mycah's life was in such danger (she was four then), I was certain of her eternity. The Bible is clear that children meet instant heaven in the case of their deaths. When a child grows to the age that he or she is aware of and understands right and wrong, she must choose to accept Jesus or reject Him. (Isaiah 7:15-16) That age is different for everyone and only God knows a heart and He is always just. And as Mycah has been given the healing and opportunity to grow in physical and spiritual age, Chris and I tried to teach her the truths of Scripture and point her to an understanding of the gospel and a relationship with Christ. However, we also knew God alone calls a heart to Himself. Content to ask God for wisdom to do our part, Chris and I waited patiently for God to do His, and we prayed ferociously she would answer His first knock.

So I didn't give it much thought when Mycah started the heaven conversation again. Many nights she would say something like, "Mom, when I get to heaven, my mansion is going to have a disco ball in it, I think. Because God knows I like to party." Then we giggle and do a party jig in her bed. But on this night, her voice was different. She sounded intense and almost fearful. "Mom, if heaven is going to be better than anything we can imagine with our minds, what will hell be like?"

Whoa.

As much as I wanted to blow it off and give her a trite answer in my weary state, my spirit caught enough within me to know better. "Well, it will be far more painful, sad, and horrible than anything we can imagine with our minds," I said now sitting straight up looking into the precious face I love so much.

"Mom, would God really make people go to hell?"

"Sweetie, everyone will live forever. It will be in heaven with God or it will be in hell without Him. The Bible is very clear on it. We all are sinners and deserve hell, but God loved us enough to give us a way back to Him so He sent His son to die and overcome hell in our place. The choice belongs to each of us where we spend eternity."

Mycah had heard the gospel hundreds of times by then, almost seven and a half years old. She completed all her Sunday school pages with correct answers. But if I've learned anything in that time, it is that God is about intimacy; and comprehension of Grace is a miracle. A miracle performed by Him alone.

She started to weep and I asked her why. She struggled to give an answer and instantly I understood. When Jesus knocks on the door of your heart, the feeling is as heavy as a load of stone. You suddenly feel the full weight of the sin He carried for you. Sensing she needed me to speak, I said, "Mycah, God is very patient and abounds in love. (Exodus 34:6, Psalm 86:15) If you are not ready to accept Jesus as your Savior, He will wait, I feel certain. But if you want Him to be your Savior, you can settle that right now."

"I want to ask Jesus to come into my heart," she said assuredly though quietly.

She called Daddy into the room. He came and together we held hands as Mycah wept and prayed this prayer I helped her say: "I know I am a sinner and without you I can do no good thing. I confess with my mouth and believe with my heart that Jesus is LORD. He died and was buried and rose again. God, You have chosen me and tonight I choose you back. Fill me with Your Spirit and help me love and serve You all of my days. In Jesus name, Amen."

As simple as that, she became not only my daughter, but my sister for all eternity. If you've not ever prayed that prayer, I do not want to miss the opportunity to encourage you to do so. It is of extreme eternal importance. If you want to be adopted into the family of God, it starts with a prayer and a belief as simple as that of a child. It can be done, sealed for all eternity, in the quietness of this moment where you sit. You can be born again into God's plan for redemption but don't think for a moment, He won't want you to begin growing in the new life He delights to create in you. Find someone to tell about your decision and make haste to ask God to help you seek out a community of believers who can encourage and strengthen your faith through solid Biblical teaching.

Mycah asked for unleavened bread and grape juice while her daddy and I were consumed with laser levels and knick knacks. We were unaware that she was pondering, listening to the call of her First Love and wrestling with a decision of eternal importance. But He was stooping low. He saw every taste, noticed every sip, favored her every move toward His loving call as she partook of an eternal covenant.

When we weren't really looking, God was watching over His Word and fulfilled it before we slept on that very night. No sooner had the adhesive set on the acrylic words Chris just hung on the wall in the dining room, "As for me and my house, we will serve the LORD" did God make it so. All of the Nichols' family has chosen to serve the Lord. But the thing I just can't stop thinking about is His way of obscene goodness. *"Give, and it will be given to you. A good measure, pressed down, shaken together and running over, will be poured into your lap.* (Luke 6:38) He is a God of lavish abundance.

I pray I might point many women to their Savior and personal promise lands, helping them to understand and use their God-given armor, teaching them to fight like women of valor until they come to the other side of their valley of shadowy death. I feel that calling on my life. And it is only because I've crossed over ahead of them, that I know the blood, sweat and tears are worth it. I count myself a hollow failure if I fell completely for Jesus without inspiring my own daughter, who sees me at my best and at my worst, to behold with her eyes the face of the One who made the way straight. She was once my idol. I thought God should surely take her from this faithless mother. Instead He called me to repentance through blood and exchanged His for hers. . . .and mine. In a heaping overflow of miracle — five loaves and two fishes style — a turn of events provided I got to be the one to lead her to His loving heart. Mycah is alive and well and had the chance to choose Christ for herself. Glory to our God!

We know man is by nature a sinner but it is hard to believe that a young child has the type of sin in her life that would require a Redeemer. But sin is sin and it all separates us from a Holy God and consequently, means death. I can clearly recall making the decision to accept Christ as my Savior when I was seven. In fact, the Bible I received from my parents to mark the occasion is one of the items

I recently placed in my dining room. It sits on the table in a bread basket lined with a fabric cover with the words, "Give us this day our daily bread" embroidered on it. I truly believe that at the age of seven, I understood the sacrifice of Jesus for my sins. I wanted Him to live in my heart and I wanted to go to heaven.

There is something deeply endearing and innately sweet about seeing a child become aware of the love of her Savior. Jesus loved and welcomed children. He even said, *"I tell you the truth, anyone who will not receive the kingdom of God like a little child will never enter it.* (Luke 18:17) Faith appears to come easy to children. We tend to think it is because they are simple and have vivid imaginations that it is feasible for them to accept the love of God. I suppose that is true. But I wonder why as we grow, we think it helpful to trade those qualities for realistic reason and the need for visible proof. The longer we live in this brutal, fallen world, the more time the enemy has to hurl assaults at our simple hearts. And in time, a heart once tender and simple can become complicated and stone cold, demanding visible proof of an infinite, invisible God. Still, there is nothing like child-like faith. It is humble, pure and innocent — everything God loves.

Paul wrote in 1 Corinthians 13:11-13, *"When I was a child, I talked like a child, I thought like a child, I reasoned like a child. When I became a man, I put childish ways behind me. . . Now I know in part; then I shall know fully, even as I am fully known. And now these three remain: faith, hope and love. But the greatest of these is love."* There came a time in my life when the faith and hope I had in my child-like understanding had to be overshadowed by full-bloom love. This book is largely the story of that "coming-of-age" journey for me. I believe Mycah will experience her own trials and thrills as she matures in Christ. But as the Song of Solomon warns, *"Do not arouse or awaken love until it so desires"* (Songs 3:5) and *"there is. . . a time for every purpose under the heavens"* (Ecclesiastes 3: 1 KJV) — the timing belongs to God.

Search your heart, sister. Is this the season? Is this your time to come to a deeper understanding of the Lover of your soul? Is He wooing you to arise and come with Him? If so, it is my prayer you invest with everything inside yourself and pursue Him with a life and death urgency. If not, my prayer is you will know when the time is right. But I have a feeling, as your eyes read these words in this moment, perhaps a sovereign Love's desire has called you here for such a time as this.

Here is a true statement: Innocence and purity are prerequisite to a mature experience of intimacy and perfection (completeness) with Christ. God absolutely requires a pure bride for His beloved Son. Please don't fret that you are neither innocent nor pure. None of us in our own flesh are. But once we are cleansed in the blood of the Lamb, we are as clean, pure, and innocent as new fallen snow. Our sins are not only forgiven. They are forgotten. (Isaiah 43:25) Jesus Himself, because of His righteousness given to you by the cross, qualifies you as a pure virgin fit for a royal union. In fact, one of His most divine abilities is bringing something new from something old. This concept is more than a line from a traditional wedding poem, it is godly by design, found many times throughout Scripture, and deeply meaningful to you and me. It is also the focus of this chapter.

But before we get too far, we have to set something straight in our minds and hearts regarding the character of God. Would it surprise you to hear that God loves a good party? It might be difficult for you to think of God, Almighty sitter-on-a-throne in heaven, as One who loves to celebrate. It was for me. Before I got to know Him, I

221

thought the Christian life boring. I believed it to be a life of restrictions and "thou shalt not's" and devoted followers of Jesus must be the squarest people on the round planet Earth. I'll admit it. I wanted to be a Christian, but I really wanted to enjoy life too and I didn't know how those two things matched up.

Sister, I once was blind, but now, oh, Glory, but now I see. It's only been a little more than three years since I've been living as a devoted bride, but I am convinced if we are not celebrating in high style, laughing with reckless abandon, dining on the richest of fare while clothed in beauty, and seeing obscene evidence of His ridiculous love in our lives on a regular basis, we are doing it WRONG! God's riches and the world's idea of riches are not the same so it takes a spiritual eye to recognize and enjoy God's abundance. He alone can open our eyes to see those things for their value in the spiritual realm. Here are a few examples to consider.

- God gave us one day a week to do no work. (Leviticus 23:3) It is "His day" and we are to keep it holy and rest. But that doesn't mean it has to be a snooze fest. It is a day of refreshment to look at the week's accomplishments in Christ, kick back and say "it is good" just as He did when He completed all of creation. I bet He celebrated His handiwork, don't you?
- God instituted seven feasts a year. (Leviticus 23) The feasts were times for taking a break from the daily grind and worshipping God. Some of them required a journey to Jerusalem in which families traveled together and fellowshipped. There was good food, wine and merriment.

- God even instituted the Sabbath year—every seventh year, the land was to rest and no one was to reap or sow the fields and vineyards. (Leviticus 25:4) And the Jubilee year—every fiftieth year, in which everyone was to go home to their own property and do no work, debts were to be forgiven and captives were to be set free, and God's miracles would be particularly manifest. (Leviticus 25:10) Sounds like a reason to celebrate to me.

- Jesus performed His first miracle at a wedding! He turned water (something old) into fine wine (something new and better). He did so with great abundance. (John chapter 2)

- God's master plan of redemption culminates in a wedding supper accompanied with the shouts of a great multitude in heaven, "Hallelujah!" (Revelation 19)

God invented celebrations, times of rest and refreshment, weddings, music, dancing, and worship. It is to be for His glory and the splendor of His name when we take the time to plan, prepare, and attend a party in His honor and for His pleasure. In fact, I really think that if we are not participating in good celebrations on a regular weekly, monthly, and yearly basis, we are missing a big part of the experience of knowing and loving the Almighty God.

With that in mind, let's check back in with the ancient Jewish bride and groom's wedding celebration for a bit of a review and then a preview of what is coming next in the display of God's glorious plan for us as we look at the Feast of Passover and how Christ used the occasion to create something new out of something old. Finally, we will look at the abundant character of God toward you through

Christ's first miracle. Something old, something new, something abundant, something you. . . .

Ancient Jewish tradition provided the bride and bridegroom entered the bridal chamber (huppah) alone and consummated their union during the *Nisuin* or "hometaking." The best man stood outside the door and waited for the groom to inform him that the union was complete in all aspects (wink, wink). The best man then announced the good news to the wedding party and close family who were waiting in attendance. Then the wedding feast commenced. Following the hometaking, additional family and invited guests joined to celebrate and rejoice at the groom's father's house for seven days with fine food and wine. All the while, the newlyweds remained alone together in the bridal chamber for those days. This gave them focused and uninterrupted time to learn about one another personally, make plans for their future, and seek God's blessing during the first days of their new life as a married couple. After six days in the wedding chamber, the bride and bridegroom emerged and participated in a final feast with friends and family.[29] This meal is called *Seudat Mitzyah*, a "festive meal!" It was the culmination of a week-long joyous celebration and it concluded the wedding festivities. This event was the first time the bride appeared without her veil in public, for all to see, since her betrothal. I image the groom was thrilled to finally stand as a proud husband with his radiant wife, delighted to put her in a place of honor in his father's home. This feast was the culmination of his desire and extravagant efforts on her behalf.

Yes, I believe God loves a celebration, but make no mistake, He is romantic from Alpha all the way to Omega. Genesis begins with God creating a paradise setting for the first wedding, breathing life into a man and then a woman who was bone of her husband's bone and flesh of his flesh. They were united, becoming one flesh, naked and without shame. (Genesis 2) His plan of redemption of fallen mankind will culminate in the Wedding of the Lamb where the bride is given her wedding dress by God Himself and everything will be made new. The old order of things will be passed away and He will wipe every year from our eyes. (Revelation 19 and 20) He makes "all things new." (Revelation 21:5 KJV) That is the kind of romance I want in on. If you do as well, let's pull our chairs up to the table, sit up straight and receive our portion of grace and even abundance with gratitude.

In the previous chapters, we've participated in preparing the field, planting the seed, waiting for the harvest. We threshed it, sifted it, made a deal for the threshing floor, accepted a betrothal offer, and entered into the holy bridal chamber built upon the stony place. Let's all say it together: "It's about time for a FEAST!" But before we get to our present party, let's look back at an ancient feast, thirty-five centuries old. Passover is the foundational feast of the LORD and His other six feasts are built upon it.[30] It is absolutely essential to understanding Christ's New Covenant as well as our place at His nuptial table.

Remember the Feast of Passover was the first of the spring feasts. It is a memorial of the time God brought His people out of Egypt. God spoke to Moses from a burning bush, *"I have indeed seen the misery of my people in Egypt. I have heard them crying out because of their slave drivers, and I am concerned about their suffering. So I have come down to rescue them from the hand of the Egyptians and to bring them up out of that land into a good and spacious land, a land flowing with milk and honey. . . .And now the cry of the Israelites has reached me, and I have seen the way the Egyptians are oppressing them. So now, go. I am sending you to Pharaoh to bring my people the Israelites out of Egypt."* (Exodus 3:7-10)

The Lord brought plagues to the Egyptians in an effort to persuade Pharaoh to let His people go. Pharaoh's hard heart made him resistant until the final plague of the firstborn. God instructed Moses and his people in the all important requirements for the salvation of their first born children and of their flocks. He told them to choose a year-old male lamb without defect and slaughter it at twilight. *"Then they are to take some of the blood and put it on the sides and tops of the doorframes of the houses where they eat the lambs."* (Exodus 12:7)

"On that same night I will pass through Egypt and strike down every firstborn – both men and animals. . .I am the LORD. The blood will be a sign for you on the houses where you are; and when I see the blood, I will pass over you. No destructive plague will touch you when I strike Egypt." (Exodus 12:12-13)

The Hebrew people have celebrated the Feast of Passover for centuries to remember God's rescue from Pharaoh and the deadly plagues. In a traditional Jewish home, painstaking preparations take place. The Passover service is quite long as the Passover story must be told according to God's instruction. *"And when your children ask you, 'What does this ceremony mean to you? Then tell them, 'It is the Passover sacrifice to the LORD, who passed over the houses of the Israelites in Egypt and spared our homes when he struck down the Egyptians.'"* (Exodus 12:26-27) Let me just interject something here. If you have a personal Passover story where Jesus covered your sins and spared you punishment, then do as God instructed His people and tell your children about it. It is the legacy of their faith, the evidence of His power in their personal family.

226

The traditional Jewish Passover ceremony dinner, called a Seder (meaning 'order'), includes songs, prayers, and narrative readings completed in a particular order. It began when the mother of the house lit the Passover candles and gave the blessing: "Blessed art Thou, O Lord our God, King of the Universe, Who has set us apart by His Word, and in whose Name we light the festival lights." Then the first of four cups of wine (symbolic of the joy of harvest) was taken during the Passover service to reflect the four fold joy of the Lord's redemption (Exodus 6:6-7):

1. I will bring you out
2. I will rescue you from bondage
3. I will redeem you
4. I will take you as My people

The first cup was extended while the prayer of sanctification "Kiddush" was said. Then everyone washed their hands as a symbolic act of purification. Then everyone present took some green vegetable (karpas) and dipped it into salt water symbolizing Passover occurs in springtime and the salt symbolic of the tears of pain and suffering shed by the people in slavery. Next the leader of the home breaks the middle piece of three pieces of unleavened bread (matzah) and then four questions are asked by the youngest at the table. These questions prompt the telling of the Passover story. Then the second cup of wine is poured. In preparation of the meal everyone present washes his hands a second time for ceremonial cleansing. The matzah is then broken and passed around the table and distributed to everyone. It is eaten with a mixture of horseradish and apple as a reminder of the sweetness of God's redemption in the midst of their bitter slavery. Dinner is served next; roasted lamb with bitter herbs and matzah. Dinner is followed by the third cup (the Cup of Redemption). Then the Fourth cup or the Cup of Acceptance, or Praise is poured and taken. Last a hymn is sung at the ending of the Passover meal. The Passover service is woven with rich symbolism and is a picture of the redemptive story of Jesus.

God's timing is always perfect. It came about that Jesus celebrated the Feast of Passover with His disciples the night of His betrayal. Jewish holidays begin at sunset so Jesus partook of the Passover meal the night before His crucifixion. Jesus died on the day of Passover as fulfillment of the Passover Lamb slain to give deliverance for the people in Egypt. He also died as the Passover Lamb to save us from death as well. The timing was not a mistake, nor a coincidence. It was God's plan and a clear message. Just as in the days of Pharaoh, there is still no deliverance without the Lamb.[31]

The authors of the four gospels, Matthew, Mark, Luke, and John, record this night with different details. Three of the four men were present at the meal and penned their accounts from different perspectives. We are going to use all four accounts to piece the night's events together. Imagine that night.

"On the first day of the Feast of Unleavened Bread, when it was customary to sacrifice the Passover lamb, Jesus' disciples asked him, 'Where do you want us to go and make preparations for you to eat the Passover?'" (Mark 14:12) Jesus gave instructions and his disciples obeyed and found the location just as Jesus told them. *"When the hour came, Jesus and his apostles reclined at the table. And he said to them, 'I have eagerly desired to eat this Passover with you before I suffer.' While they were eating,*

Jesus took bread, gave thanks and broke it, and gave it to his disciples, saying, 'Take it. This is my body given for you; do this in remembrance of me.' Then he took the cup, gave thanks and offered it to them, and they all drank from it. 'All of you. This is the blood of the covenant, which is poured out for many for the forgiveness of sins. I tell you the truth, I will not drink again of the fruit of the vine until that day when I drink it anew in my Father's kingdom.'" (From Matthew 26:26-29, Mark 14:22-26, Luke 22:14-20)

Jesus performed the centuries-old Passover service, showing His disciples how He came to fulfill the task of the Passover lamb. But He also changed the old order of things to instate a new tradition for a New Covenant. *"For Christ, Our Passover lamb, has been sacrificed."* (1 Corinthians 5:7b) Jesus taught His disciples to partake of unleavened bread and wine in remembrance of Christ's death on the cross for our sins. They were symbols of His body and His blood. He died to fulfill the Old Covenant's prophesies regarding the promised Messiah. He also died so you and I might accept the offer of His New Covenant. Essentially Jesus brought something new (the New Covenant) from something old (the Passover of the Old Testament). It is a beautiful display, perfectly orchestrated in time and circumstance to show God's glorious plan of redemption.

However, I think there is more. For the abundance seeker, we can look closely with our spiritual eyes and see not only was Jesus instating the New Covenant out of the Old Covenant in the present moment, but He spoke of the Wedding Feast to come. Jesus appears to be taking the Passover tradition and marrying it with the Jewish wedding customs.

As the evening progressed, Jesus comforted His disciples, saying: *"Do not let your hearts be troubled. Trust in God, trust also in me. In my*

Father's house are many rooms; if it were not so, I would have told you. I am going there to prepare a place for you. And if I go and prepare a place for you, I will come back and take you to be with me that you may be where I am." (John 14:1-3) You'll remember these are the words from the Jewish Wedding Rite customarily said by the bridegroom to his bride to reassure her of his return for her when his preparations for their life together are complete.

Think about how the prospective bride washed herself at the betrothal ceremony (mikvah) and how Jesus washed the feet of His disciples on the very night He took Passover with them in the upper room. *"The evening meal was being served. . .He [Jesus] got up from the meal, took off his outer clothing, and wrapped a towel around his waist. After that, he poured water into a basin and began to wash his disciples' feet, drying them with the towel that was wrapped around him."* (John 13: 2a, 4-5)

Also think about Jesus' offering the cup of the covenant to his disciples. They all sipped from it to bring about a New Covenant tradition, or The Lord's Supper. But it is also reminiscent of a bridegroom extending the betrothal cup to his bride. Her acceptance of the betrothal contract was signified in her sipping from the offered cup. Likewise, the disciples (except for Judas who already left to carry out his betrayal) drank from Christ's cup.

Consider His words, *"I tell you, I will not drink of this fruit of the vine from now on until that day when I drink it anew with you in my Father's kingdom."* (Matthew 26:29) In other words, Christ was telling them, as well as us, that this dinner was *to be continued* in the coming age. When the entirety of God's redemptive plan is complete, we will celebrate at the wedding feast and Jesus will finally drink again of the fruit of the vine and receive the praise He is due. Jesus instated the tradition of the LORD's Supper or Communion for us to partake of until He returns. The bread and wine serve as touchable reminders of His loving redemption. Fickle flesh requires frequent recollection. Not so for Him. He thinks of nothing apart from His love and desire for you. *"Blessed are those who are invited to the wedding supper of the Lamb!"* (Revelation 19:9)

The Passover of old was made into a New Covenant symbol of Christ. The partaking of the bread and wine became a remembrance of His work on the cross until we see Him face to face in God's kingdom at the wedding feast! I don't know about you, but the knowledge of Christ's ability to make something old into something new makes me feel like I have a prepared place at that table! Because He has made in me a new life out of an old sinful one, I am included among those He is promised to come back and take to be with Him. And it's not just any old place either, but a place of honor and abundance as His bride.

Speaking of abundance, John Chapter 2, versus 1-11 gives us a peek into Jesus' first miracle. I hope by now you are not surprised. It was at a wedding!

[1] *On the third day a wedding took place at Cana in Galilee. Jesus' mother was there,* [2] *and Jesus and his disciples had also been invited to the wedding.* [3] *When the wine was gone, Jesus' mother said to him, "They have no more wine."* [4] *"Dear woman, why do you involve me?" Jesus replied. "My time has not yet come."* [5] *His mother said to the servants, "Do whatever he tells you."* [6] *Nearby stood six stone water jars, the kind used by the Jews for ceremonial washing, each holding from twenty to thirty gallons.* [7] *Jesus said to the servants, "Fill the jars with water"; so they filled them to the brim.* [8] *Then he told them, "Now draw some out and take it to the master of the banquet." They did so,* [9] *and the master of the banquet tasted the water that had been turned into wine. He did not realize where it had come from, though the servants who*

had drawn the water knew. Then he called the bridegroom aside [10] *and said, "Everyone brings out the choice wine first and then the cheaper wine after the guests have had too much to drink; but you have saved the best till now."* [11] *This, the first of his miraculous signs, Jesus performed at Cana in Galilee. He thus revealed his glory, and his disciples put their faith in him.*

At first glance, one might think this story insignificant and wonder why John was inspired to include it in his gospel, aside from the fact that it was the first miracle Jesus performed and should be written for the record. No one was demon possessed or cold in the grave, or even terminally ill. Perhaps Jesus needed to start with a simple miracle until His powers had fully developed. I doubt it. Instead, I think if we look harder we might be able to glean some sweet details about the character of our Bridegroom. I think it will whet our appetite for the wedding feast to come.

1. Jesus creates something new from something old. He turned water into wine because changing one element into another symbolized covenant and more specifically, marriage. It's what He does. Here we see it in His first miracle — the one by which He revealed His glory. Let's love the fact that it was at a wedding! I just adore the whole picture God is painting in this scene. The eternal Bridegroom is invited to a wedding. And He is needed to solve the problem at hand but also to gloriously display God's redemptive plan for His people. He is still fully capable of doing both in our lives today. There is so much here, we could study for days just on these eleven versus. But here's what I want us to savor and digest: Christ has the power

to take the ordinary and change it into something entirely new and unexpected. He did it when changing water to wine and He desires to do it in your earthly vessel too. I often wonder how the glorious, splendid riches of His kingdom can be displayed through me — someone who on most days can be found in ragged pajamas mid-morning, vacuuming, cleaning toilets, or engaged in some other ordinary task. The enemy loves to tell me in those times I am too dirty, too regular and common to be used for God's kingdom. I'd bet money Satan has fed you some of that disgusting trash too. It's time we spat those lies out in his ugly face. Through the blood of our perfect Lamb, we are qualified for holy, glorious use.

2. Christ creates new glory in abundance. In this particular instance, Jesus turns the water from six stone jars (normally used for cleaning purposes), holding 20 to 30 gallons each into choice wine. If my math is correct, that means we are talking well over 120 gallons of wine! Seeing the text tells us the bridegroom is present at the festivities, we know this is most likely the evening of the last day of the week long wedding feast. I think Jesus was making sure there were plenty of leftovers for the new couple to take to their new home. Jesus left a generous gift with the new couple! Abundance is His way. He is gloriously lavish. Don't think for a second that abundance isn't in your future if you walk with Him, invite Him to it, and obey Him for it. Not only is He capable of turning five loaves and two fishes into a filling meal for thousands of people, complete with baskets full of leftovers, He can make the wine to go with it! If these are the things He did while here on earth,

can you stand to even imagine what His personal wedding feast will be like? We better get ready. The harvest He brings about in your life will go toward a feast like none have ever thought or imagined!

3. He celebrates! Oh, don't miss this one. It might appear Jesus was almost grumpy to do His mother's bidding at this particular wedding in Cana. He says to her, *"Dear woman, why do you involve me? My time has not yet come."* (John 2:4) Well, we know He ultimately does what she asks Him to do and saves the reputation of her family friends by providing abundant wine when they were fresh out. But it seems that perhaps He did it unwillingly or reluctantly, suffering her request. Not so. I really think He was sending them and us a more meaningful message. Take a look again at His words to the disciples in the upper room at the last supper, *"I tell you the truth, I will not drink again of the fruit of the vine until that day when I drink it anew in the kingdom of God."* (Mark 14:25) His *"time has not yet come,"* (John 2:4) *"until that day when I drink it anew in the kingdom of God."* (Mark 14:25) What time? What day? His wedding day! His mind was ultimately and always set upon the fulfillment of His greater task. He is continuously, intimately involved with bringing His bride into His kingdom to dine with Him for eternity. His mind was at all times consumed with it. His time will come when His bride is seated beside Him, unveiled, in a place of honor at His wedding. Make no mistake, when the day comes, He will celebrate. Finally, He will raise a glass and drink of the cup of praise due Him. Brides, we will party like The Rock's stars.

I want to leave you with this. It is the prayer of my heart this morning in light of all He taught me about Himself through these unchangeable, solid Biblical truths. It is my prayer for you as well.

"Blessed are You, the Lord our God, King of the Universe, Creator of the fruit of the vine. Hosanna, do it again today. Let there be no shame in my bold request. Your hands are the Potter's. They mold with pressure and compassionate release. So spin me. Dance me upon your wheel. Take this dry clay, this ordinary vessel, this woman used for cleaning. Fill me with Living Water. Cleanse me by the washing with water through the Word and make me holy as You are holy. Mark me with Your blood. Breathe warm life over cold, cleansed flesh and make me anew. I know: for now it is a hint, like a view through a darkened glass. My earthen body cannot stand to bear Your full glory. But in that day — Your wedding day — I shall behold, face to face, Your eyes fixed on mine. Until then, take my heart's only offering. Your Word on my lips, "How much more pleasing is Your love than wine." Ah, Sovereign Lord, You are wild and sweet from *once upon a time* to *everlasting eternity*."

If ever you've reason to celebrate, this is it: you are your Lover's and your Lover is yours.

Cheers, sisters.

> *"On this mountain the LORD Almighty will prepare*
> *a feast of rich food for all peoples,*
> *a banquet of aged wine —*
> *the best of meats and the finest of wines."* (Isaiah 25:6)

"In that day," declares the LORD, "you will call me 'my husband';
you will no longer call me 'my master.' (Hosea 2:16)

Chapter 11

The Bridal Chamber

While out shopping one day recently, I spotted a beautifully framed and matted presentation of this saying: "Life isn't about waiting for the storm to pass, it's about learning to DANCE IN THE RAIN." Chris was doing a bang-up job tolerating my weekend shopping outing. I don't believe I heard so much as a sigh or saw him even glance at his wrist watch. An ultimate gentleman in a number of home décor or "girlie stores" as he calls them, he particularly endeared himself to me. When my hyper-man who wears down even youths of mere teen years calms himself to shop with me in the "breakable stuff aisles" (his words again), I am a happy wife.

I pulled him over and pointed my batting eyes toward the piece. He stood in front of it and moved his lips as he read the words. Then he looked in my direction with absolve and said in the dreamiest manly melody. "Babe, we're not leaving this store without it. You must have it. It is so you."

Do I have to tell you my reaction?

Swoon!

This time, it was almost I who had to buy it because I nearly broke it fainting ever so gracefully to the floor. Not really. I didn't faint, but that would've been cool.

Learning to dance in the rain has been the theme, in many aspects, of my season of late. Walking with the LORD in the last few years has entailed everything from painful pulling, dead stops on my knees, clumsy stumbles, and countless do-overs. But every now and then, Jesus pulls back the veil of these earthly eyes, rains down His unspeakable glory, and I get just a glimpse of the girl He sees in the hope of my calling.

Let me tell you of one such time.

It was a clinic day for Mycah. She had been sick with a virus and delayed the previous week from receiving her chemo. On this day she was feeling better and didn't have fever. After a check of her lungs, the oncologist determined her healthy enough to move forward with her treatment protocol. It took several hours for her to receive chemo, undergo a spinal tap and a monthly breathing treatment she hates and in turn makes me and her daddy miserable. When we got home, I tended to the everyday chores of our household while Mycah had a snack and watched afternoon television to fully recover from anesthesia. Chris returned to work.

As I had every week for the previous two years, I called my mom with the news of our clinic visit. While recounting the burdensome routine, I walked onto the front porch to consider the small, dark rain cloud that, from my point of view, appeared to shadow just our home. With a heavy sigh, I mumbled, "how fitting." I pressed 'end' on the phone and stood barefoot, denying the dry bones of weariness I was too young to possess. Still.

Rolls of gentle thunder awakened my senses to God's scary powerful goodness leaning heavy upon my soul. Flashes of lightning, rolls of thunder, Revelation 4:5 pierced my awareness and I began to echo back quietly as I bent to sit on the front step, *"Holy, holy, holy is the LORD God Almighty, who was, and is, and is to come."*

Somehow I could almost sense it. He was loving on me.

Just then. . .one. Just one. The sloppiest, fattest, wet drop I've ever seen plopped down near my feet. It left a mark on the hot sidewalk the size of a chicken egg. I giggled. Then slowly more fell and speckled the grey concrete. I stretched my legs out in front of me and fell deeply into the soothing sensation as He washed my weary feet. He is the First and Last Gentleman. . .a servant at heart.

After a moment of stillness between me and my Savior, Mycah walked out the front door dressed in the pink froggy nightgown we put on her following a warm bath to help remove the bandages from her port and spinal puncture.

She sat down next to me and told me she heard the thunder and was afraid. I wrapped her under my arm and told her not to worry. God was loving on us. She stretched her sweet little feet in front of her to match mine. Our hot pink toenails wiggled and we laughed at the juicy raindrops tickling our faces.

Now unafraid, Mycah got up and walked tentatively into the yard. The tempo of the rain sped as she tip-toed. Then she turned and mused the words I've pasted to the wall of my heart's memory for eternity.

"Mom, I think He wants us to dance!"

The rain drops falling on my cheeks disguised my tears, and I got up and twirled with my woman-child beauty. There we were. Two years into cancer treatment. On chemo afternoon. Spinal tap day no less. Up since 5:30 am. Beat down from the stressful whipping that just is cancer clinic day. And we were dancing in the rain.

In that moment, I realized if my LORD is singing over me (Zephaniah 3:17), I wanna dance. Neither circumstance nor anything or anyone in heaven or earth has the right to enter into the private love between me and my Jesus. (Romans 8:39)

See, a bridal chamber is made for two—just me and Him. And at any time and in any circumstance, I can go to our secret place hidden away inside my heart. The place He has bought, built, and prepared for me; the place where His love tends to my soul and we dance as one complete Spirit.

Last chapter we learned about the celebration of the ancient Jewish wedding feast. We covered both the ancient custom as well as its shadow of the things to come in God's Kingdom story. In the pages to come, we've got to talk about what happens in that bridal chamber. Yes, it's time we talk intimacy. It is scandalously holy, pure and righteous. And much is at stake. Feeling awkward? Yeah, me too. Lord, help us.

But you know, I can't help but wonder if it was awkward for the ancient Jewish bride and groom too. Come on. Admit it. You were thinking the same thing. Perhaps the bridegroom tugged at the collar of his cloak and unnecessarily cleared his throat to break the sound of crickets chirping. Maybe the bride's cheeks flushed red and hot as she averted the piercing stares of her family and friends. I bet someone might have cut the painful social discomfort with nervous laughter like a knife through the top tier of a wedding cake. Did the men elbow one another in congratulatory awareness? Did the women blush and then giggle behind their hands and hush suddenly when they were caught? Did the children look around, tug on their mothers' party sashes and ask aloud what they were missing?

I guess we can only speculate as to what happened in the first moments when the Jewish bride and groom finally made an appearance at their own wedding feast. According to the ancient custom, the wedding celebration had been in progress for six days in the groom's father's home following the huppa ceremony before the couple joined in the festivities on the seventh day. As the family and guests partook of food, wine, and music, the newly-wed couple spent every bit of their time in the solitude of the bridal chamber. Within the private setting, years in the making, they made their union complete in the most intimate privilege of the marital experience.

Still, I can't help but wonder if the bride took extra care to smoother her tussled hair as it might give her away once she emerged from their chamber. But perhaps that is just because I have a twisted view of intimacy. Maybe you do too.

I mean, in our modern, anything-goes culture few things are sacred anymore. We are barraged in images of inappropriate material on television, movies, magazines, and the internet. Mostly though, we walk right past, giving little thought to the life-sized poster of a young, curvy woman posing in her underwear while standing in an open field of wild flowers. We don't question how in the world she found herself without clothes in the middle of nowhere. Neither does the logic of displaying her near-nudity in public cross our mind. Yet somehow it deals a mighty-gasp shock to think of a couple spending their first six days of marriage holdup alone together. Meanwhile their own mothers, fathers, sisters, brothers, great-aunt Ruths and friends filled their plates and toasted the couple's most sacred act of love while joining in the ancient Jewish version of the chicken-dance just outside the door. I wonder at what point in the days between that ancient Jewish bride to you and me, did it become normal to expose and display sexuality but real righteous intimacy is embarrassing — even shocking?

Paul said in Colossians 2:16-17 that the Jewish feasts and celebrations were a shadow of the things to come through Jesus Christ. So I ask you, what would happen if we got to know the God who created sacred intimacy between a covenant-committed man and woman all the while throwing a great banquet as the setting for such a joyous and private consummation? Perhaps a lesson in the righteous things that cause us to gasp is highly over-due.

You'll remember the ancient Jewish wedding customs included two different parts — the betrothal and then the "nisuin" or home-taking. For a man and woman to be married, both were necessary and equally important. First, the betrothal was a covenant commitment, unbreakable in the eyes of the law and the LORD. Then the "huppah" ceremony took place one to two years after the betrothal. The groom claimed his bride on an unannounced night and brought her to his father's home where he previously prepared a bridal chamber for their first night and days together as man and wife. The best man stood vigil outside the door of the chamber, waiting for word the all-important second part of the wedding ceremony was complete. At that time the couple was considered "married."

In a previous chapter we discussed the betrothal ceremony. Then we learned about the preparations the bride and groom made for their coming union. Last chapter, we learned about the wedding feast. We saw how it is the celebration of the glorious beginning of a new life as two lives become one. It is the festival of a promise fulfilled. We discovered all of these earthly traditions speak to us of God's plan of redemption and of Christ's love and desire for His bride, the Church. Well, sister, I love a good party. But I've also gotten to know the LORD of glory well enough by this point in our journey to know I don't want to just participate as one outside the door. I want to be in that bridal chamber. I want holy intimacy. What about you?

The Word of God records the events of Mount Moriah and tells us the temple of Yahweh God was built upon that holy mountain upon the threshing floor. We likened those truths to our personal lives in this modern day. Often God allows the circumstances of our lives to take us to a personal Mount Moriah just so He can purchase the threshing floor of our heart to build and prepare a personal meeting place for us there upon it. It is the temple of His glory in our very person. We likened the Holy of Holies to a bridal chamber—a secret and most sacred room built within the Father's house. You'll remember, in the actual temple in Jerusalem there was a heavy veil or curtain separating the Holy place from the Holy of Holies (the two times holy place). No one was to enter except the high priest. (Numbers 18:7) It was where the presence of God rested on earth. God and man were separated by a veil of sin. But when Christ cried out in a loud voice and gave up his spirit to death on the cross, Matthew 27: 51 tell us, *"At that moment the curtain of the temple was torn in two from top to bottom."* Christ, our high priest, died in order to tear the veil and now invites us to enter into the Holy Holy place.

Can your mind and heart bear up against the impact of that kind of Love? Do we dare desire to know a Savior who tore the curtain in His Father's holy house that He might invite His bride to her chamber of intimate one-ness with Him? Do we dare not to? I hope you've begun to see you can enter the holy, holy chamber through a torn veil to discover the place has been prepared with all the intricate details of a Lover wooing His beloved.

Romans 8:19 tells us, *"the creation waits in eager expectation for the sons of God to be revealed."* Like the anticipation of the best man and the waiting wedding party, creation is eager for word of the joyous union of Christ and His bride so it may be brought into the glorious freedom of the children of God. There will be a day when Christ returns for His Church and those of us in Christ will be seated with Him at His wedding feast as His bride. It will happen. But here's what I am asking you to consider. Until that day, could it be that you can experience the intimacy of oneness with Him within the private inner temple room He built in your heart through His Spirit? Could it be there is a torn veil and an extended nail scarred hand beckoning you to a personal and unique relationship likened to that of a married man and woman? As all the while God celebrates? If that could be reality, how would it change you?

For it is said, "The two will become one flesh." But [she] who unites [herself] with the Lord is one with him in spirit. (1 Corinthians 6:17)

"Now it is God who has made us for this very purpose and has given us the Spirit as a deposit, guaranteeing what is to come." (2 Corinthians 5:5)

Okay, hold up. If we are going to have a conversation and study about intimacy within our personal relationship with Jesus, we've got to get something straight. We need some ground rules, if you will. Jesus said, *"The Spirit gives life; the flesh counts for nothing. The words I have spoken to you are spirit and they are life."* (John 6:63) We are talking about spiritual oneness in this chapter. Our focus is not on "one flesh" physically, or the sexual oneness between man and wife. We have got to understand that the physical is a representation (a picture, object lesson, or foreshadow) of a spiritual concept. It is hard for our human minds to understand this godly concept. But plainly, a sexual oneness between a pure, devoted man and his faithful wife is meant to show us the in physical realm the loving character of the Lord toward his faithful followers and their expression of love in return to Him in the spiritual.

It is essential at this point to understand a mature and righteous relationship with Christ has little to do with our earthly experiences of the flesh and mostly to do with God's holy design for marriage and its representation of a *spiritual* oneness. God designed earthly marriage to display His love for His people. He intended for one virgin (holy pure) man to love, cherish and care for one virgin (holy pure) woman as if she were his own body. We can read of this concept many places in Scripture. Genesis chapter 2 shows us the first union between Adam and Eve. Verse 25 says a man will leave his father and mother and be united to his wife, and they will become one flesh. And then it goes on to say, *"The man and his wife were both naked, and they felt no shame."* Ezekiel chapter 16 gives an allegory of Jerusalem as God's wife. Verse 8 says, *"'Later I passed by, and when I looked at you and saw that you were old enough for love, I spread the corner of my garment over you and covered your nakedness. I gave you my solemn oath and entered into a covenant with you, declares the Sovereign LORD, and you became mine."* Paul speaks of God's design for marriage as a display of Christ's love for the Church in the New Testament, as well. In Ephesians 5:22-32, he taught that wives should submit to their husbands as to the Lord because the husband is the head of the wife as Christ is the head of the Church. He teaches husbands to love their wives just as Christ loved the church and gave Himself up for her. He refers to Genesis 2:24 saying, *"For this reason a man will leave his father and mother and be united to his wife, and the two will become one flesh.' This is a profound mystery – but I am talking about Christ and the church."* He was certainly right. This is a profound mystery.

Think for a minute. Sex and sexual pleasure are designed by a holy God. We know that. Many would agree the sexual experience is outside any other human experience. There is nothing like it. It is a shared experience, so intense and euphoric, that one cannot compare it to anything else on earth. That is precisely why it is used as a metaphor for an intimate, spiritual relationship with God. Our spiritual connection with Christ should be so far above anything else we've ever experienced that it powerfully affects everything else in our lives. It should be beyond anything we can explain or experience in any other way.

Earthly marriage was meant to display the love of God for His people or the love of Christ for His Church with that type of intensity. However, the enemy and fallen man have distorted the concept so much we don't dare compare intimacy between a married man and woman with Christ's love for His bride. Sure, we can accept a study on marital sex according to God's Word, but when was the last time we heard a lesson on how marital intimacy teaches us about what our relationship with Christ can be? We don't dare compare sexual intimacy with our relationship with Jesus. It seems twisted. But, lady, I am telling you. This is a concept we need to understand. I think God possibly included these precepts in His word precisely because He knew we women would get it. So much of the Bible is written by men and appears to be for men. We know that is not the case. All Scripture is for both sexes. However, the whole "bride of Christ" thing is not a concept many men will grab onto and find a lot of passion for. But we women do! We get this and it speaks to every one of our princess identities we've got deep inside our female chromosomes. Let's love it! It is a beautiful precept of God's Word meant to fulfill the longing we have for a hero on a white horse. A "happily ever after" love was God's plan for you all along.

I love to read Revelation 19:11-16. Check out our Hero. *"I saw heaven standing open and before me was a white horse, whose rider is called Faithful and True. With justice he judges and makes war. His eyes are like blazing fire, and on his head are many crowns. He has a name written on him that no one knows but he himself. He is dressed in a robe dipped in blood, and his name is the Word of God. The armies of heaven were following him, riding on white horses and dressed in fine linen, white and clean. Out of his mouth comes a sharp sword with which to strike down the nations. "He will rule them with an iron scepter." He treads the winepress of the fury of the wrath of God Almighty. On his robe and on his thigh he has this name written: KING OF KINGS AND LORD OF LORDS."*

I hope you'll forgive me. But that is sexy to my spirit. Can I say that in a book for church ladies? Please tell me there is something such as a holy swoon! He is the perfect king for you and for me. Come, Lord Jesus.

Sadly though, this side of heaven, we can only attempt to have a fore-shadow of the romance to come. Even the best marriages and the men and women who valiantly strive to follow the Bible's model of marriage fall short. I am sure many of us have failed in obtaining the type of earthly relationship God planned and intended to display His love. Pre-marital sex, extra-marital sex, homosexuality, sex outside of a marriage covenant, and love-less, dysfunctional marriages are just the beginning. Many have been abused, sold, objectified, molested, even raped. All manner of perversion and depravity have marred the beauty God intended. We are broken, injured, hurt, marginalized, left feeling like so much less than what God requires. If you are one broken, please hear this: It should not have been. It was not God's way or His will that you were treated like anything less than His highly valued, flawless beauty — His beloved. If you are one who lost your way and engaged in things beneath your royal standing, He died, arose and lives to forgive and restore.

Yes, we know a good and solid Biblical marriage gives the closest representation of godly intimacy. But let's get real for a minute. So few of us have ever experienced that for ourselves or grew up in homes where that was our example, we desperately need to trust God for our own healing and restoration in this area before we can ever hope to experience it in our relationships. I am convinced God's priority for us is to learn about spiritual intimacy with Him. He can restore marriages, liberate from sexual addictions, save spouses, give us a godly man. But I think, for the most part, those things happen after we realize and accept our need for Christ. His priority will always be our spirit intimately one with His, because He puts the spirit above the flesh. We have to lay our souls bare and ask for His touch. God alone can reclaim our perception of intimacy for His holy and righteous glory. He can restore our hearts and minds to righteousness, clean and pure so we might experience holy intimacy through the Spirit until we see Him face to face in glory.

Ours is a generation assaulted by a very sly enemy. Satan knows if he can control the conversation on this exquisite human experience meant to illuminate God's intention for relationship with His people, he wins. He can steal our bridal chamber right out from under us. He can keep us from the one thing that can make us more than we can be on our own. He has twisted a woman's need for something spiritually healthy, meant for holiness into something of ugly flesh, empty, and hurtful. It makes me so mad. But a oneness within your relationship with Jesus is something Satan fears. A bride radiant from an intimate encounter with Jesus is one powerful creature. Second Corinthians 3:16 says, *"And we, who with unveiled faces all reflect the Lord's glory, are being transformed into his likeness with ever-increasing glory, which comes from the Lord, who is the Spirit."* See, when we spend time with Christ in an authentic intimate relationship, we reflect the Lord's glory. The enemy knows a glorious bride who looks and smells an awful lot like Jesus in her nature and character is napalm destructive to his dominion of darkness. He will do almost anything to keep you from the private relationship of the bridal chamber.

Jesus is about leading you to it. Many have followed Jesus into a mature and close relationship, allowing them to be used mightily by Him. I am positive none of them would say it was by chance or accident they came to it. The journey to our bridal chambers can be long and dangerous, filled with hard choices and difficult tests. No two individual's journey will be alike. And although you have no business in my bridal chamber and I have no business in yours, we can help one another along the way to them. More mature brides can and should teach the younger ones. Paul said as much in Titus chapter two. So let's take the time to look at a few of the characteristics of an intimate relationship with Christ.

It may seem obvious, but it is important and worth repeating. **The bridal chamber was made for two (2).** Just two — the bride and groom. What happens inside is intimate, beautiful. . .and private. So it is in your personal holy place. It is for you and the LORD. No one else can have access. One of the things I love most about Jesus is He writes on every human DNA the innate knowledge of Himself — a God who loves and lives for only one. And the one is you. Yes, He loved the whole world and gave His life so that *whosoever* believes in Him will have everlasting life. (John 3:16) However, He has this divine ability to invite all to His love but meanwhile maintain a personal and unique relationship with each. He is infinitely focused on His beloved to an extent each can know He would have died just for her (or him), even if she were the only one. In His love, you are the only one. And so am I. He can do that. ". . .*My dove, my perfect one, is unique. . .*" (Song of Songs 6:9) ". . .*I have found the One my heart loves.*" (Song of Songs 3:4)

A spiritual relationship of intimacy with Christ is also not to be compared with someone else's. When we look around at others and their relationships with Christ, we take our eyes off of Him. We will trip every time. Believe me. I'm the one with scrapped knees. We won't spend a lot of time on this truth, but it is one we cannot overlook. John 21:15-22 records the events after Peter's three time denial of Jesus the night of His arrest. Jesus reinstates Peter as His faithful follower. The resurrected Christ gives Peter three chances to proclaim his love for Him. Then Jesus simply tells Peter to follow Him. As they walked along, "*Peter turned and noticed the disciple whom Jesus loved*

(John) following them and asks, "Lord, what about him?"(v.21) Notice the Scripture tells us specifically, *"Peter turned. . ."* (v.20) I am convinced if Jesus Himself had not been right at his side, Peter would have had to deal with some nasty bruises from a stumble. Jesus told Peter, *". . .what is that to you? You must follow me."* (v.22) His message was clear to Peter and it should be clear to us. "You, follow me." When we turn from a steadfast eye-lock on Christ and start comparing our spiritual gifts, beauty, and blessings received in alone time with God to those around us, we are headed for a stumble. Fix your eyes on Jesus and let your gaze linger.

One in an intimate relationship with Christ is not clothed in shame. Genesis chapter two tells it straight forward. *". . .they will become one flesh. The man and his wife were both naked, and they felt no shame."* (Gen. 2:24c-25) I can't help but be a bit shocked when I come across words like 'naked' in Holy Script. You? I think somewhere along the way we've turned God into a prude who somehow created men and women with sexual appetites and then expected us to never acknowledge them. It's not true. He gave us desires but knew they could be easily used against us and thus be harmful. So He gave us commandments for our good. He set the parameters of marriage so the desires and pleasure we find in the opposite sex can reflect His good purpose. An intimate relationship with Christ should be honest and without shame as well. It is a place to safely lay bare our true selves. We can be spiritually naked and feel no shame before Him.

Let's look to Scripture for a good example of this concept. Luke 7:36-50 gives the beautifully scandalous account of a sinful woman who learned Jesus was eating dinner at the Pharisee's house in her town. She brought an alabaster jar of perfume and stood behind him at

His feet weeping. Her tears wet his feet and she wiped them with her hair, kissed them and poured perfume on them. When the Pharisee objected to her presence and her sins, Jesus reprimanded him. Then He honored her by saying publically that she loved much and thus her sins were forgiven. Jesus speaks directly to her saying, *"Your faith has saved you; go in peace."* (v.50) What we might miss from this account read from our modern day perspective is that her actions were publically scandalous towards Jesus. She obviously had a reputation for sinful living but here we see her come before the Lord boldly. A woman in that culture at this time in history did not let her hair down in public. Nor did she kiss the feet of a man who was not her husband. These were things only to be done behind closed doors between husband and wife. Jesus did not seem one bit concerned about the appropriateness of her actions. Rather He knew she was showing Him a pure and honest love. Jesus knew He was her Bridegroom. He even honored her by saying she loved much. No one else understood her actions, but He did. In His presence there is no shame. You can be spiritually bold and bare-naked before Him. He gets you.

Intimacy is meant to bring pleasure. Within any relationship there is bound to be conflict, it is never *all* sugar and spice and everything nice. However, in a relationship with a perfect God, the conflict never has to do with His faults or shortcomings. When there is conflict within my relationship with Christ, it always has to do with my doubting soul, sinful flesh, my finite mind. So in the day to day struggle to follow Jesus, some conversations are difficult. Some questions are hard. Some things are frustrating to obey. Many days, there is not a bridal chamber climatic experience within my spirit. But the more I believe and trust, and the longer I walk with Him and learn His ways, the more I realize it is just a matter of time and submission. He will always be waiting. When His authority meets with your understanding, trust and willingness to receive, expect a rush of power and a thrill that will rock the socks right off your soul.

God proclaimed this of Himself, "*The LORD, the LORD, the compassionate and gracious God, slow to anger, abounding in love and faithfulness, maintaining love to thousands, and forgiving wickedness, rebellion and sin. . .*"(Exodus 34:6-7) He has made a way through the Holy Spirit for you to know His character and to be filled with His presence. It is a powerful thing and it brings intense pleasure to your spirit.

I wonder if you've experienced it for yourself. Have you been so overwhelmed by His compassionate grace and loving faithfulness you were almost unable to bear it? There have been times when He has revealed Himself to me in little bits, perhaps for days at a time and then all of a sudden, my understanding of His revelation for me leaves me shouting, "Mercy!" Let me give you one recent example as I prepared to write this chapter. In my devotional time I read Zechariah 4:10. The latter part of that verse is a parenthetical sentence. "*(These seven are the eyes of the LORD which range throughout the earth.)*" Then I read in a Christian publication the next day 2 Chronicles 16:9, "*For the eyes of the LORD range throughout the earth to strengthen those whose hearts are fully committed to him.*" Two Scriptures in a row that spoke of God's eyes sort of made me wonder if He was developing a message for me. By the next day when I read Zechariah 2:8-9 where God speaks of His vengeance upon the nations that oppressed His people, I knew something was up. The Scriptures in Zechariah chapter two say whoever touches one of His touches the "apple of his *eye*." It made me think of another Scripture in 2 Chronicles chapter seven. Verse 15 says, "*I have chosen and consecrated this temple so that my Name may be there forever. My eyes and my heart will always be there.*" By now I am asking God, "Your eyes? What is the deal with your eyes? What are you trying to say? You saw me? What did I do? I know you see everything. You see all my fears and failures. What is it that I need to fix?" Over and over again during the next days, I kept seeing these Scriptures about His eyes and I begun to have a bit of a holy freak-out. I started to search my Bible, hoping He might point me to an answer in His Word. I happened to flip open to a page in Psalm where I previously made a note about a particular translation of a verse. This is what is written on the page in my handwriting: *"I will counsel you with my eye upon you."* (Psalm 32:8 ESV) Suddenly I got the image in my head of Jesus pointing at his eyes with two extended fingers and then pointing them toward me in a signal of "I'm watching you." Holy fear went through me like a lightning bolt. I thought to myself I'd better start watching myself a little more carefully and keep myself from acting up so much. I think it was the very next day, while in the shower rinsing bubbles from my hair and singing off key to one of my favorite praise songs, out of nowhere, I heard the still small voice in my heart I have finally begun to recognize. *"I can't take my eyes off of you."*

It took a minute for Living Water to rinse away my confusion. The sweet breath of my First Love whispered understanding into my spirit. "He can't take His eyes off of me? *You can't take your eyes off of me!*" I laughed like a teenager rapt in puppy love. Just like that, I knew He had been taking His time, letting pleasure build from frustration, carefully leading me into a new revelation of Himself in answer to a deep longing in my soul. He is altogether lovely. And He thinks I am too.

Now that may or may not sound like an exciting thing to you but let me just frame it a bit. Only He knew my need, my secret request. I asked Jesus privately, "Do you really notice me? Do I hold your attention? Am I beautiful to You?" So when He responded, "I can't take my eyes off of you," there left no doubt it came from Him. No one else was in the bridal chamber! (In case you wonder if the enemy can hear what you've spoken to God within your private relationship, I believe our Lord is certainly capable of keeping that serpent liar out of His bridal chamber.) When the Holy Spirit speaks regarding something you've asked of Him in the deepest most intimate places of your heart, not only does it answer a longing and desperate need no one else could know or understand, it exceeds your expectations and is more than your eyes have seen or your mind has conceived. He blows your mind! It's His way. (1 Corinthians 2:9) When you realize the Creator of the stars is making Himself known to little old you, it can cause your earth to quake with joy unspeakable. He is a skillful lover.

But here is something I bet will shake your core. It sure did for me. Receiving blessing and revelation from the Almighty maker of Heaven and Earth is absolutely the most thrilling thing I have ever experienced and I live for it. He brings me pleasure at the slightest hint of Himself. But consider this. Did you know we can have the same affect on His Spirit? I am completely convinced of it. The Word of God says it plainly many times. See Isaiah 62:4-5. *"No longer will they call you Deserted, or name your land Desolate. But you will be called Hephzibah, and your land Beulah; for the **LORD will take delight in you,** and your land will be married. As a young man marries a maiden, so will you Builder marry you; as a bridegroom rejoices over his bride, so will **your God rejoice over you.**"* (emphasis added) Here is something He laid on my heart one evening. It popped out as if I received a text message straight from the throne. Things like that do not happen often, but when it does, I sit and stare in awe because I know it could never come from my own invention.

Every day for endless millennia, the earth revolves the sun, turns in perfect harmony ~ pirouettes with moon's moods and star's years of light in time and space you cannot fathom. The fields produce and feed the creatures who dwell there, to each every need met. The storm and lightening obey and pour where appointed to produce food for the eater and seed for the sower. He whispers: "Why would I expect anything else from you, Beloved? You are the prize of all creation. You were made – for this time and place – to know, obey and worship Me. But the difference between you and the lightening? You are free to choose, free to accept the Bread of Life or refuse your Creator. . .and that, to Me, is the beauty of your heart freely given over to Grace. . .and precisely why I am enthralled with you."

Oh, the thought of it! He knows it is hard for you to put your faith in Him. He knows you cannot see Him or touch Him or hear Him in the physical. To put your life in His hands is something He does not take lightly. It is absolutely precious to Him. It endears you to His heart in a way that makes you irresistible to Him! In loving submission and obedience, you have the ability to arouse His actions toward you and cause His Holy Spirit intense pleasure. The intimate relationship between Christ and His bride is mutual. It is ebb and flow, inhale and exhale, offering and acceptance meant for the delight of both.

I hope by now you are thoroughly convinced you are the leading lady in a truth-tale God penned just for you and His Son-king before the creation of time. He wants you to follow Him to an adventure that will rock your world and cause great gains for His kingdom. This life is brutal. It is all out war. We are well served in this life and the one to come to fight for the side of Good against evil.

But do not lose sight of this. Above all, you were created to love and worship the KING OF KINGS AND LORD OF LORDS. You've got to learn to let Him tend to you. Let Him love on you uniquely. You have to learn to let Him love you — intimately — through the Spirit. There are no shortcuts or step-by-step directions. Ask Him to help you find the way to your bridal chamber. He will lead, you must follow. Go often.

Let the King bring her into His chambers. In embroidered garments she is led to the King. Within His everlasting arms, she can rest between His shoulders. She loves Him. He loved her first. His Words on her lips are kisses. Her honest worship and living offering of praise arouse His compassion and mercy and her heart begins to pound for Him. Deep calls to deep in the roar of His waves. When they rise up, He stills them until there is only breathless ecstasy in the calm of her soul. In the private chamber there is found strength for another day in the fray because His voice is true, "Yes, I am coming soon." Let the Spirit and the bride say, "Come!"

"[S]He that dwelleth in the secret place of the Most High, shall abide under the shadow of the Almighty." (Psalm 91:1 KJV)

Let us acknowledge the LORD;
Let us press on to acknowledge him.
As surely as the sun rises,
He will appear;
He will come to us like the winter rains,
Like the spring rains that water the earth." (Hosea 6:3)

Chapter 12

A Fruitful Bride

As I begin to write the last chapter of this book, it is Christmas time. Our family is about the business of decorating, shopping, wrapping and baking. Parties and events fill our schedule. As you know, Christmas has a way of taking over your normal routine and pushes you head-long into the hustle and bustle of the season. On this year Mycah is obsessed with helping in each of the details. She decorated the Christmas trees, painted a set of new plaster Nativity figures, helped stir-up the family's traditional peanut butter fudge, picked out gifts for cousins and chose the perfect stuffed toy to offer an unknown child whose mother needs help providing Christmas gifts for her children. It is absolutely precious to see my child healthy and happy, growing to learn and participate fully in the traditions of our family. My heart was pricked with joy—so profound it caused physical pain—to watch my mother's tan, furrowed hands gently cover Mycah's pudgy white fingers on the rolling pin while baking pies for our family's Christmas meal. Mom guided Mycah's hands to just the right pressure for rolling out a beautifully smooth pie crust. Then she demonstrated how to fold it with the gentleness of one holding fine porcelain or a baby bunny and unfurled it into the pie plate. Mycah watched wide-eyed and then practiced her own version until she proved successful in her own right.

All these activities spoke not of the importance of the material details, but of glory. The glory of when God became a baby boy. His once infant hands were pierced by the nails of the world's sin and He saved us all. When the glory of that kind of self-less love is reproduced and on display in the members of my family, Christmas comes to live in my very presence. It is where heaven and earth meet and an explosion of love breathes life into my soul. And then I know. He is here. And there is so much more than what my eyes see. When the spiritual marries the terrestrial, we get a glimpse of the unseen God of unapproachable Light. It is magical. It is a joy so great there are no human words for its description; just a groaning that can only be communicated through the interceding Holy Spirit from me to Him.

I am so comforted by the traditions and heritage of my family's faith. Please do not hear that I believe we are a perfect family. Certainly we are not. We hurt one another, neglect each other, and all the rest. But one thing we continue to learn is to forgive each other, bear with each other, and deliberately remember to forget things that don't matter in the end.

But still, there is just something about the ways of my mother. Everything she does seems to echo the booming love-chant of the generations before her. She is the most visible evidence of their lives as they continue to pour into hers through the memories and lessons she learned from them. Shortly after Mycah was born, my mother wrote the story of our family's female legacy in a journal. I love it because it is penned in her familiar hand-writing and is laced with old photos of the women of our family, generations back—right up to ones of me with baby Mycah.

Apparently, a love and gift for the written word is one of the many traits she's passed on to me. You'll see because I'd like to share a bit of what she wrote for Mycah here with you.

"It had to have begun many generations back. At least that is how I see it in my mind's eye. We started as a pioneer woman of average build. She most likely had a clean, average kind of pretty about her, a normal brown color to her hair, green, blue or maybe hazel eyes, strong hands, full lips. Her convictions were strong, and in her generation she would have been called stubborn. She had no ideas about setting the world on fire, no yen to sail away and settle exotic lands or become the first woman governor in the territory. Her strengths, her vision lay in a much higher calling.

To describe that calling as simply family or love would be understating her life's work grossly, on the order of labeling the Grand Canyon a riverbed. That average pioneer woman gave us more than that, as generation after generation of her daughters grew sure and confident in the world they occupied."

My mother then penned the story of each of the women of her childhood. From my great-grandmothers, Josephine Bentley Law and Margie Overbey Morren to her mother, Billie Doris Law, Mom detailed the stories of her memories with them. She recounted stories of romance, death, war, deployments, caring for children with special needs, the Depression. They are stories of faith and strength, and most importantly, love. Then she chronicled her own story of youth and first love. She tells Mycah a bit about the time she met and fell for a tall, ruddy-cheeked, baby-faced sweetheart named Roy. They met around Halloween and were engaged by Christmas. Then she tenderly recounts how Mycah's Grandpa Roy died in a plane crash. She shares that losing him was devastating but that she and her young children (my brothers and I) grew stronger and closer as a result. And then she shares her own take on my romance and ensuing marriage to her daddy, Chris. Page after page is tangible love penned by one woman for the many in our lineage. It ends like this:

"And so time marches on, years pass, but one constant always remains — I am devoted to my mother; my daughter and I are best friends, and she now has a daughter — you, Mycah. Your mom is blessed with generations of women who understood the secret of being a mother. . .and you are heir to a legacy that virtually ensures you will someday be best friends with your own mom and your daughter will be devoted to you in turn. It is a circle, a gift handed down from daughter to daughter in our family. You are in good hands, Mycah. Your mom will guard well the lessons she's learned, add her own special flavor to the mix and love you with all her heart."

It is impossible to express what this journal means to me. My mother's profession of confidence in my ability to be a good mother meant more to me than precious jewels when she placed it in my young hands. You might imagine how it increased in value when Mycah was diagnosed with cancer four years later. I wondered if the circle would be broken with me. I feared Mycah wouldn't live to grow and pass on the love copiously invested by the women of our family before me. When I was faced with the magnitude of storm the women of my family faced in previous generations, I was sure I'd break. Somehow my mother knew better and believed God delighted to bless even this woman to withstand the squall when I leaned on Him. I am so thankful I've been taught by my mother, who was taught by hers, and so back the history goes, to lean fully. I imagine their wise counsel would sound something like this, "Darlin', lean so hard on the Everlasting Arms that your feet no longer touch the stony ground of your dessert place. Let Him carry you on to the Promised Land. He knows the way. He is the Way."

Oh, the gift of learning to lean on Jesus. Perhaps it is most readily learned from a mother swept up in Passion's arms. Perhaps the lessons are most easily seen in one who has conceived, delivered and nurtured fruitful life for Almighty God's purpose within her unique and present circumstance.

That's what this chapter is about. A fruitful bride. If you are not married, or if you are not a mother in the physical realm, don't fret, Darlin'. God created women to be a powerful helper. In the Eden garden God said, *"It is not good for the man to be alone. I will make a helper suitable for him."* (Genesis 2:18) He created woman with the high calling of life-giver and nurturer. It is in you to flourish in those roles, regardless of your earthly marital status or if you've birthed a baby. If you've trusted Jesus as your Savior, You are the bride of Christ, and it is to His Father's glory that you bear much fruit. (John 15:8)

As I said earlier, as I begin to write this chapter, it's the Christmas season. And I am thinking so very much about Mary. Yes, that Mary. Mary, the virgin mother of Jesus. Something similar happened before. The Christmas I spent pregnant with Mycah, I found myself captivated by her. Feeling the flutters of the baby inside my womb awoke a new awareness of the precious and fragile life I loved without restraint or condition. I knew already I would die for this child I had not even seen. Pondering Mary made me realize the pain she endured. She held the Christ-child in her womb, then in her arms. She watched Him grow and nurtured His curious and loving nature. I am certain she would have died to save Him one moment's pain. I can't begin to comprehend her heartbreak as she stood at the foot of her baby boy's cross as instead, He died to save her one moment's condemnation. What child is this?

Once again, in this particular year, I find myself captivated by her. I think our mother of Christ has much to teach about being the bride of Christ. How I would love to call her up for a mid-morning chat. Or better yet, for her to show me how to roll out unleavened bread while telling me all about the day Gabriel called upon her. The angel said, *"Greetings, you who are highly favored! The Lord is with you."* (Luke 1:28) The Scriptures penned by Luke tell us Mary was greatly troubled and wondered what kind of greeting an angel could have for her. *"But the angel said to her, "Do not be afraid, Mary, you have found favor with God. You will be with child and give birth to a son, and you are to give him the name Jesus. He will be great and will be called the Son of the Most High. . .his kingdom will never end." When Mary questioned how this could be since she was a virgin, the angel answered, "The Holy Spirit will come upon you, and the power of the Most High will overshadow you. So the holy one to be born will be called the Son of God. . . ."* (from Luke 1:26-37)

Can you even imagine? I am sure she was overwhelmed with a flood of emotion. I am almost certain she had a million questions to ask the angel but simply replied, *"May it be to me as you have said."* (v.

38) I have so many questions for her. Did she wonder if she imagined the whole thing? Did she doubt that she understood correctly? Did she wonder if perhaps Gabriel had the wrong house? The wrong girl?

A simple girl from Galilee given the high honor and favor to bring forth the Holy One—the Son of God. What she undoubtedly learned in her Jewish household about the ancient prophet's telling of the coming Messiah was to be fulfilled her daily reality. A truth she learned growing up of God's plan of redemption surely seemed true enough to her faithful mind and heart. But I wonder if when God's master plan collided with her morning chores she, all of the sudden, questioned its validity. How could she be the mother of the Son of God? With a heart full of questions and possibly a multitude of doubts threatening, she sang a song of praise and rejoiced in a plan she could not possibly fully understand. Wow.

Mary sang a song of praise to the Lord. (Luke 1:46-55) I can't help but wonder if the Word made man she carried in her womb was an answer to the doubting questions she previously brought to the Lord in her alone moments with Him. Gabriel told Mary she found favor with God, indicating, most likely, she had a relationship with Him prior to this appointed announcement. She begins her song, *"My soul glorifies the Lord and my spirit rejoices in God my Savior, for he has been mindful of the humble state of his servant. From now on all generations will call me blessed. . ."*(v.47,48) Had she discussed her humble state with Him? Had she taken her insecurity to the throne? I wonder if she prayed about the longing in her heart to be more than the regular girl she saw reflected in the mirror. Did she ask to be used by God for holy purposes? How'd I love to listen wide-eyed to all the details from her lips. Eternity will provide all the time I desire, no doubt.

Just as I love to read and ponder the words my mother penned for Mycah of our family's heritage, I long to search the Scriptures to see the handwriting of the God who traced His plan of love from Eden to Bethlehem and all the way to my Texas address. There is divine calligraphy from Eve, the mother of all the living to Mary, the mother of the Son of God to me and you. May it be a burning desire to follow the script and scribbles discovering lessons from the women of our rich heritage. And like Mary, may we allow our souls to glorify the Lord and rejoice in God our Savior, even when we cannot fully understand His plan. I pray the reality of His Holy presence interrupts our daily lives in such a profound way that there are no other words to be said of us save, *"Blessed is she who has believed that what the Lord has said to her will be accomplished!"* (Luke 1:45)

I am not a Bible scholar and I am in no way trying to present doctrine to you today. I would only darken His counsel with words I know not. But it is my prayer that something akin to the events in Acts chapter four when Peter and John were speaking before the elders and rulers of the people can loosely apply here. Obviously they were unlearned and ignorant men but their boldness displayed they had been with Jesus. The disciples said, *". . .we cannot help speaking about what we have seen and heard."* (Acts 4:20) My heart echoes their message. I am most certainly unlearned and ignorant. However, I can tell you boldly that I have been with the Lord in a recent season of great difficulty because of my daughter's cancer. And He made Himself so clear to me, I cannot help speaking about what I've seen and heard.

In the Old Testament, we can read of several mothers who brought forth children who later were filled with the Holy Spirit of God and accomplished mighty things for Him. One of my favorites is Hannah who asked God for a son and received one after many years of infertility. (1 Samuel chapters 1 & 2) She named him Samuel, a name that sounds like the Hebrew words for *"heard of God,"* because God heard her request. Samuel grew to be a man who listened to God and ministered before the Lord. Both Rahab and Ruth are women listed among a litany of the men in the genealogy of Christ. (Matthew chapter 1) Women were never listed in genealogy in that day. However, Holy Script records their names as women honored by God to bring forth His Son. One was a former prostitute; the other a widow, both foreigners who married into the Jewish nation. I hope these women give you a measure of hope as they do for me. God's prerogative is to consistently use unlikely people to carry out His divine plans.

I wish we had time to study each of them in detail here. I am certain God has blessings for each of us in their stories. However, what I want us to see for our current purpose is that these women were very much chosen and used by God. They brought forth life as mothers and became permanent marks in the script of history and more importantly, His story. They fulfilled their roles of helper, life-bearer, and nurturer. They did those things through the law of flesh. In other words, they conceived through the flesh and actually birthed real-life children according to the laws of nature and God's design. These women all lived, carried out their roles, and died during the times of the Old Testament or the covenant of the law. Their flesh gave birth to flesh. Mary conceived in her flesh through the Holy Spirit. (Matthew 1:18) Essentially, she became the transition between the Old and New Covenant as the mother of the Mediator of the New Covenant. Her flesh conceived through the Spirit. And through the child she bore, there is a new law of the Spirit at work. Spirit gives birth to spirit.

"Flesh gives birth to flesh, but the Spirit gives birth to spirit." (John 3:6)

The Old Covenant had to do with the law and the New Covenant has to do with the Spirit. (Romans 8:2, Galatians 5:18) You'll remember we discussed in the previous chapter, through His law, God gave physical marital intimacy as a foreshadowed picture of spiritual intimacy between Christ's spirit and yours as His bride. Just as a married couple comes together as one and a woman becomes pregnant with the fruit of their love and brings forth life in the flesh, an intimate, covenant relationship between Jesus and the Church brings forth spiritual fruit and new spiritual life. Through His Holy Spirit, we can have spiritual one-ness with Christ in the private and intimate "bridal chamber" of our heart. Consequently, our spirits conceive His seed and bear fruit for His glory. Jesus instructed His disciples as He sent them out, *"What I tell you in the dark, speak in the daylight; what is whispered in your ear, proclaim from the roofs."* (Matthew 10:27) The life He gives us through His Word in our private moments, we are to proclaim publically in order to birth His life in others.

Consider Romans 7:4, *"So, my brothers [sisters], you also died to the law through the body of Christ, that you might belong to another, to Him who was raised from the dead, in order that we might bear fruit to God."* (emphasis added) And the words of Jesus Himself, *"This is to my Father's glory, that you bear much fruit. . ."*(John 15:8) You and I have a place in God's lineage of Love. We are the daughters of Eve, living in a fallen and sinful world, but Paul teaches in 1 Timothy 1:15

that *"women will be saved through childbearing – if they continue in faith, love and holiness with propriety."* Christ has been born in the flesh to a virgin mother and died to offer us the grace of His redemption. We who believe in His death and resurrection can be made perfect again. Free of condemnation and as clean as new fallen snow — so perfect that we are qualified to be united with the King of kings in an eternal union as His bride in the spirit. Consequently, that union of spirits will conceive new life.

Because I believe this truth to be spiritual but also practical, let's look at the prophet Isaiah's words in Isaiah 53 of the Old Testament. These prophecies were written by Isaiah about the coming Messiah many, many years before Christ's birth. Matthew Henry wrote, "This chapter is so replenished with the unsearchable riches of Christ that it may be called rather the gospel of the evangelist Isaiah than the prophecy of the prophet Isaiah."[32] In other words, this chapter of the Old Testament reads as if it were written by one of the gospel authors who actually walked with Jesus on earth, not a prophet who died ages before Jesus set His holy foot on terrestrial ground. Isaiah was dead-on in his foreknowledge of the Messiah. Verses 10 and 11 say this about Jesus: *"Yet is was the LORD's will to crush him and cause him to suffer, and though the LORD makes his life a guilt offering, he will see his offspring and prolong his days, and the will of the LORD will prosper in his hand. After the suffering of his soul, he will see the light of life and be satisfied."* (emphasis added) As the bride, through the Holy Spirit, we can individually become pregnant with the LORD's purpose in our days on this earth and play a role in His lineage for the kingdom plan at large. It is how His will is done on earth as it is in heaven through you and me.

As the bride of Christ, the Church bears spiritual offspring to the glory of God the Father through Jesus. Sister, you and I have an important role in the plan. We, as spiritually mature followers, are called to be mothers who give birth to *spiritual* life. The old lady in the shoe may have so many children she doesn't know what to do, but be as spiritually barren as the dust under her soul. A woman who dies never experiencing the beauty of pregnancy and birth in her natural life may have a full quiver of heirs in the spiritual realm, where her role of life-giver begets a more eternal legacy and carries a far greater inheritance. Children are a blessing and a reward from the LORD (Psalm 127:3) and should be brought up in the Truth of the God of the Bible. But let's not neglect the high honor of bearing spiritual fruit. A spiritually mature woman is never too old to conceive. Her womb is never infertile and life can be born through her in every season.

> [7] *"Before she goes into labor,*
> *she gives birth;*
> *before the pains come upon her,*
> *she delivers a son.*
> [8] *Who has ever heard of such things?*
> *Who has ever seen things like this?*
> *Can a country be born in a day*
> *or a nation be brought forth in a moment?*
> *Yet no sooner is Zion in labor*
> *than she gives birth to her children.*
> [9] *Do I bring to the moment of birth*
> *and not give delivery?" says the LORD.*
> *"Do I close up the womb*

when I bring to delivery?" says your God.

[10] *"Rejoice with Jerusalem and be glad for her,*

all you who love her;

rejoice greatly with her,

all you who mourn over her.

[11] *For you will nurse and be satisfied*

at her comforting breasts;

you will drink deeply

and delight in her overflowing abundance."

[12] *For this is what the LORD says:*

"I will extend peace to her like a river,

and the wealth of nations like a flooding stream;

you will nurse and be carried on her arm

and dandled on her knees. (Isaiah 66:7-12)

Love, marriage, and being a mommy served as primary aspirations to me as a child. I pretended to be the bride most every day, turning cheerleader pompoms into my bridal bouquet. But make no mistake. I had a baby doll stuffed up my shirt pretending to be pregnant the next moment. Ladies, it is in us to mother. I love using the word 'mother' as a verb. If you are a mother, or if you've had the privilege of being under a mother's care (whether or not she was your biological mother), you know 'mother' is an action word. Mothers mother. Many times women just can't keep themselves from mothering. Even if her own children are grown and moved out of her home, or if she never birthed or adopted a child of her own, sometimes a woman just has to mother something or someone. Even a pet or a stray child riding a scooter in her neighborhood can be the victim

. . .I mean recipient of her unique gift of mother-ness. Mothering is a desire of our hearts placed there by a loving Father. He never needed human souls to carry out His plans, but He mercifully invited us. We were created to partner with Him as His help-meet. Do not miss out on the truth of Immanuel—God *with* us. Please come with me to another feast. The Feast of Tabernacles.

You'll remember we learned there are seven Feasts of the LORD. According to God's design, they depict the entire redemptive career of the Messiah. The four spring feasts have been fulfilled in Christ's first coming. The three fall feasts will be fulfilled in Christ's second coming. The feasts were taught and experienced in the days of the Old Covenant by the law. I believe the precepts of the feasts can be experienced by us, under the New Covenant, by the Spirit.

I experienced a personal Feast of Trumpets as well as a personal Day of Atonement. Mine were ordained by God to coincide with the actual Jewish dates, I believe, just so I understand He is still in the business of redemption according to the master plan. He showed His people in antiquity by their law-required participation in the feasts, and He is still teaching this modern mom the truths of those feasts in my personal circumstances through His Holy Spirit. You may not have an exact experience to mine, but I believe He is the same yesterday, today, and tomorrow and He desires to teach you about His redemptive goals for your life within your circumstances in equally profound ways.

When God first outlined the chapters and message of this book, The Feast of Tabernacles (the final Feast of the Jewish year) was a subject not included. God put on my heart the final chapter, A Fruitful Bride, and I believed it to be a chapter including the concept of bearing fruit to God and coming full circle on the agricultural wheat-cultivating theme. While it is just that, many months later, God literally floored me with the Feast of Tabernacles. He had no intention of leaving His final feast out of the scope of this message. He tied in its meaning with an umbilical line from heaven to me.

On a September afternoon, I drove I-35 toward Children's Hospital in Dallas. Mycah in the backseat, we sang our way to her clinic appointment at the cancer center. We headed there for a regularly scheduled follow-up appointment because her hospital continues to monitor her closely even after her cancer treatments completed. A normal day, a normal drive, like countless other trips we made to the hospital in the previous three years, when out of the cloudy sky, I KNEW within my spirit—as clearly as I can see with my own two eyes—I had conceived of the Holy Spirit. This normal cancer mom, late for her daughter's appointment, was appointed to bear fruit to His glory in a life-giving way. An awareness of being pregnant with the LORD's purpose consumed my mind while filling out insurance papers and discussing my child's health with her oncologist. When we got home, as I normally do after hearing the LORD in my heart, noted it in my journal. I wrote the date, the details of the experience, what I felt in my spirit the LORD communicated, and a list of questions I wanted to seek in Him through His Word. September 23, 2010. I began to pray and ponder, taking my myriad questions to the LORD. You will have to try to imagine my shock as I went to the calendar and discovered that this very day was the Feast of Tabernacles according to the Jewish holiday calendar for 2010. I didn't know what that meant to me for sure, but I knew it was a definite holy convocation for this housewife. God again used my personal circumstances and His Holy Feasts to get my attention.

I am not presuming my experience to be the magnitude of Mary's Gabriel moment, but when one suddenly becomes aware of the Lord of Angel armies talking to her, it causes quite the quake in one's soul. My soul was rocking off the Richter scale.

So I had to find out about the Feast of Tabernacles. What is it? What did it mean? What might it mean for me? He already showed me the beauty of the Feast of Trumpets in light of the Jewish wedding and the return of Christ our Bridegroom for His Church. He will come with a shout and a trump. (1 Thessalonians 4:16) I also experienced a personal Day of Atonement as He became the atoning sacrifice for me, as well as, a wedding day as His bride on the two year anniversary of the Day of Atonement, experiencing the revelation of one-ment with Him through the Spirit. The sun did not set on that very day before I read all I could lay my hands on regarding the Feast of Tabernacles.

As it is with all the Feasts of the LORD, the Feast of Tabernacles is rich with symbolism and prophecy. It is impossible to pick through even a handful of the treasure it contains in this time and space. So please allow me to bring out the aspects God revealed to me most useful to our present subject of becoming a fruitful bride.

The Feast of Tabernacles or *Sukkot* was the final feast of the Jewish year occurring in the autumn (usually late September to mid-October) five days after the Day of Atonement. It is the feast most often mentioned in the Bible. "The holiday," as it came to be called, was the most prominent of Israel's holidays as well as the most joyful and festive. The joy was twofold, for it commemorated God's past goodness and provision during Israel's 40 year wilderness sojourn, and it commemorated God's present goodness and provision with the completion of the harvest. Scripture outlined that the people were to live in booths (temporary huts) and rejoice before the Lord with branches. (Leviticus 23:33-43)[33]

"So beginning with the fifteenth day of the seventh month, after you have gathered the crops of the land, celebrate the festival to the LORD for seven days; the first day is a day of rest, and the eighth day also is a day of rest. On the first day you are to take choice fruit from the trees, and palm fronds, leafy branches and poplars, and rejoice before the LORD your God for seven days each year. This is to be a lasting ordinance for the generations to come; celebrate it in the seventh month. Live in booths for seven days: All native-born Israelites are to live in booths so your descendants will know that I had the Israelites live in booths when I brought them out of Egypt. I am the LORD your God." (Leviticus 23:39-43)-

The Feast of Tabernacles, one of the three pilgrim feasts, required all Jewish males to appear before the Lord in the temple. Upon their arrival in Jerusalem, they built leafy booths for their families to reside within during the seven day feast. Water and light are two major elements of the Feast of Tabernacles — water, due to the prayers asking for the essential rain for working the soil and the sprouting of the new season's crops. Light was a significant element because the Feast of Tabernacles begins in the middle of the lunar month when the harvest moon is full. Both the elements of water and light were highlighted with elaborate light ceremonies each evening and water ceremonies each morning of the feast. The celebrations, marked by extreme joy, carried a Messianic emphasis. The congregation waved palm branches toward the altar and sang, *"Save now, I pray, O LORD; O LORD, I pray, send now prosperity."* (Ps. 118:25 NKJV)

With some knowledge of the Feast of Tabernacles and its emphasis on light and water, the words Jesus spoke while at the Feast of Tabernacles recorded in John's gospel carry new meaning. *"On the last and greatest day of the Feast, Jesus stood and said in a loud voice, 'If anyone is thirsty, let him come to me and drink. Whoever believes in me, as the Scripture has said, streams of living **water** will flow from within him.'"* (John 7:37-38 emphasis added) It was at this same Feast that Jesus also said, *"I am the **light** of the world. Whoever believes in me will never walk in darkness, but will have the light of life."* (John 8:12 emphasis added) It is also why Jesus was greeted by the crowds shouting *Hosanna* (Hebrew for "Save now" in Psalm 118:25) and waving palm branches on His triumphal entry into Jerusalem. (Matthew 21:8-9, Luke 19:38, John 12:13) They viewed Him as the Messiah King, come to deliver ("save now") Israel in fulfillment of Psalm 118. They hailed Him with the messianic image of palm branches from the Feast of Tabernacles. It is the same imagery in Revelation 7:9-10 where redeemed saints worship, with palm branches in hand, around the throne of God and the Lamb.[34]

The Feast of Tabernacles pointed to the presence of God dwelling with man. The fulfillment of the Feast will be when Christ returns and *"the dwelling of God is with men, and he will live with them. They will be his people, and God himself will be with them and be their God."* (Revelation 21:3) But until that day, I can't help but believe we can experience this truth within our personal relationships with Christ through the Holy Spirit. In fact, it is worth mentioning it was during the Feast of Tabernacles when the Shekinah glory of the Lord descended from heaven to light the fire on the altar and fill the Holy of Holies during Solomon's reign when the newly built Temple to the Lord was dedicated. (2 Chronicles 5:3, 1 Kings 8, 2 Chronicles 7:1-10)

I am convinced that we can follow a chord God tied in Holy Script from the record of His Shekinah glory filling the Holy of Holies inside the temple to the Holy of Holies inside our personal hearts. The glory of the LORD came down from heaven with a cloud and fire so intrusive the priest could not enter the temple at its dedication during the Feast of Tabernacles. Think of the Holy of Holies of the temple as your personal bridal chamber or "tabernacle" of your heart. Then think that the glory of God can take up a position right there. Look out! A consuming fire and an enveloping cloud just might take over your reality.

Let's come around full circle now and visit Mary, the mother of our LORD again. Luke 1:35 is where we find the answer given by Gabriel to Mary when she asked how it could be that she birth a son since she was a virgin. *"The angel answered, "The Holy Spirit will come upon you, and the power of the Most High will overshadow you."* The meaning of the word 'overshadow' in this Scripture is described as such, "From a vaporous cloud that casts a shadow; the word is transferred to a shining cloud surrounding and enveloping persons with brightness; of the Holy Spirit exerting creative energy upon the womb of the virgin Mary and impregnating it; a use of the word which seems to have been drawn from the familiar Old Testament idea of a cloud symbolizing the immediate presence and power of God."[35]

Don't you just love it? The Holy Spirit exerting creative energy. The immediate presence and power of God! I am convinced He still does that! His word says so. John 14:23: *"Jesus replied, "If anyone loves me, he will obey my teaching. My Father will love him, and we will come to him and make our home (dwelling) with him."* This is a statement teaching the truth of Immanuel—God with us, or the theme of the Feast of Tabernacles.

Two distinct elements—God and [wo]man become one to form a perfect whole resulting in fruit (offspring) that is divinely God and distinctly you. It is His legacy. You can hold a position in His lineage as you bear abundant fruit to the glory of God. The spiritual life we birth will be as varied as precious children in His sight. Each is unique. A ministry, a message, a song, an art, a craft, a gift, a talent, your begotten life will be the image of your heart, with the characteristics of your Bridegroom. God with you.

Again, this is a concept that is uniquely *woman*. Yes, men can and do bear spiritual fruit, as well. But women get this concept in this particular context. Ask any mother about her experience of bringing forth life and prepare to listen to her entire story from the first onset of labor to the dramatic conclusion of holding her precious baby bundle in her arms. Mothers love to share their birth story because it is arguably the most divine event they have the privilege to encounter this side of heaven. We were created for it and the physical represents the spiritual. *"Flesh gives birth to flesh, but the Spirit gives birth to spirit."* (John 3:6)

Consider for a moment the converse of conceived life between Christ and His bride. Isaiah 64:6 says, *". . .all of our righteous acts are like filthy rags. . ."* You might have heard it preached that the original language is a bit more graphic. In fact "filthy rags" in this instance more accurately means "menstrual cloths."[36] I've heard it taught that our righteous acts are disgusting to God. While it may be certainly true— menstrual cloths are waste and meant for the garbage—the Lord set something in my heart a bit more meaningful to me as a woman. Ask any woman who wishes for a child but is unable to conceive. Ask any woman who struggles with infertility about the heartbreak she feels as she hopes with everything inside her to be pregnant but discovers a crimson stain on a menstrual cloth as opposed to a + symbol on a pregnancy test stick. Yes, perhaps disgusting. But more so, it is the evidence of un-conceived life — wasted potential. The righteous acts we produce on our own, apart from the Holy Spirit's seed, will only produce the evidence of un-conceived life — wasted potential. They are like filthy rags.

Salvation and conception are determined by God. But spiritual conception is never fruitless within an intimate relationship between Christ and His true bride. The individual members of His Church are unique in their callings, creative, purposeful, and powerful. The same power that raised Christ from the dead is at work in us. (Romans 8:11) Jesus said, *"anyone who has faith in me will do what I have been doing. [S]He will do even greater things than these, because I am going to the Father."* (John 14:12) See, through His Holy Spirit at work in us, His ministry continues. There is freedom for the captives, sight for the blind, healing for the sick, comfort for the hurting. These are the evidence of the abundant life He promises those who remain in Him.

Eve is the mother of all the living daughters. Satan most likely targeted her in the garden precisely because she was the bride and the prophetic symbol of God's love for His people.

"How long will you wander, O unfaithful daughter? The LORD will create a new thing on earth — a woman will surround a man." (Jeremiah 31:22)

Perhaps in our generation, God will redeem the sin of Eve through the Blood of Christ at work and on display upon His fully devoted Bride. When the Bride lives, moves, and has her being in the life of Jesus, she allures a lost and broken world unto herself and to Him.

A bride is breath-taking, beautiful, alluring. And she must have an answer for the hope she professes. It is Jesus. Just Jesus. Only Jesus. Instead of influencing man toward sin, we, the Bride, and the mother of Christ's continuing lineage in this generation, will influence mankind toward holiness.

It is my pleasure to place my first borne in your hands. This book is the fruit of my one-ness with Jesus conceived immaculately through His Holy Spirit. It is uniquely me and completely Him. It is a message I never invented on my own and certainly never imagined completing apart from His imminent and creative Presence.

I am a regular woman in pajama pants with a list of chores as long as my arm. I am a mom heading to pick up my daughter from school, who needs to feed the cat and the hamster. But I've been with Jesus through a season where His light has brought forth new life. It is my joy to share the testimony of my life joined with the Creator's. I pray this message is a blessing and a heritage to the LORD. I pray it will breathe new life into someone. Perhaps just one. Perhaps you, dear sister. The most amazing evidence that the season of my little girl's cancer was not wasted or in vain would be to have this message breathe life into you, my daughter. It would be the reaped sheaves of an abundant harvest and the cause for songs of joy. Praise Him!

My prayer is this book will not only feed you for a moment with the whole truth of God's Word, but you will become a fearless bride, or an even bolder one, bearing spiritual life through your calling. No, your journey won't look just like mine. But you have an equal amount of God's infinite love upon yourself. My prayer is you will learn to work the soil, plant the seed and seek God in bringing forth abundant fruit as His perfect bride — 100 times what was sown.

And so time marches on. It is a circle, a gift handed down. Cycling from seed to fruit, planting to harvesting, season after season, generation after generation. And you are heir to a legacy of One Faithful and True. The epic story continues until eternity in God's glory is attained. But something is at stake: the Kingdom in you—your page in this Love story. Don't leave it blank or scantly powerful. Don't leave your mark unmade, your song unsung, your story untold, your riches unclaimed, your position of honor forfeit, your pain wasted. For the sake of a better ending, the story continues. The thread is now tied to you. Will it be embroidered into garments of wedding splendor or left dangling as a noose?

"The LORD bless you and keep you; the LORD make his face shine upon you and be gracious to you; the LORD turn his face toward you and give you peace." (Numbers 6:24-25)

May your life cause His face to brighten and shine forth His light because when the King's face brightens, it means life, and His favor is like a rain cloud in spring. (Prov. 16:15) Prepare for a harvest, dear daughter. Be fruitful and multiply for the splendor of the Most High. It is to His glory that you bear much fruit.

Make no mistake, the Word is alive. His covenant stands. The forever conclusion is sure. This story is about a wedding coming and all eternity will be joy. And the bride? She lives. . .really lives—abundantly ever-after.

This end is your beginning:

STUDY GUIDE AND HOMEWORK

Chapter 1-Chapter 12

Whether you are studying on your own or in a group, the study guide and homework will help you grow as the Bride of Christ. For each chapter, there are four days of homework to further highlight the precepts presented. The homework is setup with the following structure to guide you in your time with the Lord and focus your heart and mind to bear fruit for the glory of God.

Prepare your Field: A question to focus attention

Plant the Seed: Scripture to read

Cultivate: Application of Scripture using further teaching from commentaries, original language study, a testimony example, etc.

Reap the Harvest: A prompt for you to apply the truth of the Scripture to your life and personal circumstance

Day 4 of each chapter's homework is a journal prompt/prayer starter.

Homework

Chapter 1: Grow-up!

Chapter 1-Day 1

Prepare your Field: Have you tasted that the LORD is good? When was the last time?

Plant the Seed: Read 1 Peter 2:1-3

Cultivate: As Christians, I think we are aware on some level that the LORD is good. We hear it all the time, "God is Good." I wonder if you know it right now as you sit reading these words. Do you know it in your current circumstance?

In the original language, the meaning of "good" as used in verse three carries the meaning of kind, gracious, easy, and *useful*.[37] In my past, there was a time I knew the LORD was good, but I didn't know Him to be useful. When times got difficult, I determined to find my own solution because I felt like He wouldn't handle things to my satisfaction. I felt He had let me down and was no longer trustworthy and thus was not useful in many ways.

Reap the Harvest: If you have tasted the LORD and have experienced His good, gracious, easy, kind usefulness, write a prayer of thanks being specific in your description of how He showed Himself good in your personal circumstance. Then pray a prayer for someone you know who could benefit from His goodness in their lives. Ask Him for direction in how to be His hands and feet to them.

Perhaps you know on some level God is good, but you don't feel it at the moment in your situation, or perhaps it has been a long time since you've had a taste of Him bringing you delicious bliss. Write a prayer asking to experience His goodness in a new and fresh way. He delights to feed His children.

Chapter 1-Day 2

Prepare your Field: What might be stunting your growth?

Plant the Seed: Read 1 Peter 2:1-3

Cultivate: According to these Scriptures, we are to 'grow-up' in our salvation. Regardless of our age in years, maturity in Christ is something we are intended to work toward by craving the pure nourishment of God's Word. The Scriptures tell us some possible causes of stunted growth: deceit, hypocrisy, envy and slander. If you haven't seen growth in an area of your life in Christ, consider what might be stunting your growth there. Perhaps you are praying over the same area of your life after many months or even years. Perhaps you are holding something or someone back from His authority. Think about if you've sought and applied the nourishment of God's Word to your circumstance. If so, consider if you are holding on to deceit, hypocrisy, envy or slander in some way. Nothing is worth missing God's appointment for your life in His plan.

Reap the Harvest: Are you holding on to sin that could be stunting your intended maturity in Christ? Do you have a personal answer to "Not _____, Lord. You can have anything but _____." Use this opportunity to get real with God about it. He can handle any fear or any anger you might need to reveal. The vital part is exposing it to His goodness.

Chapter 1-Day 3

Prepare your Field: How can you grow up into the fullness of Christ?

Plant the Seed: Read Ephesians 4:13-15

Cultivate: I was both fascinated and captivated by the original language in verse 15 of Ephesians chapter four. The phrase, "Grow up **into him** who is the Head, that is, Christ" jumped off the page. The Jamieson-Fausset-Brown Bible Commentary taught this concept as such, "So as to be more and more incorporated with Him, and become **one with Him.**"[38] (emphasis added) I don't know about you, but becoming one with Him gets my heart racing. I want that! Growing-up takes on a whole new motivation for me once I know that speaking truth in love makes me grow-up into being one with Him.

This particular section of Scripture is dealing with unity in the Body of Christ, or unity of the Church. However, I've got to know first, I, *Angie*, can become one with Him. Let's just sit on that concept for a minute before we move on to how all of us can work together. That will come as a result of our individual growth and 'one-ness' with Jesus. . .but for now, let's be a bit spiritually self-centered and go after the 'one-ness' for ourselves.

Reap the Harvest: Practice speaking the truth in love in order to grow up into Him. Perhaps you are someone who is good at speaking the truth, but not in a loving manner. Perhaps you are someone who is good at loving, but not good at confronting painful truths. Ask God to help you do both.

Think about an area of your life that is in need of God's attention. Use this time to speak truth in love to Him privately. Be specific and real. God knows when you are "candy-coating," holding back, or speaking from denial so you might as well get real. It will make things so much better.

Chapter 1-Day 4

Journal prompt: What is your love story with Jesus?

I am increasingly fascinated with my sisters' love stories with Jesus. Females are romantics at heart and the details and circumstances around a good love story captivate our senses and cause our cheeks to flush while exhaling a dreamy sigh.

Sit for a moment alone with Jesus and ask Him to remind you of an especially intimate time He showed His love for you uniquely. Perhaps you would like to write the details of your salvation experience or the account of a personal healing, rescue, or miracle. Do so here and thank Him for the way He shows up for you. If you can't think of a time, that's okay. I've been there, too! Write a prayer asking for a fresh revelation of His unique love for you and tell Him why you need it. I am convinced He is anxiously awaiting an invitation to be your Rescuer, your Redeemer, your Everything.

Chapter 1-Special Assignment

Read Psalm 45 and focus particularly on verse 10 and 11. Throughout the 12 weeks of this study, I pray you have the courage to see yourself as Christ sees you. He is enthralled by your beauty. Do you believe that truth? Do you dare?

If you did, it would change everything.

Write down a list of the things or people, the circumstances, the thoughts, the defeats, the fears that most often keep you from seeing yourself as Jesus sees you. Be as specific as you can be. Write down the opposing thoughts that rise up in your mind when you picture yourself as the pure and beautiful bride affianced to Jesus Messiah.

(Don't worry. I won't ask you to share these with anyone publically or privately.)

I want you to think seriously. Spend some time and be thorough. Ask God to help you recall what He wants you to bring before Him. Write them as offerings of a sincere heart — not to beat yourself up — but to bring to God for healing.

Then below your list, journal a prayer asking for His truth to be revealed in answer to each item you've listed. Ask Him to give you His Word as an antidote to the poison in your spirit. Over the next 12 weeks, focus on living out your beautiful identity in Christ Jesus. Commit to believe and wait upon the LORD to see Him work.

When you are done, seal it up in an envelope. Keep it in the back of the book or in another safe place you will remember.

Homework

Chapter 2: Preparing Your Field for an Abundant Harvest

Chapter 2-Day 1

Prepare your Field: If Jesus took a "soil sample," so to speak, of your heart at this season in your life, how would He find its condition?

Plant the Seed: Read Matthew 13:10-15 (Parable of the Sower)

Cultivate: In this chapter, we looked at the Parable of the Sower—both as Jesus told it to the crowd and how He explained it to His disciples in a more intimate and personal setting. Jesus used parables to compel listeners to discover truth, while at the same time concealing the truth from those too lazy or too stubborn to see it.[39] Verses 11-15 give details of a deeper kind of listening, which results in spiritual understanding. If you and I are ever going to be "good soil," we are going to need to receive the words of Jesus in this passage. Verse 15 states that those who hear but do not comprehend are those whose hearts are _hardened_ (think fallow ground). It goes on to say that such people CANNOT turn to Jesus to let Him heal them.

Reap the Harvest: I think it is interesting to note that Jesus explained the parable to the disciples in private *AFTER they asked Him* about it. (v.10) Let's do the same. Use this time to ask Jesus (in private) to open your eyes and ears. Ask for Him to soften your heart to further understand His truths. Ask Him for the healing you desire. Tell Him why you need it. Then like the disciples, sit nearby Him to hear what He has to say.

Chapter 2-Day 2

Prepare your Field: What kind of seed are you planting?

Plant the Seed: Read Galatians 6:7-10

Cultivate: To find out about what you are currently planting, it is helpful to look at what you are currently harvesting. You wouldn't expect to plant wheat seeds and harvest a crop of watermelon. Similarly, you cannot expect to plant to your own desires and harvest a crop pleasing to God. Our actions determine results. Someone who gossips about her friends will eventually lose friendships. Someone who indulges in the desires of her flesh will harvest a life of sorrow. But if you work to live and plant seeds to please the Spirit, from that Spirit you will reap joy and everlasting life.[40] 'Everlasting life' doesn't mean life after we die; it means life beginning *today* and lasting for all eternity. I love the fact that everlasting life doesn't begin when we die.

I pray you have tasted and seen that the LORD is good. So good that you desire with all your heart to please Him by bearing much fruit. (see John 15:8) Sin is a definite deal breaker to God's ability to bless your life with abundant fruit. In fact, sin keeps Him from tending your field at all. I have surely sown my share of wild oats. You? Let's get rid of the sin by asking for His forgiveness. In doing so, we allow Him to rain down His righteous favor.

Reap the Harvest: I would never ask you to write out your specific sins for others to ever happen upon and (accidentally or on purpose) see, but I do think it would be helpful to use this time to ask God to help rid your heart of anything that would hinder Him bringing forth a bumper crop in and through you. Be specific in prayer. Ask the Holy Spirit to remind you of things that might still be hindering His work. Then ask Him to rain down His righteousness, cleanse your heart and conscience, and make some rich humus of humility in which to plant the seed of His Word.

Chapter 2-Day 3

Prepare your Field: Are you just a hearer; or are you a doer also?

Plant the Seed: Read James 1:19-27

Cultivate: This particular passage in the book of James gives instruction on listening to the Word and doing what it says. If we want to be good soil, we are going to have to go beyond listening with closed ears and eyes and begin to increasingly do what the Word instructs. Verse 21 is especially useful for our study purposes. "Therefore, get rid of all moral filth and the evil that is so prevalent and humbly *accept the word planted in you*, which can save you." (emphasis added)

The word for 'accept' in the original Greek language is *'dechomai'* meaning to receive favorably, give ear to, embrace, make one's own, approve, not to reject.[41] I love the "make one's own" portion of that definition. Don't you love when there is something you can make your own in the rich treasures of God's kingdom? So what James is writing to you here is that you should accept the Word of God and MAKE IT YOURS! Say to yourself, because God says so, IT IS MINE! Your actions will be different from the world's if you truly own what God says in His Word.

Reap the Harvest: Write out Psalm 36:7 -9

Now own it as James 1:21 instructs. Make it yours and live knowing it is true. Personalize it by inserting your name and personal pronouns in it:

How precious is your unfailing love, O God!

_____ *finds shelter in the shadow of your wings.*

You feed_____ from the abundance of your own house,

Letting _____ drink from the river of delights. For you are the fountain of life,

the light by which _____ see. (personalized paraphrase of Psalm 36:7-9 NLT)

Are there fallow (inactive, unproductive) areas in your circumstance? Name them and ask God to tip the water jars of heaven (Job 38:37b) over it. Write a prayer and ask God to show you a seed from His Word you can claim as yours to plant in the mud. When He does, be sure to write the Scripture here or somewhere handy and revisit it often until it is yours.

Chapter 2-Day 4

Journal prompt: In this chapter, we learned how there is great hope for an abundant harvest in the mud.

At one point in my own difficult season of Mycah's cancer, I felt as if I genuinely sought the LORD. I felt I confessed my sin and turned from my evil ways and destructive habits. However, I also *still* felt as if I was buried and in a yucky, sticky situation, still facing childhood cancer in my only child. I wondered why I hadn't experienced the abundance the Word promises when abiding in Christ.

God taught me that bearing fruit in a life is a process. He showed me that in order to bring forth much fruit, it was necessary to break up the hard places of my heart with repentance. However, I couldn't skip the steps of sowing the seeds in the mud (reading and applying Scripture), maintaining a field free of weeds (sin), or waiting upon the LORD for harvest time.

If you find yourself frustrated that you sought the LORD, repented from sin, and possess the gracious righteousness of His forgiveness, but still feel bogged down ankle-deep in the drudge of life, take heart. It may be that you have been *blessed* with mud. There is great hope for an abundant harvest.

Sister, are you in the mud? Give Him thanks! How can you start sowing the true seed of His Word? Are your hands dirty from diggin' in with Christ? Write your thoughts.

Homework

Chapter 3: Cultivating an Abundant Harvest

Chapter 3-Day 1

Prepare your Field: Is your life bearing fruit or thistles?

Plant the Seed: Read Hebrews 6:7-8 and Matthew 15:13

Cultivate: Here is what the Life Application Study Bible says about Hebrews 6:7-8:

"The writer uses an analogy from agriculture to make a simple point. Real seeds (the gospel) given genuine care by the farmer (God) and planted in a fertile field (your heart and life) will produce a bountiful crop (spiritual maturity). Weeds (temptations) threaten to overwhelm the crop. If the field produces only weeds, then the seeds are lost and the field ruined."[42]

A Christian's life should bear fruit. It is the evidence in which the world can know we are His.

To do better, we have to know better. I tended a weed for weeks because I didn't know it was a weed. Spiritually speaking, we sometimes tend weeds because they look like useful life to us. We just don't know better.

Reap the Harvest: Are you tending any weeds, mistaking them as fruit? What relationships might be ruining your field? What sin? What about your current circumstance appears to be life, but is really a weed choking the true seed? Ask God to help identify it for you. Ask Him to rip it from the root and replace it with the seed of His Word.

(If you do not currently have stickers in your field, write about an experience when you had to do some weed pulling in the past. Ask God for an appropriate time and place to share this testimony with someone who needs to hear something of His heart.)

Chapter 3-Day 2

Prepare your Field: Are you walking with your head held high?

Plant the Seed: Read Leviticus 26:3-13

Cultivate: In this section of Scripture we find God's teachings to the Israelite people regarding obedience. It describes the rewards for their obedience and the benefits of being set free from their captivity in Egypt. It promises that if they follow the commands of the LORD, their harvesting will continue until time to gather the grapes from the vineyards. Basically, there would be no idle time in their abundance and there would be so much harvest, that when the time came to bring in the new year's crop, they would still be eating last year's. It is speaking of abundant blessings.

In Jesus, we too are set free from our sin when we accept Christ's payment that redeems us from sin's slavery. We no longer have to hang our heads in shame, but can walk with heads held high knowing we have been redeemed and freed.

I remember after I began to believe God's promises in private, I still walked in public as one defeated. I felt that others looking at me would surely know I was being punished and the fruit in my current circumstance was evidence of my sinful life. God soon taught me that I was to walk with my head held high, even when I didn't feel like it was a true representation of my feelings during the painful circumstances. Did He ask me to "fake it?" No. Later I realized He was asking me to "believe Him for it." I didn't need to feel ashamed, but I needed to walk as a slave set free. My circumstances had nothing to do with it. I was free through the blood of Jesus and should walk upright in belief of it. Soon the fruitful evidence of the truth would begin to show.

Reap the Harvest: Are there times when you walk with your head and shoulders schlumped over in defeat? Are you still carrying a yoke of shame? Are you walking as a slave in bondage or as one set free? Write here about the shame you still carry. And then **let it go**. Sow it in the mud where it belongs and wait for God to bring His beautiful harvest.

Read Psalm 34:5 and then go do the rest of your day with head held high.

Chapter 3-Day 3

Prepare your Field: How can you feed others the Bread of Life?

Plant the Seed: Read 2 Corinthians 9:10-15

Cultivate: In this chapter, we discussed how farmers in Old Testament days needed to harvest enough seed to **feed** their family, **plant** for next year's harvest, and **save** for years when the harvest was less plentiful. According to research, insufficient crops happened as frequently as once every three to four years.

Spiritually speaking, we want to harvest enough righteousness to feed ourselves, sustain our future, and reserve for difficult seasons ahead in life. We cannot expect to feed those around us if we have not sufficiently planted righteousness in our own lives. When we receive an abundant harvest, we are to be generous with it and bake bread to feed those in need. In these Scriptures, Paul teaches to be generous with a self-sacrificial heart. Acts of generosity result in praises to God, thus bringing an even greater abundance of glorious harvest in and through the giver.

If there are those around you who may be currently experiencing an insufficient crop—either physically or spiritually—the Scriptures charge those bringing forth abundance to be generous.

Reap the Harvest: Think of a time when someone showed you great generosity when you were experiencing a season of insufficiency. When you were in need, what did their generosity mean to you? Write about it.

Now think of someone in your circle of influence who could benefit from your spiritual abundance. Who could use a sustaining word or their physical need met? Write their name or initials. Then write verse 6 of 2 Corinthians 9 with it:

Ask God to help you sow generously so that you might reap generously for the purpose of His praise and thanksgiving. How can you begin sowing generously today?

Chapter 3-Day 4

Journal prompt: Search your heart. Is there something you hold onto with a death grip? Do you hold onto something as if it were life itself? Is there something or someone, if lost, would cause you to want to die as well—wealth, status, beauty, reputation, relationship, addiction, a secret, a grudge? Ask the Holy Reminder to bring it to your attention.

Deuteronomy 30:19b-20a states:

"Now choose life, so that you and your children may live and that you may love the LORD your God, listen to his voice, and hold fast to him. For the LORD is your life."

We have to loosen our grip—"let it go." We have to sow the very thing that appears to be life to us. Sowing it means having an empty hand. We must fill it with the LORD and hold fast to Him. "Get a grip," so to speak, onto Almighty God alone. You will find, if you continue to seek Him and endure patiently, that He is upholding you with His righteous right hand and taking your right hand into His left (see Isaiah 41:10and 13). Think about that for a minute. In the position the Scripture speaks of, you are in a dance hold with the LORD. Would you ever hold onto something so relentlessly you forfeit dancing with the Alpha and Omega? What are you holding onto? Is it keeping you from dancing to joyous songs of abundant harvest? How could letting it go be better for you?

Homework

Chapter 4: The Threshing Floor

Chapter 4-Day 1

Prepare your Field: What affect does your acknowledgement of God have on Him?

Plant the Seed: Read Psalm 139: 1-18 and Psalm 91:14

Cultivate: In Psalm 139 you see how fully known you are by God. He knows everything about you from beginning to end, inside and out, near and far, light and dark, word, thought, and deed—everything. He knows.

In Psalm 91:14 you see God's response to *your* knowledge of *Him*. "Because [she] loves me," says the LORD, "I will rescue [her]; I will protect [her], for [she] acknowledges my name."

The word for 'knows' and 'acknowledges' in these Scriptures is '*yada*' in the original Hebrew language.[43] It is the same in both Psalm 139 and Psalm 91. It stuns me to think about this! God knows me. He knows everything from my name to the number of hairs on my head, to my every thought. He is the God of heaven and He knows my name! Now contrast that thought with Psalm 91:14—because I love

Him, *because I acknowledge His name*, He will rescue me. Does that not blow your mind?

It is a big deal to be known by the God of heaven. Such knowledge is too wonderful for us. But don't miss it. Psalm 91 says it is a BIG DEAL for God when we acknowledge Him. He is all knowing, but I suspect He reserves the right to be somehow blown over when one of His children lays down her life for a God she has never seen. When we show our love for Him by obeying Him and acknowledging His name, it stirs Him to act for our protection and in our rescue.

Reap the Harvest: How does it make you feel to know He is moved to act on your behalf because you acknowledge His name? What are a few of your favorite names for God? Acknowledge Him by writing a few of them in your response.

Chapter 4-Day 2

Prepare your Field: How do you endure hardships? Do you see it as discipline? Perhaps a test of your faith?

Plant the Seed: Read Psalm 139:23-24 and Hebrews 12:7-12

Cultivate: The Psalmist invites God to test him to see if there is any offensive way inside him in order to be led in the way everlasting. The writer of Hebrews 12:7-12 instructs us to endure hardships as discipline, because it produces a harvest of righteousness and peace for those who have been trained by it. Testing isn't always prompted by sin, but testing proves us and trains us as we grow spiritually. Testing upon the threshing floor is the training ground for Christian maturity. God disciplines those He loves. It may be painful at the time, but will produce a harvest if we allow it.

Reap the Harvest: Are you on the threshing floor? If not, have you spent a season there before? Consider:

How am I responding to it?

What am I learning from it?

How does my response demonstrate faith, commitment and love for God and for others, and Christ-like character?

Chapter 4-Day 3

Prepare your Field: Does your faith show in your actions?

Plant the Seed: Read James 2:14-25

Cultivate: It is imperative to note: We cannot earn our salvation by serving and obeying God. Salvation is a free gift we receive by faith (Ephesians 2:8-9). However, faith without action, once we are saved, is useless. Many claim an intellectual agreement with Christian teachings, but never act in faith according to those teachings. True faith requires action verb belief in God's Word. Abraham acted on God's Word and it was credited to him as righteousness. We have to choose. When the rubber meets the road, will we act in faith or be paralyzed by fear? It is very hard to believe God's Word over the appearance of circumstances, other's opinions, and your own gut feelings. However, God asks us to trust Him in faith over all other factors.

Reap the Harvest: Have you faced a decision where God's Word was contradictory to what you wanted? What did you decide? What was your action? (Remember, even doing nothing is taking an action.) What was the result?

It is important to know that God allows re-takes on His tests. . .in fact, often He will not allow you to move on in your walk until you pass. (Lamentations 3:22)

What do you think God is teaching you in your current circumstance? Ask Him to train you to act in faith with action-verb belief.

Chapter 4-Day 4

Journal prompt: Read 1 Peter 1:3-9. I love verses 6-8. Suffering may come because of various trials, but these come so that our faith can be proven genuine and result in praise, glory and honor when Jesus Christ is revealed. I especially love verse 8: "Though you have not seen him, you love him; and even though you do not see him now, you believe in him and are filled with an inexpressible and glorious joy. . ."

Soon after we made the decision to trust God with Mycah's clinical trial decision, He kept reminding me over and over about Abraham and Isaac. It was like every time I turned around, He was reminding me. On radio broadcast sermons, my daily devotional readings, in discussions with other Christians, blogs, everywhere! I finally asked Him, Why? What am I missing? Why do You keep bringing this up?

I was brought to tears when I realized He wanted me to know. He wanted me to know it was a BIG DEAL to Him. He knew it was the most difficult decision to make for a God I'd never seen. Our acts in faith are precious to Him.

He knows we are dust. (Psalm 103:14) He knows this life is hard. He knows how hard it is to believe in someone we've never seen. He highly esteems us when we prove faithful by believing anyway.

What is He asking you? How can you lay down your life for another? How can you believe a God you can't see to be trustworthy with even the most difficult decisions? How have you seen His faithfulness even when you couldn't see His face? Your "Once upon a time. . . ." begins on the threshing floor of your heart. Begin writing the rest of the story with Him today. Ask Him to make the threshing floor of your heart into the foundation for the temple of His glory in you.

Homework

Chapter 5: Sifted as Wheat

Chapter 5-Day 1

Prepare your Field: Do you believe God can turn any curse (trial) into a blessing for you?

Plant the Seed: Read Romans 8:28-38 (Even if you've read this passage a million times, read it now as if it's the first)

Cultivate: I think it is easy to see in hind-sight, in our own lives and in the lives of others, how God can turn difficult circumstances into blessings. It is not as easy to feel that truth when in the midst of tragedy or suffering, especially when we might have been the cause of it. Satan loves to exploit guilt to convince us we are worthless.

I imagine Satan celebrates his success when one of God's children gives up on a bold and dynamic life in Christ because of his accusations. If he can convince a believer she is all chaff (trash), he can cause eternal loss. God has things no eye has seen, no ear has heard, and no mind has conceived prepared for those who love Him. (1 Corinthians 2:9) If Satan can debilitate your ability to claim them in Christ, he wins. He might not have your soul for eternity, but he can steal the abundant and fruitful life Christ promises you. We will either believe Christ and claim the abundance He has for us, or we will believe Satan's lies and forfeit them.

Romans 8:37 says we are more than conquerors through Him who loved us. He has given you the power to defeat the enemy, because He already has once and for all. Put on your superhero cape, sister! (See Isaiah 61:10) This trial you are under is your blessing. Claim it!

Reap the Harvest: What is Satan trying to steal from you? What lie has he been getting you to buy lately? What is he accusing you of?

What are you forfeiting by believing him?

Look at Matthew chapter four. Jesus was tempted by Satan for 40 days. He resisted through fasting, prayer, and applying the Word of God. Notice THEN he began His ministry preaching. Have you considered your ministry might be on the other side of temptation, trial, or suffering? Take this time to talk to God about it.

Chapter 5-Day 2

Prepare your Field: How can you begin to see and hear what your eye has never seen and your ear has never heard? (1 Corinthians 2:9)

Plant the Seed: Read Acts 4: 1-21

Cultivate: We looked closely at Peter's sifting experience in this chapter. Just before Christ was crucified and laid behind that stone, he denied Jesus three times. We then saw Peter forgiven, reinstated, and given instructions for a future ministry of feeding the LORD's sheep. In the reading today (Acts 4:1-21), we see Peter living a bold life for Christ, healing a crippled beggar, leading others to belief in Jesus, and speaking courageously to his accusers.

I love verse 13: *"When they saw the courage [boldness] of Peter and John and realized that they were unschooled, ordinary men, they were astonished and they took note that these men had **been with Jesus.**"* (emphasis added)

Does it not blow your mind to know that in Christ, we can be bold and courageous? It does not take seminary degrees, professional training in speaking, or a formal education to cause kingdom gain with your life. It just takes "being with Jesus." If you've walked with Him and taken His teaching to heart, you are fully equipped to astonish.

Reap the Harvest: Have you failed in your walk? In what ways? Have you sought forgiveness? Have you heard Jesus make a call on your life for His kingdom?

Are you astonishing people (or perhaps yourself) with your boldness?

313

If you answered yes to all the above, thank Him for an abundant life! If you answered no or are not sure, ask God to begin moving you toward boldness. Ask Him to create in your life and testimony the ability to say like Peter and John, *"For we cannot help speaking about what we have seen and heard."* (Acts 4:20)

Chapter 5-Day 3

Prepare your Field: How can you stand against the enemy's schemes and accusations?

Plant the Seed: Read Ephesians 6: 10-18, Revelation 12: 9-11, Isaiah 54:16-17

Cultivate: Here we see some very powerful tools to use in our struggles against evil:

- The full armor of God: belt of truth, breastplate of righteousness, boots of the gospel of peace, shield of faith, helmet of salvation, and the sword of the Spirit which is the word of God (Ephesians 6:13-17)
- The blood of the Lamb and the word of your testimony (Revelation 12:11)
- A heritage and vindication from the LORD (Isaiah 54:17)

God has given us every tool we need to defend ourselves against the enemy. He has already won the war on our behalf. We just have to believe and obey Him for our victory.

Reap the Harvest: *"They overcame him [the accuser] by the blood of the Lamb and by the word of their testimony. . . ."* (Revelation 12:11)

What is your testimony? Is there something you've seen and heard in your own life that you just can't help but speak about? Write about it.

I have felt the flaming arrows of accusation from the enemy over and over while preparing this study. He has gotten in some good hits. But I know because of Isaiah 54:17 that no weapon forged against me will prevail. I find it completely AWE — -SOME when I speak a word of my testimony and the flaming arrows fizzle in the living water of Christ at work in me. Let's find relevant and appropriate ways to speak a Word to someone else in need. Not only will we be strengthening a brother or sister, but we will be overcoming the enemy! That is our vindication from the LORD.

Let's do boldness. Start talking! Write it first to help you practice. Now look for a situation in which you can share it.

Chapter 5-Day 4

Journal prompt: Sifting is an all out attempt by the enemy to destroy you and cause you to quit. He aims to convince you that you are all chaff (trash).

Write down some of the negative feelings you've had recently about your own life and character:

(I'll put a few of mine here as an example to get you started)

I'm ugly. I'm a failure. I misunderstand the Word. I am a fake. I am a liar. My work is meaningless/incorrect. I am alone. I could never be the person Jesus wants me to be.

Now you go.

Write 1 John 3:1.

We are God's children! He lavishes His love on us.

Now write down some of the ways you have experienced His love lately:

(I'll go first again)

I opened my eyes to a new day this morning. I saw a single bird sitting on the cross of the steeple of the church across from Mycah's school when I dropped her off. I think somehow it was there for me. My daughter had a great report at the cancer clinic on Thursday. I get to peek into the beautiful hearts of other women who love the Lord each week.

Now you go.

Whom do you believe? Do you believe the lies Satan tells you or do you believe the evidence of God's love in your life? Do you believe Jesus about you? Why or why not?

How would your actions be different if you walked in the secure knowledge of lavish Love? You are Christ's eternal *BRIDE.* How are you living today in that truth?

Homework

Chapter 6: His Extravagant Purchase

Chapter 6-Day 1

Prepare your Field: Have you neglected your own heart?

Plant the Seed: Read Song of Songs chapter 1

Cultivate: Song of Songs, or Song of Solomon, is a short book of the Bible with only 117 verses. With no explicitly religious content, the *Song* is often interpreted as an allegorical representation of the relationship of Christ and the church, as husband and wife. Look especially at verse six of chapter one.

> *My mother's sons were angry with me*
> *and made me take care of the vineyards;*
> *my own vineyard I have neglected.*

We learned in the first session of this study that the Bible often uses the symbol of land, fields or vineyards to represent the heart. We see the Beloved (or the prospective bride) reveal that she has neglected her own vineyard because she had to care for other's vineyards. As females, we OFTEN neglect our own needs and hearts to take care of someone else's.

Reap the Harvest: How have you neglected your own vineyard, your heart? Why?

As noble, honorable, and even necessary, as the tasks at hand are, when you tend to the needs of others in your life, it is important to let Christ tend to your heart. Look now at Hosea 2:15-16

The NIV states it as such:

"There I will give her back her vineyards,
and will make the Valley of Achor [trouble] a door of hope. . .
In that day, declares the LORD, you will call me 'my husband';
you will no longer call me 'my master.'

The LORD desires to redeem and heal your heart, especially the most secret places of brokenness. He can give it back healed, because He paid for its redemption with His blood in order to establish an eternal and binding covenant with you. It came with an extravagant price tag. Write Him a love letter and thank Him for His unfailing love. If you have not given Him access to your threshing floor or feel like you are not ready, tell Him why and ask Him to answer your heart's questions.

Chapter 6-Day 2

Prepare your Field: How seriously does God take His promises?

Plant the Seed: Read Numbers 23:19, 2 Chronicles 6:14-15, Psalm 119:160, 162, and 2 Peter 3:9. If it helps you to focus and meditate, write them down so you can see them all together in writing.

Cultivate: These are just a few of the things God says about His promises in His Word. He is all about promises. Everything He does and says is based on promise, because it is impossible for God to lie. (Hebrews 6:18) Perhaps you have trusted in a promise someone made to you only to be betrayed when that person did not keep their promise. Often our experiences with humans, especially those we trust and love and who are supposed to love us, affect our trust in God. I remember feeling very convinced that God *could* heal and redeem and use my brokenness as the foundation for His glory in me, but wondered if He *would*. If we are not fully convinced of His covenant of peace, we often live as if we believe His promise for a day or two and then begin to doubt and stumble in our side of the covenant.

Reap the Harvest: Do you believe God is completely true and trustworthy to handle your threshing floor? Do you believe He will? Are you convinced He has not taken the sorrow and pain lightly and that your place of brokenness is of extreme value to Him? Have you heard a still, small whisper upon your threshing floor and doubted it as His promise? Did you think it too good to be true? Or maybe just wishful thinking by your own imagination? Take this time and place to ask

God for a personal promise of peace and/or the wisdom to know and believe His voice and His promise. (See James 1:5-6) Practice continuing to believe and living as if He is currently fulfilling His promise for you.

Chapter 6-Day 3

Prepare your Field: What is your covenant of peace?

Plant the Seed: Read Isaiah 54:1-10

Cultivate: Isaiah Chapter 54 prophesies about the relationship of Jesus and His bride, the Church. In the previous chapter, Isaiah prophesied about the suffering of Christ, and in this chapter, he speaks of the coming comfort and glory of the Bride. Verse ten tells you even if the mountains are shaken and hills removed, His unfailing love for you will not be shaken nor will His covenant of peace be removed. Remember everything God does is based on covenant and there are over 3000 promises in the Bible. Often in our most secret places of suffering and pain, He desires to make a covenant of peace.

Reap the Harvest: In your walk with the LORD, have you experienced a personal covenant of peace? Are you currently in need of a promise for your peace? Ask God to help you realize His offer of a personal and new covenant for you. Like Abraham, tell Him why you are in need of one (see Genesis 15: 3). Ask Him what your side of the covenant will be. Then devote your heart and soul to seeking the LORD your God. (1 Chronicles 22:19) He may not promise you *your* every desire. *His* **desire for you is priority**. He promises to work all things for the good of those who love Him. (Romans 8:28) I do not believe we would ever come to hold the riches of His promise in our reality and still desire our own way. His ways are always better and higher. (Isaiah 55:8-9)

Chapter 6-Day 4

Journal prompt:

Perhaps you've believed God for salvation. Maybe He has access to your heart in general, but does He own that deepest, darkest, broken place too? How do you know? Have you allowed Him to pay full price for even your threshing floor? Has He revealed it as sacred by putting His presence in it? He won't take what is yours. He insists on paying full price with His blood because you are of great value.

Casting Crowns sings a most wonderful song, *Your Love is Extravagant*. Here are some of the lyrics:

Your love is extravagant
Your friendship, it is intimate
I feel I'm moving to the rhythm of Your grace
Your fragrance is intoxicating in the secret place
Cause Your love is extravagant

Spread wide in the arms of Christ there's a love that covers sin
No greater love have I ever known; You considered me a friend
Capture my heart again[44]

How has he captured your heart with His extravagant love? Count the ways. Name them one by one.

Bonus: Ask for more! His love is unfailing and **abundant**. *"How great is the goodness you have stored up for those who fear you. You lavish it on those who come to you for protection, blessing them before the watching world."* (Psalm 31:19 NLT)

Homework

Chapter 7: Beautiful House of Glory

Chapter 7-Day 1

Prepare your Field: Have you experienced His double-portion?

Plant the Seed: Read Isaiah 62:3-5

Cultivate: *Your land will be married.* In our study we've discussed how land is often symbolic in Scripture as your heart. To enter covenant with Jesus is to become His bride, holy and consecrated for Him. His presence in your heart is a place of intimate worship and spiritual knowledge.

Look at Isaiah 61:7 *"Instead of their shame my people will receive a double portion, and instead of disgrace they will rejoice in their inheritance, and so they will inherit a double portion in their land."*

I don't know the circumstances of your personal threshing floor. However, I dare you to find better motivation than a double portion of Jesus to persevere. Holy, holy glory!

Reap the Harvest: Is there a temple of God's glory standing upon your threshing floor? Have you entered a place of double-portion relationship in Christ? Do others sense in you the knowledge and intimacy you've experienced within the sacred temple? Why or why not? What might be keeping you from entering His presence?

One way we can know that God has set His glory on our threshing floor is that it has become hallowed ground, the foundation of sacred relationship, chosen and consecrated to be holy and pure. What evidence do you find of that type of construction upon your threshing floor?

Chapter 7-Day 2

Prepare your Field: What are your intentions when you approach God in His temple?

Plant the Seed: Read Psalm 27

Cultivate: Psalm 27 was penned by King David himself. Verse four is one of my all time favorite verses of Holy Script. David (as the one who made many of the plans for the temple) was familiar with God's hand upon his own. First Chronicles 29:19 tells us how David came to know the plans for the temple. *"All this," David said, "I have in writing from the hand of the LORD upon me, and He gave me understanding in all the details of the plan."*

Jeremiah 29:11 says, *"I know the plans I have for you," declares the LORD, "Plans to prosper you and not harm you, plans to give you hope and a future."*

David's primary desire was to live in the house of the LORD all the days of His life. Jesus, the mediator of the New Covenant, came from David's family line and God trusted David with the plans for the temple. David, though imperfect, had an intimate relationship with God and in turn was given access to astounding knowledge and promises. Perhaps the key to knowing the plans God has for our lives comes from seeking Him in His temple, not so that we can gain any-thing from Him, but rather for the sheer pleasure of delighting in Him.

327

Reap the Harvest: God wants us to tell Him our needs and make requests of Him. He invites us to come to Him with anything and everything. (Philippians 4:6) However, we must not forget that there is also an appropriate time for authentic and exclusive worship. What do you desire most from God? Do you look forward to being in the presence of the LORD? Are your intentions to gain something from Him or just to be still and gaze upon His beauty? True worship and intimacy seeks no gain, yet everything is offered freely. Talk to Him about that.

Chapter 7-Day 3

Prepare your Field: What is your living sacrifice today?

Plant the Seed: Read 1 Corinthians 6:19 and 2 Chronicles 7:15

Cultivate: Using the knowledge we've gained through this week's study, we can see God's intentions toward Solomon's Old Testament temple and in turn, see His intentions toward your New Covenant temple in Christ. His eyes will be open and His ears attentive to your heart. He has chosen and consecrated (set it apart for Himself) this temple so that His Name will be there forever. His eyes and heart will always be there. Verse one of 2 Chronicles, Chapter seven says fire came down from heaven and consumed the burnt offering and the sacrifices, and the glory of the LORD filled the temple.

We no longer need to make blood sacrifices to God. Jesus did that for us once and for all. Instead, Romans 12:1 teaches to offer our bodies as a *living sacrifice*, holy and pleasing to God. It is your spiritual act of worship. In doing so, the eyes and ears of the LORD will always be on you, and the glory of the LORD will shine in your spirit like a consuming fire.

Reap the Harvest: How do you best experience true worship? Through nature, in corporate settings, music, the Bible, quiet times, etc.? In what ways do you offer your body as a living sacrifice? How have you experienced the consuming fire of God's presence filling your life? How do you reflect His glory in your actions, words, and thoughts? What affect do you believe your worship has on God? (Don't feel like you have to answer all the questions, pick the one or two the Spirit leads you to and meditate on it with Jesus.)

Chapter 7-Day 4

Journal prompt: It is amazing to realize the value of your heart to God. I love to meditate on the passion Jesus has for me that He would pay extravagantly with His perfect life for mine. However, upon realizing His riches, we must not mistake material wealth for eternal inheritance. It is also critical that as His bride, we not attempt to counterfeit our beauty. Fashion, jewelry, and material glamour are not sinful in themselves. However, they should never become an illusion or "cover-up" for authentic glory radiating from a place of intimate worship and communion with Jesus.

For me, there are few things more jaw-dropping beautiful than a woman ablaze with Christ's glory due to an intimate relationship with Him in hidden places. If there were a store where I could buy that beauty potion in a bottle, I would be first in line! However, it is impossible to duplicate, counterfeit, or "put-on."

Have you witnessed such beauty? Write about it.

How have you displayed that kind of beauty within your own relationship with Christ? When do you feel most radiant with the glory of The Beautiful One?

Second Corinthians 3:18 says that we reflect the Lord's glory and are being transformed into His likeness with ever-increasing glory, which comes from the Lord, who is the Spirit. Ask God to increase His glory within you. Ask Him for more of His beauty displayed in and through you. No purchase necessary. Your spiritual clothing comes from Him free of charge to you. (Revelation 19:8) His fashion line is called Grace. Be His supermodel!

Homework

Chapter 8: Betrothal of the Virgin Bride

Chapter 8-Day 1

Prepare your Field: If you are brutally honest, are you afraid to "go down to the threshing floor?"

Plant the Seed: Read Ruth 3:1-4

Cultivate: I love to try and imagine what was going through Ruth's mind as she prepared herself to go to the threshing floor at night, in the dark, alone, a foreign new-girl-in-town, to lie down at the feet of one of the community's most respected and noble land owners. I bet you anything she was almost physically sick with doubt and fear of rejection. Can you imagine her self-talk? *"What am I thinking? I have lost my ever-loving mind agreeing to Naomi's ridiculously dangerous plan. Lie at the man's feet? Why in the world? What will he say? What will he do? What if he exposes me for a harlot? What if he says no? Surely I am not worthy to even approach him, let alone ask him to cover me with his garment. I have no business to be near one of such status."* I guess it is easy for me to imagine Ruth's insecurities, because I have said very similar things myself. What about you?

Reap the Harvest: Do you avoid the threshing floor at all cost? Why? Do you pray even, that you won't have to "go there?" Why in the world do we avoid it as if it were not an acceptable way to experience true intimacy and the glory of Jesus? Is anything worth missing out on the abundance to be found here? Why won't we "go there" with Him?

Write down your answer to one or more of the questions that resonate in your spirit.

Chapter 8-Day 2

Prepare your Field: If you are brave enough to "go there," will you trust enough to be vulnerable when you get there?

Plant the Seed: Read Ruth 3:5-9

Cultivate: When Ruth went down to the threshing floor, she had to lay everything out, exposing her every need to the one who might be able to cover her. Not only was she asking for Boaz to buy her dead husband's land, but she was asking him to marry her and proposing he give her their first born son to carry on another man's name. She was in serious need and she went to his feet, exposed herself, poured out her heart, shed her every pretense, and laid bare every bit of her vulnerable life to his will.

If the threshing floor isn't intimidating enough, we see that we must not only "go there," but we must lay bare our every weakness, pour out our heart, and expose our soul in complete truth. The last thing I ever desired was to strip down spiritually and expose the ugly truth of myself to God Himself.

Reap the Harvest: Sister, what are you still wearing? Have you stripped off every shred of your old self and poured out the deepest secrets of your heart to Him? He can handle it. Will you risk full, honest exposure to wear His divine and glorious covering?

What is keeping you from trusting Jesus? Ask Him to help you move toward complete vulnerability upon the threshing floor. (This is a daily struggle for even the most submitted servants of Christ, and everyone's process of routinely coming before the Lord in naked truth looks different. It may feel awkward, but do not think for one moment that He is oblivious or unconcerned with your struggle. He is waiting with a warm garment of glory. He will not delay in wrapping you in it.)

Chapter 8-Day 3

Prepare your Field: Have you found refuge under His wings?

Plant the Seed: Read Ruth 3:9-15, Psalm 91:4, and Psalm 63:7-8

Cultivate: The request for covering is an intimate proposal. It symbolized marriage and the fact that she would be his. The word for garment, or skirt, in the original language is "kanaph."[45] Its meaning includes wings and is also used in Ezekiel 16:8 when God takes Israel as His own. He says, *"I spread the corner of my garment over you and covered your nakedness. I gave you my solemn oath and entered into a covenant with you, declares the Sovereign LORD, and you became mine."* In Psalm 91:4, *"He will cover you with his feathers, and under his wings you will find refuge."* Christ offers His garment as a garment of salvation. Because of His perfection, we are made perfect and pure, a fitting bride of royal status for the King of kings.

Reap the Harvest: How have you experienced the Lord's covering in the past? Has He kept you from disaster? Spared your marriage or other relationship? Granted healing for someone you love? Walked with you through a difficult season? Shown grace when you messed something up royally? Write about it and then write how that experience can help you trust Him for the future. What does it mean to you that His perfection can cover you and make you a fitting bride of royal status?

Chapter 8-Day 4

Journal prompt: If we follow the example of Ruth at the threshing floor, we are fully ready to accept the offer of betrothal of our eternal Bridegroom. God is looking for a flawless and pure bride for His Son. Although it is difficult for our minds to comprehend, Jesus has made a way for us to be perfect and complete as a bride of royal status. Ruth went to the threshing floor, submitted herself to her kinsman-redeemer, made herself vulnerable to His will, and then asked to be covered with his garment. His response, *"Do not be afraid. I will do for you all you ask."* (Ruth 3:10) If we do likewise, I wonder if we would get the same response from our Kinsman-Redeemer. Make your requests known to Him:

I love this intimate and tender peek into the heart of Christ through Boaz. Look at verse 15 of Ruth chapter three. *"He also said, 'Bring me the shawl you are wearing and hold it out.' When she did so, he poured into it six measures of barley and put it on her."* I could just bawl at the tender mercy. Not only will Christ give us all we ask for, He will pour into our hands from His rich abundance. Ruth once scraped out a thin existence from the leftover sheaves of Boaz's field. Then she became his bride and carried an abundance for which she did not have to work. It is like Him, isn't it? Look at Romans 9:23. *"What if He did this to make the riches of His glory known to the objects of His mercy, whom He prepared in advance for glory – even us. . . .?"*

You were prepared since before creation for glory. Do you know the riches of His glory? What if He wants to show you more? Will you "go there" with Him?

Chapter 8-BONUS DAY!

Prepare your Field: What is the significance of Jesus' last word spoken on the cross?

Plant the Seed: Read John 19:28-30 (The Crucifixion)

Cultivate: "It is finished." We think of this statement as Christ's last words and the announcement of His completion of the Father's will and fulfillment of the work of the cross. And it is. However, for those who look for abundance, the flawless poetry of God's Word offers a play on words. The Aramaic word (which Christ spoke on the cross) for "finished" is "kelal", meaning to complete, finish, and make perfect.[14] We know Jesus' death on the cross made us perfect and complete as He finished the task given Him by God the Father. While Jesus spoke the Aramaic word, "kelal", the Hebrew word for bride is "kallah", translated bride or spouse.[15] It comes from the Hebrew word (kalal), to complete![16] Jesus used His last breath to send a message to His bride. He paid the mohar (bride price) to complete and fulfill the Jewish law stating how He must obtain Her. You are so valuable to Jesus; He paid your mohar with His perfect life, with His very blood. The cross was for you. With His last breath, He spoke your name.

Reap the Harvest: If that doesn't blow you away, I don't know what will. I love the flawless Word of God. It is rich with meaning beyond our wildest dreams.

Have you considered your worth through God's eyes? Have you considered your extravagant price tag? Do you feel He made a wise purchase? How do your actions and attitudes demonstrate your belief regarding your worth to Jesus? What might be different about your walk with Christ knowing now that you've been unashamedly purchased at the ultimate price? Do you feel valuable knowing you are Christ's eternal bride, purchased in accordance with every law? (Don't feel like you have to answer all of the above questions. Perhaps pick one or two you feel God has pointed out to you and expand in thoughtful meditation with Him.)

Homework

Chapter 9: Preparing a Place

Chapter 9-Day 1

Prepare your Field: How does Christ see you? Are you His?

Plant the Seed: Read Psalm 45

Cultivate: Verse 13 of Psalm 45 gives us a peek at ourselves through the eyes of the LORD. The original word for "within" is *pĕniymah*, and it conveys the idea of the inner parts of a room, sanctuary, or palace.[46] *All glorious is the princess within. . .* You are glorious within, dear one. Remember God built His temple upon the threshing floor and the Holy of Holies is where the Ark of the Covenant resided. The top of the Ark of the Covenant was knows as the Atonement Cover. Jesus became our Atonement Cover when He covered us with His blood as full payment for our sins, thus taking them away forever and giving us His garment of salvation. Upon the threshing floor of your heart, God wants to build the house of His glory. In Jesus, the Holy of Holies of your heart is being prepared as a bridal chamber where you meet with Him intimately. He makes you glorious by being covered in His glory.

Reap the Harvest: What is the condition on your "within"? Is the inner place of your heart a sanctuary? Have you allowed Him to purchase the threshing floor of your heart to build a place of His glory? Does Jesus have your heart's complete devotion while He prepares a place for you within? Do you experience one-ment with Him there or is it a ramshackle or a temple to a false god?

Chapter 9-Day 2

Prepare your Field: Are you prepared?

Plant the Seed: Read Matthew 25:1-13

Cultivate: Keep watch. The moral of this parable, for me, is to always be watching for the Bridegroom. No one knows the day or the hour. We must not fall asleep or forget our faith and be caught unprepared. As the devoted bride of Christ, we must be set apart for Jesus alone, take care to make ourselves beautiful in His eyes, and gather a trousseau (treasures) for the coming age.

Read 1 Timothy 6:17-19

Paul is teaching us how to gather (lay up) treasures for ourselves for the coming age. He says to do good, to be rich in good deeds, and to be generous and willing to share. Our salvation is never "works based." Salvation is a free gift. However, to lay up treasure and always be ready for the Bridegroom to return, we should look for ways to establish a firm foundation for our eternal home with Jesus. There is a bonus here as well. In doing good deeds, we can take hold of the life that is truly life in this age.

Reap the Harvest: Ask God to help you see ways in which to lay up treasure for yourself. Who can you share with today? How can you show generosity to another in your circle of influence? What good might you do for someone else this week? Write it down and commit to following through, lest you be caught unprepared.

Chapter 9-Day 3

Prepare your Field: How does Christ describe you?

Plant the Seed: Read Ephesians 5:25-27

Cultivate: In this passage of Scripture we get a moment to see the bride as Christ sees her. Mentioned here are these descriptors: holy (some versions "sanctified"), clean, His, radiant, without stain or wrinkle or blemish, holy, and blameless. You might notice holy is listed two times. I believe in the perfect and flawless Word of Scripture and believe it is not by accident or coincidence that holy is listed twice. (The KJV uses the word "sanctified" in verse 26. In the original language both are from the same word *hagios* or "holy" used in verse 27.)[47] Remember the outer court of the temple is called the Holy place, while the inner-most place was termed the Holy of Holies (two times holy). As the bride of Christ, we are those who have offered the inner sanctuary of our hearts (the Holy of Holies) to Christ, making it "double portion" holy.

Reap the Harvest: It may feel awkward, but we have to start owning and showing our position as the bride of Christ. He gave us that title at great cost. To hide it under a bushel of doubt, fear, and false humility does not honor Him. Write the verses of Ephesians 5:25-27 as a personal statement, replacing your name with "the church" (because that is you).

My personal example: Christ loved Angie and gave himself up for her to make her **holy**, cleansing her by the washing of water through the word, and to present her to himself as radiant, without stain or wrinkle or any other blemish, but **holy** and blameless.

You go:

We may not see ourselves as He does when we look in the mirror. In fact, I saw a new wrinkle this morning. But we walk by faith and not by sight. How can you walk in the faith of this truth today? What specific action can you take in full faith that you are who He says you are?

Chapter 9-Day 4

Journal prompt: One of my most favorite revelations from researching and writing this particular session was learning about the special care and attention the Jewish bridegroom took when preparing the bridal chamber for his bride. I love imagining him searching for information about her likes and dislikes, trying to seek out the perfect furnishings, perhaps carving designs of her favorite flower into the door post, placing the room in such a way as to let her know he was eager to understand her, know her, and please her with the desires of her heart.

Jesus has gone to prepare a place for you, His bride. Until the day He comes to take us there face to face, I believe He prepares the inner chamber of our hearts, our personal Holy of Holies, as a place where He can be at one with us in spirit. He regularly writes my favorite Scriptures (His Word) upon the walls of my heart, reminds me of His faithfulness with memories of His loving work in my life as if hanging framed photos of us together, and cleans out the riff-raff, dirty sin, and lies I've believed that threaten to ruin our sanctuary.

Take this time to write some of the specific ways Jesus has prepared a place especially for you within the inner chamber of your heart. If perhaps He does not currently have access to your threshing floor, maybe this is a time to tell Him you accept His offer of betrothal and allow Him to begin preparing a place of at-one-ment for you and Him.

Homework

Chapter 10: The Wedding Feast

Okay! This week we're going to do something a bit different for homework! I believe it is party-horn obvious that the LORD loves a celebration. God instituted seven feasts each year, one day a week for down time, Jesus performed His first miracle at a wedding (turning water into wine), and the culmination of His plan of redemption is a wedding feast of all things! Our God is a God of celebration!

Some believe Christianity to be a boring life for only squares. Not so. In fact, the more I walk with Him, the more I believe that if we are not celebrating in style, in some way or another, on a regular basis, we are not doing it right. This week we are going to become one with Him in spirit and focus our time and attention to rejoicing, rejoicing, rejoicing in the Lord God Almighty! I am in the mood. What about you? Don't be a party foul. So to mark the special occasion, we will be ditching the normal homework framework and doing some things a bit different. Let's have some fun in the LORD!

Remember the bride had some very important tasks to complete before her bridegroom returned for her on the unexpected day of their wedding. We will spend this week in the spirit of the bride, practicing and celebrating preparation for our coming Bridegroom. Come Lord Jesus! (Revelation 22:20)

Chapter 10-Day 1

Set Yourself Apart

"You are to be holy to me because I, the LORD, am holy, and I have **set you apart** from the nations to be my own." (Leviticus 20:26)

"Before I formed you in the womb I knew you, before you were born I **set you apart**. . ." (Jeremiah 1:5)

Find some time today and set yourself apart from normal life. Get up earlier in the morning, stay up later than everyone else, lock yourself in the bathroom (get in the tub. . .that's always my gig), go outside and hide if you have to. Find about 20 minutes or so and sit alone with the LORD. Don't ask Him for a single thing. Just sit alone with Him, praise Him, thank Him for His hand in your life. . . .do whatever you do that makes you feel like you are pleasing Him with your very presence and effort to be there with Him. Set yourself apart for Him and only Him in that moment. If you feel led, write things He might have whispered to you in the quiet, draw what you saw or felt, or write what you feel relevant from your experience. If not, don't sweat it. . .Just celebrate that He chose you from the beginning and set you apart as His own.

Chapter 10-Day 2

Lay Up Treasure (gather a trousseau for the coming age)

Re-read 1 Timothy 6:17-19. Let's take today to live the life that is truly life! Do something for another and do it with excellence and love as if doing it for Jesus. A betrothed woman should conduct herself as one who brings honor to her bridegroom. Perhaps you might cook a nice meal for your family, maybe cook a double portion and share it with a neighbor, write an encouraging note to someone else, surprise someone with an unexpected little gift or gesture, seek out a "least of these" person in your circle of influence and fulfill a need, or do something for your husband he especially loves. Be generous. Don't do it out of obligation, need, or to earn anything in return. Do it as unto the LORD!

"The King will reply, "I tell you the truth, whatever you did for one of the least of these brothers [sisters] of mine, you did for me." (Matthew 25:40)

We are going to be accountable on this one. Not to boast in ourselves, but so that we can celebrate obedience to His Word. So write what you did here or in your journal:

Chapter 10-Day 3

Prepare your Wedding Garments (take special care of your beauty)

According to Revelation 19:8, fine linen stands for righteous acts and "fine linen, bright and clean" is given to the bride who has made herself ready.

Preparing our garments means acting righteous. Being beautiful in the eyes of Christ is to be holy, clean, radiant, without stain, wrinkle or blemish, holy (two times), and blameless (Ephesians 5:25-27)

Celebrate your beauty in His eyes. Do something special to care for your heart and spirit today. Wear something that makes you feel especially beautiful (even if no one understands why you're wearing a cocktail dress while buying groceries). Maybe go for a manicure, pedicure, or other beauty treat. Spend a few more minutes on your hair (see Song of Solomon 7:5), go buy some new lip stick, or perhaps even a new wrinkle cream! The point here is not vanity or self indulgence, so don't go using me as an excuse to spend a lot of money! The point is to put your hands to the care of your beauty with a spiritual understanding that you are to prepare yourself to be ever beautiful in His eyes. He wants us to be radiant from an intimate relationship with Him, so practice this task in your reality today. . .but know your beauty exudes from acting righteous within your relationship with Christ. He wants you to *celebrate* your beauty in Him! Strut your Jesus-glamour.

Write what you did here (or tape the receipt for the item or service!).

Chapter 10-Day 4

Ready Yourself with Rejoicing!

No one knows the day or hour. (Mark 13:32) Imagine for a moment that Jesus is coming back for His bride this day. What would you want Him to catch you doing? What would please Him most in your opinion? What would make Him throw His holy head back and laugh in joyful surprise? I bet it might be you praising Him in a way that is unique to your desire and love for Him. When I am alone, I sometimes sing like a fool in my car, ballet dance in my bathrobe for Him while getting dressed, or hum a worship melody when I am doing tasks I find especially repulsive (like cleaning nasty toilets), as well as other things I won't share. I do these things to let Him know my heart belongs to Him alone. If He were to show up in person, I think I'd see Him fall over in laughter, but I also know I am showing Him love in my unspoken thoughts and private time.

Whatever you believe would please Him most if He were to show up in person with a trump and a shout, do that today. Praise Him as only you can. Then don't you dare write a single word on this page! It is private and just for Him.

Homework

Chapter 11: The Bridal Chamber

Chapter 11-Day 1

Prepare your Field: What do you know of passion?

Plant the Seed: Read 1 John 4:10-19 and Mark Chapter 14 - Chapter 16

Cultivate: The week leading up to Resurrection Sunday (Easter) is often referred to as "Passion Week." Palm Sunday (the Triumphal Entry) through Wednesday, Jesus spent each night in Bethany, probably at the home of Mary, Martha, and Lazarus. Thursday night He spent praying in the Garden of Gethsemane (after partaking of the Passover and instituting New Covenant Communion). Jesus died on Good Friday. Friday and Saturday nights Jesus' body lay in the garden tomb. And of course Sunday He was resurrected, victorious over death so we who believe in Him will never die and death forever lost its sting. (You might want to read the four gospel accounts of the Passion Week this week in addition to your regular homework. They can be found at: Matthew 26-28, Mark 11-16, Luke 19-24, and John 12-20)

I especially love to read John's gospel. I love how John refers to himself as "the one Jesus loved." I once thought he must have been quite full of himself to write out such a title. But all Scripture is inspired by God. John wrote only what God inspired Him to say. I am thinking now that God must have known John especially needed to see the words in writing himself. It is often hard to comprehend and live in the belief of God's love. Writing it down was probably a direct instruction from God to help John believe. He loves you fiercely. You, yes you, are the object of his obsessive passion.

If you get nothing else in all of this study, get this: (and as I type this, God is leaning hard on me to get it for myself!)

HE. LOVES. YOU.

It is the bottom line of the gospel and all of Holy Script.

Reap the Harvest: Take this time to reflect on His passion for you. Don't think about your love for Him or for others through Him right now. Focus intently on **His** love for **you**. It can feel awkward and uncomfortable, but you have to learn to let Him love you. It is the center piece of His entire plan, and we will never live in the fullness of His calling until we learn to let Him love us. Be still now and know He is God. (Psalm 46:10) Quiet your chaos and let His love fall over and around you.

Now read Deuteronomy 33:12. The tribe of Benjamin was assigned the portion of the Promised Land near the temple of God. In fact, Mount Moriah, the site of the sacred edifice, lay in the confines of Benjamin. In essence, this Scripture is all about you as the temple. The one the LORD loves is you.

Be like the apostle John and see it in writing. Personalize the verse with your name and personal pronouns:

"Let _____ rest secure in Him, for He shields _____ all day long, and _____ rests between His shoulders."

In the moments you sit still in the reality of His love, what else matters?

He loves you that much. . .enough to have written all of history for you. . .for this moment when you can more fully understand His passion for you. You are the leading lady in the epic love story of your life. Are you fully convinced? Why or why not?

Chapter 11-Day 2

Prepare your Field: Is your perception of intimacy twisted?

Plant the Seed: Read Genesis 2:18-25 and Ephesians 5:22-33

Cultivate: Paul references the Scripture in Genesis "For this reason a man will leave his father and mother and be united to his wife, and the two will become one flesh." Here we see Paul teach the practical structure of godly marriage while also briefly addressing the mystery of marriage's resemblance to the union of Christ and the Church. God had precise reasons for His commands on marriage, because they signified a powerful spiritual precept. When we have access to a perfect and complete union with Christ, we will be empowered to accomplish mountain-moving works for His Kingdom. The enemy has attacked our perception of intimacy in order to malign a precept meant to bring us into a powerfully complete state with Christ through the Holy Spirit. Satan has an entire arsenal of evil directed toward this all-important experience. And as in the Eden garden, the woman seems to be his primary target—sexual abuse, prostitution, rape, assault, pre-marital and extra-marital sex, homosexuality, and sexual images avalanched in our daily lives. The beauty given women by a holy God is under brutal attack. Our perception of intimacy is often twisted way before we even get a chance to learn or experience a pure version of it. So when Christ calls us to an intimate spiritual relationship, we don't know how to react. The perception we have of His intentions are too often colored by our painful, pressured, or even shameful experiences.

Reap the Harvest: How has your perception of intimacy been twisted or maligned? What affect do you believe it plays in your feelings toward Christ? What is your reaction to thinking about a spiritual one-ness with Jesus through the Holy Spirit?

Ask God to heal you. Invite Christ to redeem and restore your perception of spiritual intimacy. Confess what might be holding you back from a spiritual one-ness with Him. Write a prayer and ask Him to make you unashamed before Him. Ask Him to open your eyes to the beauty of your bridal chamber. Ask Him to show you the way to it.

Your experiences might have been too traumatic to handle alone. Many times, women need to seek professional Christian counseling to help sort through the pain and resulting paralysis from abuse or other victimization. Do not hesitate to seek wise counsel if you feel overwhelmed by the past. Ask for God's quick and obvious direction in finding a resource.

Chapter 11-Day 3

Prepare your Field: Do you look like Jesus? How can you reflect His glory?

Plant the Seed: Read 2 Corinthians 3

Cultivate: Christ removed the veil. Matthew 27:51 tells us that when He breathed His last breath, the veil in the temple, separating the Holy of Holies, was torn in two from top to bottom. When we turn to Christ, the veil is removed and we can meet with Him in the Holy of Holies within our own heart. We then become the unveiled bride of Messiah Jesus. We are literally transformed from glory unto glory and begin to look like Him through the Spirit at work within us. When Moses spent time in the presence of God, his face was so radiant he had to cover it when he returned or he would scare the people. (Exodus 34:29-35) The glory the Spirit imparts to us is even more excellent and lasts longer than the glory that Moses experienced.

Reap the Harvest: Have you experienced someone who looked like Christ in their actions and passions? Have you spent time with someone who revealed His glory? What was your impression? Your reaction?

Have you ever been accused of looking like Christ? In what ways?

How can you walk your current journey more fully aware of the unveiled glory of Christ alive and active in you?

Chapter 11-Day 4

Journal prompt: In the homework for chapter one of this study, I asked you, "What is your love story with Jesus?" (Homework Day 4, Chapter 1) Hopefully through this study, Christ has opened your eyes to a new Word and shown you more of Himself. It is my sincere prayer you have come to see yourself as the flawless bride of Jesus, mature and complete. I hope you believe to the tips of your toes that you were chosen for this before the creation of the world. I pray you more fully comprehend in your mind and in your heart His desire for you. I hope you see every event leading up to this point in your life as the backdrop of His epic love story written just for you.

With all He's taught you in this season of life in mind, I want to ask you again.

What is your love story with Jesus?

Now compare it to what you wrote on Day 4 homework from Chapter 1. In what ways have you matured from a child of God to the bride of Christ? What impact has His revelation made in your belief of your leading role in His story?

Homework

Chapter 12: A Fruitful Bride

Chapter 12-Day 1

Prepare your Field: How can we return love to Jesus?

Plant the Seed: Write the Scriptures:

Galatians 5:6

John 14:15

Romans 5:8

Cultivate: Write the personalized version of Romans 5:8 as a response to Christ's love for you. While you were yet a sinner, He died for you. While your circumstances persist, your pain remains, your life is chaotic, etc. Do you trust Jesus?

While yet _____,

(the circumstance in your present reality)

_____ trusted Jesus.

(your name)

How can your actions prove your trust in this present time?

Living in the full reality as the mature, complete, flawless bride of Christ, your life will bear abundant fruit for His glory!

Reap the Harvest: In your alone time with Christ, complete this statement for yourself, in your current circumstance. Then plant it in faith, tend it with the Word, and watch Christ bear abundant fruit through you for His glory. I think it would be especially meaningful to actually copy your completed phrase on a separate sheet of paper, tear it up, and plant it in soil somewhere near your home, perhaps even in a planter or patio flower pot. There is nothing magical or mystical at work here. Perhaps, however, a touchable reminder of sowing the seed of His Word into the actions of our lives might cultivate a change in our hearts and spur us toward a more holy thought process and influence obedient action.

Chapter 12-Day 2

Prepare your Field: Who in your circle of influence needs Hosanna?

Plant the Seed: Read Psalm 118

Cultivate: In the days of the temple, during the Feast of Tabernacles, the congregation listened as a choir of Levites sang the *Hallel* — or the praise Psalms, 113-118. At the proper time, they waved palm branches toward the altar. "Hosanna — Save now" was the cry of their song and prayer. Verses 25 through 27 carry a significant message for The Feast of Tabernacles as they called for the coming of Messiah.[48]

Now read Revelation 7:9-10. Here we see the fulfillment of the Feast of Tabernacles.

As the bride of Christ, living in the New Covenant, we can ask Hosanna to dwell within us through His Holy Spirit. We can pray for it to be poured out like living water into our souls, for Him to light us from within with His glory. A bride living in the strength of His Holy Spirit will be powerful in bringing His life into others through her life's work.

Psalm 118:5 says, *"I called on the LORD in distress; The LORD answered me and set me in a broad place."* (NKJV) One of the meanings of the word 'distress' in the original language is 'strait' or 'narrow'[49]; as in a narrow passage between two larger bodies of water. Interestingly, it has been paraphrased and recast as a *tkhine* [prayer or devotion for Jewish women] for childbirth. In fact the traditional Jewish prayer for childbirth translates it as *"Out of the narrow place I called upon God, who answered me in spaciousness."* This draws the word picture of coming through a narrow, distressful place into an open space of freedom. With this imagery in mind, it makes this particular Scripture's message fitting for the theme of new life or childbirth.[50]

Reap the Harvest: Are you in a narrow or distressful place? Ask God to answer you with a place of spaciousness. Call upon Hosanna to save you now.

Perhaps you are in a season of your life where you are in a position to influence others in distress with the Truth given you by God. Ask for the wisdom and strength of the Holy Spirit to help you give life and nurture them in their time of need. Pray specifically for the people, group and/or nation God has placed upon your heart. Ask Him to conceive a life-giving heritage in your soul.

An idea: As you come to the end of this study, if you've found it helpful in your relationship with Jesus, think of someone you know who could benefit from the truths you learned. Give a fresh copy to a friend and pray for her to wake to her role as bride. Ask God to help you be a good "mother" to her as you nurture Life in another.

Chapter 12-Day 3

Prepare your Field: What is your heritage in the Lord?

Plant the Seed: Read John 14:23. Write it.

Now read John 15:1-17. Write John 15:16.

Cultivate: A fruitful bride is one, who by her living union with Christ through the Spirit, produces much fruit. Fruit might be soul winning, answered prayer, joy, and love (John 15: 7, 11, 12). Galatians 5:22-24 and 2 Peter 1:5-8 describe additional fruit. It is the qualities of Christian character. Keep in mind, these characteristics and the fruit conceived in Christ can never be faked or obtained apart from Him. *OUR* righteous acts are filthy rags (menstrual cloths), wasted potential fruitful life. But Christ spoke and said He chose you and appointed you to bear fruit—fruit that will last. No need for Gabriel on this birth announcement. Jesus announced it to you Himself.

Reap the Harvest: What are your talents, gifts, and fruits of your testimony and walk with God? What desire has God planted in your heart to use for His glory? If you are honest with yourself, these will probably come easily to your mind. Make a list as a thank offering.

Now write a prayer asking Christ to consume these offerings with His holy presence through the Spirit. Ask Him to cause His creative power to inhabit the work of your hands and bless the heritage of His life on this earth through you. Be specific in the requests of your heart. Then submit the product and the path to Him and His perfect will.

Chapter 12-Day 4

Journal Prompt: You, dear friend, have a calling on your life by Almighty God. He created you, chose you, and appointed you to bear lasting fruit for the glory of the Father. Through Christ, you have access to all the power, strength, and wisdom of the Holy Spirit to continue His life in your day and circumstance. Only believe and you will see the glory of the Lord. (John 11:40) Through the Bride, the Church, we should be witnessing mighty acts of His Holy Spirit. You are that bride and have a part in His plan.

As we complete our time together in this season of study, I want you to find and contemplate Ephesians 1:18-19. Really read it and reread it again. Savor every delicious word.

I am praying you see the hope of your calling in your reality. There is a glorious inheritance for you. Plus all the INCOMPARABLY GREAT POWER for you to complete the tasks He is appointing you to do. Use this time to dream with your Bridegroom. Write down the desires of your heart. What, in your wildest imagination, do you wish He would do in His Kingdom through you? What type of righteous acts, conceived in His Spirit, do you want to birth for His glory? What is your hope for your calling? Ask Him to match it with *His* hope for your calling. Be bold and ask in His Name, submitting the path and product to His pleasure. If you are structured, make this an organized list with subtitles and a section for your dreams and a section for your prayer. If you are creative, draw it out in the imagery of your soul. If you have an eye for beauty, script your heart's dreams with furls and tails. Be completely 'you' in His presence. Ask Him to conceive new life in you, through His abundant glory, for your **abundant *life.***

Chapter 12-Special Assignment:

Locate the sealed envelope you saved from the Special Assignment of chapter one. Pray and ask God what He would have you do with it. Sit and wait until you believe you feel His leading. Perhaps He wants you to open it and read the words you wrote. Maybe He will take the next several days to show you the ways He answered each doubt. He may ask you to destroy the envelope without opening it in an act of faith that you are indeed, "A new creation" — His bride. He may have you do something neither you nor I expect. Ask God to make it an intimate and personal task you do together in the privacy of your inner chamber with Him.

Dear Daughter,

May I call you that? I desire to speak words of wisdom over you such as a mother imparts on the day her grown child marries. Picture me straightening your veil and turning the mirror to let you behold a radiant vision of yourself. I am praying you are fully convinced of your capacity to move mountains, to conceive life for Jesus Messiah, and to exude a beauty that others find unexplainably alluring. I pray you have a quick answer for the hope you can't help but profess: Jesus. Just Jesus. Only Jesus. My hope is you influence those around you to know and pursue the Lover of your soul. Much is at stake. I hope I get to see you realize the hope of your call. But if I never know you personally in this life, I know we will stand together in heaven, looking full in the face of our Bridegroom. Until then, let the Sprit and the Bride say, "Come!"

ENDNOTES

1. Webster's New World Dictionary, Third College Edition (New York, NY: Simon & Schuster, Inc., 1988).

2. Borowski, Oded. *Daily Life in Biblical Times*. (Atlanta, GA: Society of Biblical Literature, 2003).

3. Blue Letter Bible. "Dictionary and Word Search for *hypomonē (Strong's 5281)*". Blue Letter Bible. 1996-2013. 31 Jul 2013.

4. Illustrated Bible Dictionary, Third Edition, published by Thomas Nelson, 1897. Public Domain.

5. *Clean House*. Gina Rubinstein (Executive Producer and Director), Niecy Nash (Host), Stan Dembecki (Writer). Style Network. 2007

6. *Mama Mia!* Director, Phyllida Lloyd. Universal Pictures, 2008. Film.

7. ABBA. "Dancing Queen," "Mama Mia," "Fernando." GOLD: Greatest Hits. Polydor Records, 1992. CD.

8. John Eldridge, *The Journey of DESIRE*. (Nashville, Tennessee: Thomas Nelson, Inc., 2000), 211.

9. Blue Letter Bible. "Dictionary and Word Search for *qodesh (Strong's 6944)*". Blue Letter Bible. 1996-2013. 31 Jul 2013.

10. Zola Levitt, *A Christian Love Story*. (Dallas, Texas: ZOLA, 1978), 7.

11. Ibid., 8-10

12. Ibid., 15

13. *Baker's Evangelical Dictionary of Biblical Theology*. Edited by Walter A. Elwell. (Grand Rapids, Michigan: Baker Books, a division of Baker Book House Company,. 1996).

14. Blue Letter Bible. "Dictionary and Word Search for *kĕlal (Aramaic) (Strong's 3635)*". Blue Letter Bible. 1996-2013. 31 Jul 2013.

15. Blue Letter Bible. "Dictionary and Word Search for *kallah (Strong's 3618)*". Blue Letter Bible. 1996-2013. 31 Jul 2013.

16. Blue Letter Bible. "Dictionary and Word Search for *kalal (Strong's 3634)*". Blue Letter Bible. 1996-2013. 31 Jul 2013.

17. Zola Levitt, *A Christian Love Story*. (Dallas, Texas: ZOLA, 1978), 13.

18. Ibid., 12.

19. Ibid., 11.

20. Ibid., 14.

21. Yeshuat Yisrael - The Salvation of Israel. "The Messiah and the Jewish Wedding" http://www.yeshuatyisrael.com/messiah_wedding%201.htm (last accessed July 31, 2013).

22. Zola Levitt, *A Christian Love Story*. (Dallas, Texas: ZOLA, 1978), 13-17.

23. Kevin Howard and Marvin Rosenthal, *The FEASTS of the LORD: God's Prophetic Calendar From Calvary to the Kingdom.* (Nashville, Tennessee: Thomas Nelson, Inc., 1997), 14.

24. Ibid., 13.

25. Ibid., 15.

26. Ibid., 16-22.

27. Ibid., 25-31.

28. Ibid., 113-114.

29. Zola Levitt, *A Christian Love Story*. (Dallas, Texas: ZOLA, 1978), 17-18.

30. Kevin Howard and Marvin Rosenthal, *The FEASTS of the LORD: God's Prophetic Calendar From Calvary to the Kingdom*. (Nashville, Tennessee: Thomas Nelson, Inc., 1997), 16.

31. Ibid., 54-62.

32. Henry, Matthew. "Commentary on Isaiah 53." . Blue Letter Bible. 1 Mar 1996.2013. 31 Jul 2013.

33. Kevin Howard and Marvin Rosenthal, *The FEASTS of the LORD: God's Prophetic Calendar From Calvary to the Kingdom*. (Nashville, Tennessee: Thomas Nelson, Inc., 1997), 135.

34. Ibid., 135-148.

35. Blue Letter Bible. "Dictionary and Word Search for *episkiazō (Strong's 1982)*". Blue Letter Bible. 1996-2013. 31 Jul 2013.

36. Blue Letter Bible. "Dictionary and Word Search for `iddah (Strong's 5708)*". Blue Letter Bible. 1996-2013. 31 Jul 2013.

37. Blue Letter Bible. "Dictionary and Word Search for *chrēstos (Strong's 5543)*". Blue Letter Bible. 1996-2013. 31 Jul 2013.

38. Jamieson, Robert; A.R. Fausset; and David Brown. "Commentary on Ephesians 4." . Blue Letter Bible. 19 Feb 2000.2013. 31 Jul 2013.

39. James C. Gavin, *Life Application Study Bible* Notes and Bible Helps. Life Application Study Bible. (Carol Stream, Illinois: Tyndale House Publishers, Inc., 1986, 2004), 1568.

40. Ibid., 1995.

41. Blue Letter Bible. "Dictionary and Word Search for *dechomai (Strong's 1209)*". Blue Letter Bible. 1996-2013. 31 Jul 2013.

42. James C. Gavin, *Life Application Study Bible* Notes and Bible Helps. Life Application Study Bible. (Carol Stream, Illinois: Tyndale House Publishers, Inc., 1986, 2004), 2096.

43. Blue Letter Bible. "Dictionary and Word Search for *yada` (Strong's 3045)*". Blue Letter Bible. 1996-2013. 31 Jul 2013.

44. Evans, Darrell. "Your Love is Extravagant." Casting Crowns. Reunion Records, 2003. CD.

45. Blue Letter Bible. "Dictionary and Word Search for *kanaph (Strong's 3671)*". Blue Letter Bible. 1996-2013. 31 Jul 2013.

46. Blue Letter Bible. "Dictionary and Word Search for *pĕniymah (Strong's 6441)*". Blue Letter Bible. 1996-2013. 31 Jul 2013.

47. Blue Letter Bible. "Dictionary and Word Search for *hagios (Strong's 40)"*. Blue Letter Bible. 1996-2013. 31 Jul 2013.

48. Kevin Howard and Marvin Rosenthal, *The FEASTS of the LORD: God's Prophetic Calendar From Calvary to the Kingdom.* (Nashville, Tennessee: Thomas Nelson, Inc., 1997), 139.

49. Blue Letter Bible. "Dictionary and Word Search for *metsar (Strong's 4712)"*. Blue Letter Bible. 1996-2013. 31 Jul 2013.

50. Lori H. Lefkovitz, Jewish Women on Life Passages & Personal Milestones. (Jewish Lights Publishing) http://mobile.myjewish-learning.com/life/Life_Events/Lifecycle_Ritual/Other_Life_Passages_101/Why_New_Ceremonies/Giving_Birth.shtml (last accessed July 31, 2013).

ABOUT THE AUTHOR

Angie Nichols is a teacher, writer, and messenger. She is the founder of Something Abundant Ministries, serving the Bride of Christ through worship and Biblical teaching. The ministry serves mothers with children with cancer, as well as ministering to hurting women through the message for the Bride. Her speaking engagements have taken her as far away as Africa and as near as her own east Texas backyard. She is married to Chris and they have one daughter Mycah, who is healthy and growing to the glory of God. Angie's passion is for women to experience the abundant life of knowing Christ as Bridegroom. For more information, to book speaking events or women's retreats, and to read Angie's blog, visit: www.somethingabundantministries.org

CPSIA information can be obtained
at www.ICGtesting.com
Printed in the USA
FSOW02n0550040515
6871FS